FOOD AID AND THE DEVELOPING WORLD

FOUR AFRICAN CASE STUDIES

CHRISTOPHER STEVENS

CROOM HELM LONDON
in association with
THE OVERSEAS DEVELOPMENT INSTITUTE

© 1979 Overseas Development Institute
Croom Helm Ltd, 2–10 St John's Road, London SW11

British Library Cataloguing in Publication Data

Stevens, Christopher
    Food aid and the developing world.
    1. Underdeveloped areas – Food relief
    I. Title   II. Overseas Development Institute
    338.1'9'1724   HV696.F6

    ISBN 0–85664–622–9
            0–7099–0036–8 (pbk)

Printed in Great Britain by offset lithography by
Billing & Sons Ltd, Guildford, London and Worcester

CONTENTS

TABLES AND FIGURES

Tables

Figures

ABBREVIATIONS

BAMB	Botswana Agricultural Marketing Board
BCEAO	Banque Centrale des Etats de l'Afrique de l'Ouest
CAP	Common Agricultural Policy (EEC)
CARE	Co-operative for American Relief Everywhere
CCC	Commodity Credit Corporation
CDC	Commonwealth Development Corporation
CES	Conservation des eaux et des sols
CFA	West Africa franc
CNSS	Comité national de solidarité sociale
CRS	Catholic Relief Services
CSB	Corn soya blend
CSD	Consultative Sub-committee on Surplus Disposal
CSM	Corn soya milk
DAC	Development Assistance Committee, OECD
dc	Developed country
DG6	Directorate-General for Agriculture, EEC
DG8	Directorate-General for Development, EEC
DSM	Dried skim milk
FAC	Food Aid Convention
FAO	United Nations Food and Agriculture Organisation
GMV	Grands Moulins Voltaiques de Banfora
HER	Service de l'Hydraulique et de l'Equipement
IFP	Institutional Food Programme
INS	Institut National de la Statistique
LCSD	La lutte contre le sous-développement
ldc	Developing country
oda	Official development assistance
MCH	Mother and child health (Mother/pre-school child)
Minrudev	Ministry of Rural Development
OCT	Office des Céréales de Tunisie
OECD	Organisation for Economic Co-operation and Development
OFNACER	Office National des Céréales
ONH	Office National de l'Huile
ORD	Organisme Régional de Développement
SCF	Save the Children Fund

Abbreviations

SIDA	Swedish International Development Authority
SOVOLCOM	Société Voltaique de Commercialisation
UMR	Usual marketing requirement
UNDP	United Nations Development Programme
URN	Unité de Récupération Nutritionelle
USAID	United States Agency for International Development
USDA	United States Department of Agriculture
WFP	World Food Programme
WHO	World Health Organisation
WSB	Wheat soya blend

ACKNOWLEDGEMENTS

An indispensible requirement for authorship is the capacity to be a pest and a bore. Research inevitably means imposing upon the time of many people who have plenty of better things to do, and this book, which involved fieldwork in seven countries, is no exception. The number of people to whom I am indebted is very great. So this can only be a very partial list both because of the limitations of space and because some people I would particularly like to thank are officials and might be embarrassed by public mention.

However, I must express gratitide to the Ministry of Overseas Development which financed the study through its Economic and Social Committee on Research (ESCOR). I owe much to my advisory group whose members set me in the right direction, read innumerable drafts, and saved me from many major and minor errors. The group was chaired by my Director, Robert Wood, and included Professor Hans Singer, Hal Mettrick, Paul Richards, Mark Bowden and officials from government and donor agencies. I received every assistance during my fieldwork from my host governments and from the donors. Indeed, I have been struck by the way all of those involved with food aid are conscious of the need to improve performance wherever possible even if they disagree with my own prescriptions. This book has benefited from being written at the same time that Professor Hans Singer and Simon Maxwell were compiling an extensive and rigorous analysis of existing literature on the subject. Their work has made it more easy than it would otherwise have been for me to place my case studies in a broader context. My colleagues at ODI helped by creating the stimulating and happy atmosphere in which I was lucky to work. I must mention particularly my secretary, Shamsi Assef, who bore with fortitude all my messy drafts and numerous tables. Obviously any remaining errors result from my own obstinacy and stupidity.

I hope that those who use this book will find it easy to read. If they do, they should thank my wife, who taught me to write clearly in English, and Robert Wood, who taught me to write clearly in economics.

London, September 1978

SECTION ONE: INTRODUCTION

1 WHYS AND WHEREFORES

To some people food aid is as close to an ideal form of aid as we are likely to find in an imperfect world. It achieves a happy union between the interests of the recipients and those of farmers in the donor countries, and it is a way of channelling assistance direct to the starving millions who need it, while bypassing the rich elites in developing countries (ldcs). The evidence of recent literature (although not necessarily of opinion polls) is that this view is rapidly losing ground to its polar opposite: that food aid is particularly pernicious since it exists largely to help sustain inefficient agricultural policies in developed countries (dcs) and to increase the leverage that its donors can exert on poor countries, and that furthermore it not only fails to benefit the recipient adequately to compensate for these costs but it actually puts ldc farmers out of business, leads their children to adopt exotic tastes that can be satisfied only by imports, and enables their governments to neglect agricultural reform.

Such a stark conflict of views should be reason enough for a book that examines how food aid has actually been used and the impact it has had in four of the countries receiving it. Further justification is provided by food aid's importance in the aid scene — it currently accounts for 15 per cent of official aid[1] — and recent interest in the world food situation provoked by the spectacular food shortages and associated price increases of 1972/3 when poor countries found that they could not count on food aid in the years when they needed it most. From a parochial perspective, Britain has a particular interest in the subject at the present time. In the past, opinion in the UK has been rather negative on the grounds that since Britain does not have an agricultural surplus any food aid it supplies has to be purchased with hard cash on the world market, and that it would make more sense simply to give the ldc the money. Since joining the EEC, however, Britain has had a voice in the disposal of an important and growing food aid programme.

Although food aid may be an important subject for study, analysis of its impact is not as straightforward as might at first sight appear. Aid can be divided into two sets of categories which can be labelled modes and sectoral types. The term 'modes' refers to the form in which the aid is supplied: soft financial loans, financial grants, food aid grants, etc.

'Sectoral types' covers the uses to which the aid is put: educational aid, infrastructure aid and the like. It is sensible to measure the impact of sectoral aid, for example to primary education or to smallscale industry. It is also sensible to consider the impact of aid as a whole or from specific sources to specific recipients as has been done in a number of Overseas Development Institute (ODI) case studies.[2] However, when considering the various modes of aid it is not normal to consider impact as such because end-uses are not known. How can one assess the impact in general terms of 3 per cent cash loans with five-year grace periods? Similarly, while one may assess the efficiency, flexibility or political acceptability of food aid as a mode of transferring resources compared with other possible modes, it is not clear how its impact in the recipient country may be measured since food aid can be put to a multitude of different uses. Will not the impact vary between food aid to primary education and food aid to smallscale industry?

The conventional answer to this problem is that because food aid is provided in kind and because all recipients produce food themselves it will have a certain set of effects in addition to any that may arise from the circumstances of recipient countries or specific uses to which it is put. However, while it is true that food aid must react in some way on food production in recipient countries, it is not clear that it is so very different from other modes of aid. Although it is conventional to express financial aid agreements in cash terms, transfers of free foreign exchange are rare. By the time it is implemented, financial aid has usually been transformed into goods and services that flow from the donor to the recipient. Thus, while it is true that food aid may compete with the recipient's domestic agriculture, similar considerations apply to, say, technical assistance supplied under financial aid. Under technical assistance, rich country personnel (arguably in surplus supply) are sent to poor countries where they may compete with local people, sap the government's will to adopt 'realistic' manpower policies, and introduce Western tastes unsuited to local conditions. Similarly, rich country machinery sent under financial aid agreements may compete with local technology and may depress the income of those involved in indigenous industry.

These distinctions are important both as a guide to the boundaries of this study and as a help in evaluating some of the general comments increasingly being made about food aid. First of all, food aid has been attacked on grounds that effectively make it a surrogate for the concept of aid as a whole. The idea that aid is a good thing can certainly be queried on several counts: on the grounds that it weakens the resolve of ldc governments to mobilise domestic savings, that it largely benefits rich elites and enables them to remain in power, or that it ties the Third World to the apron strings of the West. Judgement on these issues is inherently a balance-of-probabilities affair because data are lacking, because aid has numerous second and third round effects that can only be weighted subjectively, and because it has indirect effects. With a couple of relatively minor exceptions, food aid may be assumed to suffer from all the defects of aid as a whole. That is not really at issue. What is at issue, and what this book is designed to illuminate, is whether food aid is also subject to other defects, and if so how common and how serious they are. This study therefore considers food aid as a mode of aid to be compared with other modes, and for its purposes food aid can be given a clean bill of health if it can be shown to be as good as, or no worse than, financial aid even though, obviously, when considering aid from a broader perspective other problems have to be addressed as well.

This approach may be illustrated in relation to the criticism levelled at food aid that it has been used extensively as a foreign policy tool to assist favoured regimes and to build up a dependent relationship between recipient and donor. There is plenty of evidence in favour of at least the first part of this proposition. It is clear from the figures in Chapter 3 that the distribution of food aid is highly skewed in favour of a very small number of countries. It has been calculated that 14 ldcs closely linked to the USA, which accounted for 23 per cent of the population of low and middle income food aid recipient countries in 1973, obtained 81 per cent of all the US food aid supplied to that group.[3] Similarly, in 1974 South Vietnam, Cambodia, Jordan, and Israel received 63 per cent of the total Title I programme.[4] Between 1968 and 1973 South Vietnam alone received 20 times the value of food aid that the five African states most seriously affected by drought received during the same period.[5]

By itself, however, such data say little about the merits of food aid as a means of development assistance. An African state will find it of little help in deciding whether to accept food aid and how to use it to know that South Vietnam received a more than proportionate share. Food aid is open to particular criticism only if it can be shown that it is inherently more liable to be used as an adjunct of foreign and military policy than are other forms of aid. There is one area in which this may be the case. There is evidence that in a number of years since 1973, the US Administration has used food aid to compensate regimes favoured by the Executive but not by Congress for congressionally imposed cuts in financial aid. This has been possible because PL 480 country programmes* are not subject to annual congressional appropriations. The budget submitted is only an estimate that can be changed without congressional approval.[6] Nonetheless, while such practices may be undesirable from several points of view, they reflect more on internal US politics and budgetary procedures than they do on food aid itself.

The second part of this criticism, that food aid is used to create a relationship of dependence, is perhaps more worrying. If true, it would certainly cast doubt on the desirability of food aid. It is difficult to see, however, how one could show that food aid was creating dependence. One method favoured in critiques of dc food trade and aid policies is to cite statements of donor country politicians. Thus Hubert Humphrey in 1957 claimed:

> I have heard . . . that people may become dependent on us for food.
> I know this is not supposed to be good news. To me that was good
> news, because before people can do anything they have got to eat.
> And if you are looking for a way to get people to lean on you and
> to be dependent on you, in terms of their co-operation with you, it
> seems to me that food dependence would be terrific.[7]

This approach reverses Oscar Wilde's dictum that no one will believe a man who boasts that he will devote his life to sin, but everyone will encourage a person who pledges his life to good. A statement by a donor politician that his country's aid policy is determined solely by philanthropic motives is normally received with considerable scepticism, and rightly so. By contrast, the sceptics seem to throw caution to the winds and accept quite uncritically a statement to the opposite effect. At the very least, we need to know to whom such remarks were addressed. Normally, such statements show merely that politicians tend to pitch their remarks according to their audience, and that there are multiple motives to many state actions.

What is important is not whether a donor sees in food aid a way of creating dependence, but whether it actually succeeds. In what ways is food aid likely to increase the power of leverage of a rich country above that which it obtains by virtue of its wealth alone? Countries that are not selfsufficient in food are dependent on those that have a surplus. However, this dependency need not be onerous for a rich country like Britain; what is onerous is when a food shortage is combined with

* See Chapter 2, section on the USA for a description of the PL 480 programme.

poverty. Such dependence could be alleviated by an increase in
domestic food production or an increase in income. Food aid *per se*
does not affect the position either way, unless it has an impact on one
of these two variables. If food aid depresses the recipient's domestic
agricultural production it may increase dependence, but by no more
than any other factor that hits local agriculture. Similarly, if the resource
transfer implicit in food aid results in a long-term increase in the
recipient's income it may reduce dependence, but not to any greater
degree than other resource flows with the same effect. The task is
therefore to find out which, if either, of these two situations obtains.

A related argument is that bulk food aid sold on the open market is
a major source of revenue for some recipient governments which hence
are vulnerable to pressure from the donor. Again, however, food aid
should be singled out only if it gives a donor more potential for
leverage than other kinds of aid. As a general proposition, it is doubtful
whether this is the case. Although food aid is less often project tied
than financial aid and therefore more often adds directly to general
revenue, even project tied aid can increase a recipient's general revenue
if it releases local financial resources. To the extent that it provides
special favours, all aid has an inherent potential to make the recipient
dependent. Whether these risks are worth accepting depends on the
observer's views on the likelihood of dependency, the overall motives
of donors, the effectiveness of aid today in creating income tomorrow,
and the extent (often exaggerated) to which rich countries can bully
poor countries.

Even within the limits established for the study, however, the
breadth of the food aid mode creates numerous problems. Food aid is
one, often small, input into a complex food production and
marketing system. As such, it is often difficult to establish lines of
causality, and to discover precisely what effect food aid has had. Thus,
for example, food aid can be criticised because sometimes it is
distributed only in the urban areas and so does not reach the rural
poor direct. However, although it may not reach the rural areas direct,
it may have an indirect effect on them. If, for instance, the urban
population is politically strong, the 'normal' course of events may be
for the government to extract from the countryside enough food to
feed the cities, even though this may mean that not enough is left for
the rural population. In such an example, the real impact of food
aid might have been to reduce the urban depredations of the countryside and to leave the farmer with more food. A similar example
concerns smuggling, which occurs extensively in the Sahel. If an input

of food aid into Upper Volta is matched by an equivalent amount of food smuggled out ito neighbouring Ghana, does this mean that it is wasted? The answer will depend on who ends up with more food and/or more cash at the end of the day. Frequently, such second, third and fourth round effects are virtually impossible to quantify, or even to evaluate qualitatively so that they can be weighed against each other. This study tends, therefore, to concentrate on the more immediate effects of different types of food aid on those who receive it (individuals and governments).

Although the generalised impact of food aid raises conceptual problems, the impact of its different sectoral types is a more straightforward subject to consider. 'What is the impact of food aid used for preventive health measures, or for infrastructure development' are questions that can be addressed and answered. Similarly, the impact of food aid as a whole on specific recipient countries is something that can be assessed, and an attempt can be made to discover whether the food aid mode is more suited to some types of recipient than to others. For this reason the study concentrates on the impact of food aid in Africa, an area which is relatively neglected by the literature on this subject.

There is a fairly extensive literature on food aid, much of which is concerned with measuring the effects of American aid on agricultural price levels and production in recipient countries. However, it concentrates mainly on South Asia and, to a lesser degree, on Latin America. This is justifiable to an extent since South Asia has received a major share of the food aid that has been supplied over the past quarter century. But it is far from clear whether the conclusions from such studies can be generalised for other food aid recipients. Researchers face a perennial problem in judging the extent to which generalisation is justifiable and it is always necessary to find an acceptable position between extremes of global theorising on the basis of very limited empirical research, and of insistence that no generalisations at all are possible. The problem is particularly severe, however, in the case of food aid because it is a mode of aid with characteristics that can vary considerably depending on how it is used and to whom it is supplied. To take India as an example: food aid has formed a high proportion of imported foods, but food imports as a whole have accounted for only a small proportion of total supplies. In Lesotho, by contrast, the situation is quite the reverse: imports are much more important in total supplies, but food aid forms a smaller proportion of them.

Similarly, the administrative structures and marketing policies that have been used or are possible in India are often simply not feasible in parts of Africa.

This study therefore seeks to throw more light on the possible impact of food aid by examining the experience of four African countries with widely differing backgrounds, size, rates of growth and prospects. They are Botswana and Lesotho in Southern Africa, Upper Volta bordering the Sahel in West Africa, and Tunisia in North Africa. One characteristic they all share, however, is that they are 'good of their kind'. Thus although the administrative capacity of the four varies greatly between Tunisia, the best, and Upper Volta, the worst, the situation in Upper Volta compares well with that in its neighbours. There is, of course, a danger that because we have studied countries that tend to cope with problems better than others in a similar position the potential adverse effects of food aid will appear to be smaller than they actually are. It was decided not to consider a country that was 'bad of its kind' to provide a better balance because the object of the book is not simply to show whether food aid can have negative effects since it is perfectly clear that it can and sometimes does, but to establish whether or not such mishaps are more likely with food aid than with financial aid and, if so, how much more likely. To achieve this it is important to know something of how the food aid has been used. The pages that follow are full of laments for the inadequacy of the data that exist even in countries that are 'good of their kind'. It is more than likely that a study of a 'bad' recipient would simply have prevented any conclusions being drawn on this issue. In any case, because the study considers four countries at very different levels of economic and political development, it is possible to show that what is feasible and innocuous in one may be quite unfeasible and potentially harmful in another.

Because food aid is a mode of aid and has been used in a host of different ways, the study has had to concentrate on a limited number of sectors in which it has been used or on which it may have had an impact. Three areas have been selected as being particularly likely to have been affected with especially serious consequences. They are nutrition, consumer prices, and agricultural production. It is conventional to distinguish between direct and indirect effects, although in practice the two are hard to separate. Possible direct effects of food aid on, for example, nutrition include, on the positive side, an improvement in nutritional levels, better nutrition education, and higher attendance at clinics, or on the negative side, the introduction of alien tastes, undermining local self-reliance, and health hazards. The indirect effects are seen to occur via food aid's impact on government policy. Thus, nutrition oriented food aid could spur a receiving government to take an interest in a formerly neglected subject, or it could have the opposite effect and reduce the urgency for reform of the system that creates the malnutrition. Both direct and indirect effects are considered in this book. Ideally, the direct effects should be charted through empirical observation, although the indirect effects require a high level of qualitative analysis. Unfortunately, although a surprisingly large amount of data has been collected it is not sufficiently coherent or reliable to form the basis of an economic model to simulate the direct effects of food aid on, for instance, agricultural prices and production. This is in contrast to the situation in South Asia where econometric models have been used extensively although, arguably, to the neglect of the indirect effects. The methodology adopted therefore has been pragmatic, and related to the type and quality of data available and it has resulted in the creation of a mosaic of small chunks of data. In practice, this is how decisions are made on a wide range of issues in ldcs with poor statistics.

This study considers the wisdom of supplying and receiving food aid on a continuing basis as a means of development assistance. However, in addition to its use in this way, food aid is also supplied to alleviate suffering following emergencies, such as a severe drought or an earthquake. Although the dividing line between emergency and development aid is often blurred in practice, there are important differences between them. Emergency food aid is considered only to the extent that it alters the framework within which development food aid has to operate. One reason for selecting Upper Volta as a case study is its location bordering the Sahel and the fact that it received a considerable amount of emergency relief during 1973-5. However, this relief is not considered in its own right, but only to the extent that it doomed certain kinds of development food aid to failure. The reasons for excluding emergency relief are not that it is unimportant or problem free. Clearly neither of these is correct, and indeed some of the worst cases of food aid misuse are to be found in emergency campaigns. The reasons are simply that the problems of emergency relief are quite different from those of development food aid, and that the rationale for supplying it is also different. No doubt, horrendous difficulties arise when an attempt is made to supply large quantities of possibly unfamiliar and in some circumstances dangerous food to landlocked countries with an inadequate physical and administrative infrastructure, to a population suffering from social dislocation and impoverishment. Not least of these are weaning the recipient government away from food aid once the emergency is over and, indeed, in establishing whether or not there really is a food shortage after a disaster. It has been argued, for example, that food aid sent to Guatemala after the 1976 earthquake was dysfunctional because there was no local food shortage.[8] Lesotho provides an example of how emergency relief can cause problems even if supplied on a fairly small scale to a relatively minor emergency. Following a drought in 1972/3, Britain offered Lesotho emergency food aid. The Lesotho response was that it could absorb 1,000 tons of wheat. However, when a firm offer came from the UK it was for 6,000 tons of wheat. The Lesotho Government accepted the increased amount even though adequate storage facilities did not exist, and at the same time received as emergency food aid over 1,000 tons of Belgian wheat flour instead of the 662 tons originally requested, as well as its normal development food aid deliveries. In addition, and contrary to expectation, the 1973/4 harvest was particularly large. The result was the diversion of Lesotho government personnel away from the management of routine food aid into the task of finding ways of storing and disposing of the surplus wheat, the construction of six new storage sheds at a cost of R45,000, and the loss through rotting of many bags of wheat.[9] The justification for risking these problems is presumably that, despite the desirability of long-term solutions, when an emergency strikes something has to be done. The justification for development food aid is different and has to be assessed in relation to its own problems.

This book is divided into three sections. The remaining two chapters of Section One supply some background data on the donors and recipients under consideration in the case studies. They also sketch in broad strokes the wider context of food aid. Readers well versed in the folklore of food aid may skim these chapters without any great loss, except for the last section of Chapter 3 which touches on the thorny subject of how food aid flows are to be valued. Section Two shows the main ways in which food aid has been used in the four countries studied. It both provides the bricks and mortar for the following section and suggests that there are certain broad patterns characterising the many and varied ways in which food aid has been used. Since food aid has been accorded many, often conflicting objectives it is essential to clarify what these really are if its success or failure is to be assessed. Section Three considers specifically the impact of food aid on nutrition, consumer prices, and agricultural production in the four countries. It also attempts to isolate important effects of food aid in other areas and to explain the reasons for the wide gulf that exists between the views of the supporters of food aid and those of its critics.

Notes

1. Official development assistance (oda) as defined by the Organisation for Economic Co-operation and Development (OECD).

2. See Bibliography: Morton (1975): Holtham and Hazlewood (1976): Jones (1977); and Wood and Morton (1977).

3. P. Wallensteen, 'Scarce goods as political weapons; the case of food' in V. Harle (ed.), *Political Economy of Food* (Tampere Peace Research Institute, 1976), Table 9. Cited in Singer and Maxwell (1978), p. 32, (see Bibliography).

4. J. Power and A.M. Holenstein, *World Hunger* (London, 1976), p. 60; cited in ibid.

5. See Bibliography: Lappé and Collins (1977), p. 337.

6. Lappé and Collins (1977), p. 338.

7. Cited in George (1976), p. 211, (see Bibliography).

8. *New York Times,* 6 November (1977). See also J. Rivers 'Disaster Relief Needs More Research', *Nature,* vol. 271, 12 January (1978), p. 100.

9. Further details of the UK Government end of this saga are in *Fifth Report from the Committee of Public Accounts, Session 1976–77* HMSO, (London, 23 June 1977), paras 839–925.

2 THE DONORS

Food aid has seen many changes since 1954 when the United States began systematically to export food on concessional terms as part of its policy to cope with growing domestic agricultural surpluses. Begun as a scheme designed primarily to assist rich-country farmers by disposing of surplus commodities, it has become an instrument of the development aid agencies and not only is it no longer restricted to foods in surplus supply, it actually utilises exotic concoctions that have been developed especially for food aid and do not exist outside its domain. The general trend has been to shift the emphasis from surplus disposal to development. The 1974 World Food Conference set three main objectives for food aid: to provide emergency relief; to combat hunger and malnutrition; and to promote economic and social development. Different donors give different priorities to these goals, but all now attempt to justify their aid within a development framework. However, the changes in emphasis have brought their own problems. The farmers have been joined by the blended food processors as a powerful donor lobby with interests that need not necessarily coincide with those of the recipients. Emphasis on the poorest ldcs has caused administrative headaches. Thus, a congressional directive that 75 per cent of PL 480 Title I aid should go to states with a per capita GNP of under $300 had to be amended to set the limit at $550 because there were too few takers. However, this chapter is concerned less with the philosophy of food aid than with its size and distribution.

Table 2.1, page 24, shows that, using the donors' valuation,[1] food aid has accounted for 12-16 per cent of OECD (Organisation for Economic Co-operation and Development) total net official development assistance (oda) since 1971. While this is slightly down on the levels achieved in the 1960s (22 per cent in 1965) the table suggests that although the abrupt change in the world food situation in 1972-3 from relative abundance to relative scarcity may have affected food aid in many ways, it has not caused a major, permanent reduction in the proportion of oda disbursed in this form. Nevertheless, there was a sharp fall in the quantity of food aid supplied in the early 1970s, particularly with respect to cereals. Table 2.2, page 24, indicates that between 1964 and 1973 the volume of cereal food aid disbursed fell by 63 per cent, while the real value of food aid in all commodities (at 1968

23

prices) fell by 60 per cent. Since then, however, flows have increased. In 1975/6 cereal aid totalled 9.1 million tons, which was not far short of the annual target of 10 million tons set in 1974 by the World Food Conference.[2] Dairy food aid has also been increasing, albeit erratically, and now probably accounts for some 10-15 per cent by value of total food aid.[3]

Table 2.1: OECD Food Aid, 1965 and 1971-6 (in $ million, net)

Year	Bilateral Grants	Loans	Multilateral grants	Total food aid	Total official aid	Food aid as % of oda*
1965	1,298		13	1,311	5,895	22
1971	1,050		167	1,217	7,759.3	16
1972	1,014		262	1,276	8,653.5	15
1973	430.5	419.8	282.1	1,132.4	9,376.0	12
1974	604.4	461.3	457.3	1,523.0	11,315.6	13
1975	826.3	805.1	497.9	2,129.3	13,585.1	16
1976	846.1	601.8	342.3	1,790.2	13,656.2	13

* Official Development Assistance.
Source: OECD, *Development Co-operation* (various years, Paris).

Table 2.2: Nominal and Real Value of Total Bilateral and Multilateral Food Aid Disbursements and Cereal Volumes Received under Food Aid

	1964	1966	1969	1972	1973
Nominal value ($m)	1,529	1,329	1,147	1,276	1,130
Real value ($m at 1968 prices)	1,390	1,278	1,236	1,129	553
Cereal volume Received (million tonnes)*	16	14	13	11	6

* Estimate.
Source: OECD, *Development Co-operation: 1974 Review* (Paris, November 1974), Table V—1.

Two features of the food aid scene since the early 1960s have been the declining share of the USA (although it is still the dominant supplier) and the increasing proportion that goes through multilateral channels. The shift in the position of the USA from provider of 96 per cent of all food aid in 1963 to 58 per cent in 1975 (see Figure 2.1, page 25) is partly the result of determined American pressure for 'burden sharing' among the rich countries, and partly because of the emergence of the EEC as a surplus producer. However, the share of food aid in total aid still varies considerably between the main donors, and in 1973 it constituted about 25 per cent for the USA, 19 per cent for Canada and 5 per cent for the EEC states.[4] The growth of multilateral food aid (see Table 2.1) reflects the increasing importance of the UN/FAO World Food Programme (WFP) and of the EEC.

Not all food aid donors fall within the sphere of interest of this

Figure 2.1: Per Cent Shares of Main Donors in Total Food Aid, 1963, 1966, 1969, 1972, 1975

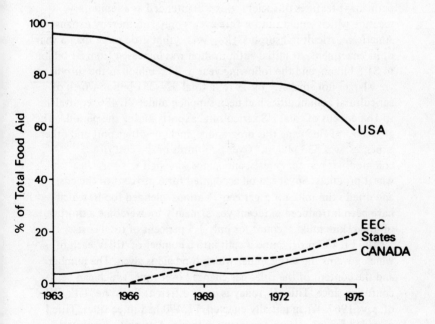

Source: OECD, *Development Co-operation: — 1974 Review,* Table V—3; *Development Co-operation: — 1976 Review,* Table VI—13.

book, although the largest do. The four African states that have been studied have received development food aid from the USA, both direct and via voluntary agencies, the WFP, the EEC, Canada and France. The remainder of this chapter provides some background information on each of these donors.

USA

The USA created food aid as we know it today, has supplied the over-whelming bulk of the aid that has been given, and has a major voice in world food aid policies and practices. Although US food aid can be traced back to before World War 2, it is generally accepted that its present form dates from June 1954 when the US Government approved Public Law 480: the Agricultural Trade Development and Assistance Act, better known by its now ubiquitous initials – PL 480. Like many permanent features of society, this was intended as a temporary measure which would run for three years only and thereby exhaust the American agricultural surplus. However, within little more than a year of its enactment, its initial authorisation was increased from $1 billion* to $1.8 billion, and the following year to $3.5 billion as the surpluses grew larger not smaller.[5] By 1975, a total $24.251 billion-worth of agricultural commodities had been supplied under PL 480, equivalent to 16 per cent of total US agricultural exports during the period.[6] The gross cost of financing this programme, including transport and other expenses, was $33 billion.[7] Over two-thirds of the cost of commodities was for cereals, and almost one-half was for wheat and wheat products. Soyabean oil accounted for 6 per cent of the cost, and dried skim milk for 5 per cent. Various 'blended foods' which have been introduced in recent years, mainly to overcome a shortage of dried skim milk, account for only 1.5 per cent of total costs.

The PL 480 programme is split into a number of 'titles' each of which governs the terms under which food aid is given. The number and the content of the titles has changed over time, which can be confusing since 'Title III' today is quite different from the 'Title III' of, say, 1967. When initially enacted, PL 480 had three titles. Title I provided for the sale on concessional terms of surplus agricultural commodities for payment in the local currency of the recipient, which could then be used either for US purposes or for mutually agreed economic development projects in the recipient country. Title II covered grants for emergency relief, community development, school feeding and other economic development purposes. However, Title II

* The term 'billion' is used throughout the book to represent thousand million.

assistance could not replace Title I or other sales. Title III authorised
domestic donations of surplus commodities as well as overseas
donations via US voluntary agencies and multilateral organisations, and
it also covered food exports to finance barter trade.

Title I was the most important of the three, and indeed accumulated
counterpart funds of local currencies faster than they could be spent.
Partly as a result of this, sale for foreign currencies has been replaced
by dollar sales. This change was authorised initially by a new Title IV
enacted in 1961, but since 1966 long-term dollar credits have been
subsumed under Title I and no new local currency sale agreements
have been concluded under this title since the end of 1971.[8] Nonetheless, substantial amounts of foreign currency continue to be made
available through repayments of earlier loans. There are currently five
countries in which the supply of US-owned currencies arising from
PL 480 is in excess of requirements, and until recently Tunisia fell into
this category.

In 1966, PL 480 was revised substantially. The requirement that a
commodity must be in 'surplus supply' to be used as food aid was modified to being 'available', and although the new term was hedged with
restrictions, the change resulted in greater flexibility.[9] Furthermore, the
USA gave notice that it would produce agricultural commodities specifically for food aid. Under the revised law, Title III was confined to
barter deals and lost its responsibilities for providing food to multilateral
organisations, which now fall under Title II.

Yet further changes were introduced by the International Development and Food Assistance Act of 1977. Title I has been amended so
that 75 per cent of sales must go to countries which meet the poverty
criteria established by the International Development Association
(IDA),* and also so that it is now possible for the US Government to cut
off food aid to states that violate human rights. A further amendment to
Title I allows high protein and blended or fortified foods to be sold to
the recipient country at prices which discount the cost of processing;
this is the first time that sale at anything other than prevailing world
market levels has been permitted. The act has created a 'Food for
Development' programme as part of an extended Title III under which
funds derived from the local sale of commodities supplied under Title
I need not be repaid if these are used in agricultural and rural development projects. Thus, whereas American food aid used to be in grant

* The International Development Association is an affiliate of the World Bank
(IBRD) which promotes economic development by providing finance on more
flexible terms than conventional loans.

Table 2.3: Gross Cost of Financing Programmes Carried out under the Agricultural Trade Development and Assistance Act of 1954, Public Law 480, 83d Cong., as amended, 1 July 1954, through 30 June 1975 (in millions $)

Fiscal year ending 30 June	Title I		Title II, donations abroad		Title III	Total
	Sales for foreign currency	Long-term dollar and convertible foreign currency credit sales	Famine and other emergency relief	Voluntary agency programmes	Bartered material for supplemental stockpile	
1955	129.5	—	86.9	214.5		430.9
1956	624.2	—	93.6	271.2	—	989.0
1957	1,396.4	—	124.9	234.1	217.3	1,972.7
1958	1,144.7	—	121.4	254.3	83.9	1,604.3
1959	1,113.3	—	97.9	178.7	314.7	1,704.6
1960	1,308.0	—	95.5	130.8	192.4	1,726.7
1961	1,557.3	—	198.6	169.3	200.5	2,125.7
1962	1,606.1	29.0	241.9	191.7	193.3	2,262.0
1963	1,739.4	80.3	215.6	238.8	99.7	2,373.8
1964	1,636.2	65.1	228.2	341.6	37.7	2,308.8
1965	1,505.8	211.0	147.2	174.6	40.6	2,079.2
1966	1,287.8	274.6	222.5	148.3	25.8	1,959.0
1967	1,067.8	221.7	335.9	34.2	32.5	1,692.1
1968	784.8	350.0	344.6	—	25.9	1,505.3

Table 2.3 continued

Year	a	b	c	d	e	
1969	373.0[a]	495.4	364.2	—	1.7	1,234.3
1970	335.3	560.0	351.0	—	0.2	1,246.5
1971	225.2	625.9	395.7	—	0.1	1,246.9
1972	155.0	614.9	524.4	—	—	1,294.3
1973	8.2	736.3	396.1	—	—	1,140.6
1974	0.3	577.8	384.8	—	—	962.9
1975	4.6	767.9	460.4	—	—	1,227.7
Total	17,997.7[a]	5,609.9[b]	5,431.3[c]	2,582.1[d]	1,466.3[e]	33,087.3

a. Represents the gross cost to CCC of financing sales of US agricultural commodities for foreign currency. Includes commodity and other costs, ocean transportation costs, and interest costs.

b. Represents the gross cost to CCC of financing long-term dollar credit sales of US agricultural commodities. Includes commodity and other costs, ocean transportation costs, and interest costs. The export value of commodities financed and ocean transportation costs (except ocean freight differential) are repayable by the importing country or private trade entity.

c. Represents CCC's investment value in commodities made available for donation abroad under Title II of Public Law 490, ocean transportation costs for such donations and for foreign currency for use in self-help activities. Also includes gross cost of foreign donations through non-profit voluntary agencies beginning 1 Jan. 1967.

d. Represents CCC's acquisition cost value, plus the cost of any processing and packaging performed after acquisition, for commodities donated through non-profit voluntary agencies under authority in sec. 416, Agricultural Act of 1949. This authority was repealed by the Food for Peace Act of 1966, Public Law 89–808, and such donations consolidated into new Title II of such act, effective 1 Jan. 1967.

e. Represents the value at which barter materials were transferred to the supplemental stockpile.

Source: USDA, *Food for Peace: Fiscal Year 1975* (Washington, 1977), Table 6.

form only if supplied under Title II, it is now possible for shipments under Title I to be grants as well. However, to qualify for a Food for Development programme, a country must undertake steps 'to improve its food production, marketing, distribution, and storage systems'. The act specifies that a minimum of 5 per cent of Title I funds are to be allocated to Food for Development in 1978, and that this proportion will rise to 10 per cent in 1979 and 15 per cent in 1980 and following years.

The Title I sales programme is the responsibility of the US Department of Agriculture (USDA). Thus, liaison in the recipient country is maintained by an officer in the US Embassy. Title II is a joint responsibility of USDA and the US Agency for International Development (USAID), and liaison in the recipient country is through the USAID office (although, of course, this office is formally attached to the Embassy). The USDA determines the types, quantities and values of the commodities available, while USAID manages the programme design and monitors implementation of the projects. With both titles, the mechanics of purchasing and overseeing the logistics of the food is the responsibility of the Commodity Credit Corporation (CCC), which is part of the Foreign Agriculture Service of USDA.

Title II activities are carried out by a variety of 'co-operating sponsors' who propose programmes for USAID consideration and have responsibility for their implementation. There are three types of co-operating sponsor: (a) non-profit voluntary agencies, both private such as CRS, CARE and CWS,* and intergovernmental like UNICEF; (b) friendly governments operating under bilateral agreements with the USA; and (c) the World Food Programme (WFP). The four recipient countries studied in this book have experience of all three types of co-operating sponsor; all have received WFP aid, and all except Botswana have CRS missions, while in addition Tunisia has experienced Title II food channelled through CARE and on a bilateral government to government basis. Although CRS and CARE obtain most of their food aid under PL 480, the USA is not their sole supplier. Both voluntary agencies have their eyes on the EEC milk supplies.

The changing size of the various titles over the years is shown in Table 2.3, pages 28/9, while the cumulative size and geographical distribution of the Title I programme is conveyed by Table 2.4, page 31, which gives the quantities supplied between fiscal years 1955 and 1975. The largest recipient has been India which has obtained 25 per cent by value f.o.b. of the commodities supplied over this period, while

* Catholic Relief Services; Co-operative for American Relief Everywhere; Church World Service

Table 2.4: US Public Law 480 Title I – Cumulative Quantities Programmed under Agreements signed between Fiscal Years 1955 and 1975* (by region of destination, in thousands)

Region	Wheat and wheat products (bushels)	Feedgrains (bushels)	Rice (cwt)	Cotton (bales)	Tobacco (lb)	Fats and oils (lb)	Dairy products (lb)	Other (lb)
Europe	532,354	152,474	498	3628.3	177,818	3,493,666	46,297	380,813
Africa	157,986	23,900	11,505	458.6	33,559	1,210,305	41,529	49,604
Near East – South Asia	3,485,064	596,436	68,040	3520	138,306	6,947,406	329,187	99,459
Far East – Pacific	522,109	117,286	194,088	8565.6	303,306	638,326	580,400	254,654
Latin America	541,872	47,662	4,006	275.2	34,382	916,353	37,104	59,240

* Quantities shown reflect a combination of quantities shipped under agreements for which all activity is complete, plus quantities programmed in signed agreements for which activity is not complete.

Source: USDA, *Food for Peace: Fiscal Year 1975*, (Washington, 1977), Table 9.

Pakistan, Vietnam and Korea have each received 7-9 per cent.[10] Africa
has received only 3.6 per cent by value overall, but it has received more
than this proportion of fats and oils and of dairy products (8 per cent
and 6 per cent respectively). The geographic distribution of Title II
food aid during this period is given in Table 2.5, below. Again, India
has received the largest share, with 12.5 per cent by value, but generally
Title II is less concentrated than Title I. Tunisia has received 3 per
cent of shipments by value, the same proportion as Egypt, the
Philippines and Vietnam.

Table 2.5: US Public Law 480 Title II — Total Commodities shipped
from 1 July 1954 to 30 June 1975 (by region of destination, weight
and Commodity Credit Corporation dollar value)

Region	Quantity (thousand lb)	Value (thousand $)	Value as % of total value
Europe	9,458,366	1,097,995	16
Asia	31,378,095	2,503,200	36
Near East	24,886,741	1,733,546	25
Africa	6,284,397	458,250	7
Latin America	10,159,610	1,110,817	16

Source: USDA, *Food for Peace: Fiscal Year 1975* (Washington, 1977), Table 18.

These cumulative figures do not indicate changes in emphasis over
time. Figures for the value of Title II food aid shipped in fiscal year
1975 show that while Africa still receives less than some other regions,
its current importance is greater than the aggregate data would suggest.
It accounts for 21 per cent of total shipments, compared with 44 per
cent for Asia, 16 per cent for the Near East and 18 per cent for Latin
America.[11] However, figures on Title I programmed under agreements
signed in fiscal year 1975 suggest that Africa is even less important
than hitherto, since it accounts for only 1.75 per cent by value of the
total.[12]

The European Community

Although the EEC's food aid programme does not have its origins in
the food mountains thrown up by the Common Agricultural Policy
(CAP), there can be little doubt that, as in the USA, the existence of
commodities in surplus supply has profoundly influenced the
Community's policy. The origins of an EEC food aid programme

separate from the bilateral undertakings of its member governments is
to be found in the 1967 Food Aid Convention. The Convention was
the most solid part of the International Grains Arrangement (1967) and
persisted in a modified form when the latter was replaced by a more
limited International Wheat Agreement in 1971. As such, it was
originally regarded as a negotiating concession to the USA related to
the 'Kennedy Round'.[13] As a signatory to the Convention, the EEC was
committed to supply 1.035 million tonnes of cereals food aid annually,
increasing to 1.278 million tonnes in 1973/4 with the enlargement of
the Community. These figures covered both the bilateral commitments
of member states ('national actions') and EEC commitments
('community actions'). The relative proportions of national and
community actions have changed over time, with the latter gradually
rising from 29 per cent in 1968/9 to 55 per cent in 1975/6. The EEC
programme of food aid in dairy products began in 1970, and consists
entirely of community actions. Dairy food aid is supplied outside the
framework of any international agreement, and the stimulus for its
inception and continuation owes much to the EEC's persistent
surpluses. As a result supply has 'remained very much linked to the
levels of availability of these products on the Community market' and
'the Community has not been able to pursue as regular and continuous
a policy for these products as in the field of cereals'.[14] The size of the
European food aid effort is indicated in Table 2.6, page 34, and its
geographical distribution in Table 2.7, page 35. As with PL 480, Asia
has received the largest share, but Africa including the Maghreb has
been the second biggest recipient of cereals, and is currently also the
main recipient of dairy products.

In theory, the EEC applies three criteria when selecting beneficiaries:

(1)   there must be a food shortage which cannot be covered
      through normal commercial channels for various reasons;
(2)   per capita annual income has to be less than $300;
(3)   there must be a balance of payments deficit.

However, in practice the criteria are not very helpful: although aid is
not sent direct to countries that do not satisfy these conditions, they
are not used for priority ranking and rational distribution of food aid
between eligible countries. The general practice appears to be that a
major part of each year's programme is allocated to India and Bangladesh
(together about 60 per cent by quantity), Pakistan and the Sahel, while
the rest is distributed to other countries according to some arbitrary

Table 2.6: Breakdown of EEC Food Aid Commitments by Programme, Product, Quantity and Value (Estimate at World Price)

Cereals programme (commitments)

	1968/9	1969/70	1970/1	1971/2	1972/3	1973/4	1974/5	1975/6	1976/7
Quantity (tonnes)									
Community schemes	301,000	337,000	353,000	414,000	464,400	580,000	643,500	708,000	720,500
National schemes	734,000	698,000	682,000	621,000	696,600	707,000	643,500	579,000	566,500
Total	1,035,000	1,035,000	1,035,000	1,035,000	1,161,000	1,287,000	1,287,000	1,287,000	1,287,000
Value (million units of account)									
Community schemes	19.6	21.9	30.7	29.4	71.0	110.2	86.87	97.9	81.2
National schemes[a]	47.7	45.4	59.3	44.1	106.6	134.3	86.87	80.1	63.8
Total	67.3	67.3	90.0	73.5	177.6	244.5	173.74	178.0	145.0

Other products (commitments)

	1970	1971	1972	1973	1974	1975	1976
Quantity (tonnes)							
Milk	127,000	—	60,000	13,000	55,000	55,000	150,000
Butteroil	37,000	—	15,000	—	45,000	45,000	45,000
Eggs	—	—	500	—	—	—	—
Sugar	—	—	6,150	6,062	6,094	6,100	6,094
Value (million units of account)							
Milk	73.4	—	39.1	8.9	46.0	30.2	76.98
Butteroil	57.9	—	19.6	—	61.1	64.1	68.95
Eggs	—	—	1.2	—	—	—	—
Sugar	—	—	1.6	1.9	3.7	2.3	2.33
Financial contribution	—	—	1.6	1.6	3.8	2.6	1.00
Total	131.3	—	63.1	12.4	114.6	99.2	149.26

a Calculated at the same average per tonne as for Community schemes.

Sources: *The Courier*, No. 47, Jan./Feb. (1978), p. 77; *Information: Development Co-operation* (165/77E) (EEC Commission Information Directorate-General, September 1977).

Table 2.7: Geographic Distribution of EEC Food Aid (% by Quantity)

Cereals	1968/9	1969/70	1970/1	1971/2	1972/3	1973/4
Europe	17	15	10	—	1	3
Maghreb	7	10	19	18	5	4
Africa	9	19	11	16	23	28
Middle East	—	9	18	13	7	10
Asia and Far East	62	46	32	41	46	37
Latin America	—	—	4	3	12	3
International organisations	6	1	6	9	7	16

Dairy products [a]	1970		1971		1972		1973		1974	
	DSM[b]	Oil	DSM	Oil	DSM	Oil	DSM	Oil	DSM	Oil
Europe	—	—	2	—	—	—	—	—	—	..
Maghreb	11	14	4	14	6	10	5	..	..	..
Africa	3	5	21	8	14	6	36	2	17	13
Middle East	25	37	22	43	22	30	20	61	2	6
Asia and Far East	50	19	39	29	31	40	33	24	21	29
Latin America	10	25	11	7	27	14	6	14	..	2
Other	1	—	—	—	—	—	—	—	59[b]	49[b]

— = zero.
.. = negligible.
a. Regional figures include flows through international organisations except in 1974.
b. DSM = dried skim milk.
c. Included in this figure is the contribution to international organisations for which the regional breakdown is unknown.
Sources: *Memorandum on Food Aid Policy on the European Economic Community* (EEC Commission, 6 March 1974), Table 7; *Information: Development and Co-operation* (EEC Commission, Information Directorate General, November 1974), pp. 7—9.

rule of thumb.[15] Apart from 'normal' bilateral allocations, part of each annual programme is distributed through multilateral and voluntary institutions and 10 per cent is reserved for emergencies and disasters. The proportion channelled through institutions ('the indirect flow') varies from year to year and between products. The bulk of cereal aid is disbursed bilaterally ('the direct flow') with only 6-13 per cent going through institutions; however, almost half of the dairy products aid is indirect.[16] Cynics might argue that this difference reflects the different supply position for the two commodities: cereals are a valuable resource for which the Community wants to obtain the maximum political kudos whereas with dairy products a major consideration is how to reduce the embarrasing mountains. Possibly for the same reason, the European Council of Ministers has been more responsive to requests from the Commission to increase the scale of the dairy products programme than it has towards similar efforts for cereals.[17]

Unlike US food aid, EEC aid is all in grant form. However, the provisions for transport vary between different recipients. In theory, 'normal' aid is supplied f.o.b., so the recipient has to pay all transport costs. However, with aid defined as 'emergency aid' which despite its name often resembles development food aid as understood in this book, the EEC may pay external transport costs to the recipient country and even internal costs to the final distribution point as well. Hence, in practice transport costs are often paid. For example, all EEC food aid to Upper Volta has been classified as emergency aid.

The EEC's procedures for processing requests for normal aid are convoluted and time consuming.[18] Getting food aid from the EEC is a lengthy and uncertain enterprise. The two main reasons for this are that the Council discusses and approves the smallest details of each allocation, and that food aid has to be requested and supplied annually. There is a conflict between the Commission and the Council on both scores, with the former pressing for more autonomy and long-term programming. Under current arrangements, requests for normal aid go through three phases before the food arrives in the recipient country. The first phase concerns the compilation and approval of an annual programme; the second involves drafting country agreements; and the third covers the actual supply and transport of the food. In October each year, the Commission starts to prepare separate programmes for cereals, milk powder and butteroil. Requests from ldcs cannot be dealt with individually but must be incorporated into the annual programmes; thus countries that request early must wait for those who request late. The draft programmes prepared in the Directorate-General for Development (DG8) have to be approved consecutively by the 'Ad Hoc Group for Food Aid', which comprises delegated experts of the member-state governments, by the Committee of Permanent Representatives, and by the Council of Ministers. The draft may be rejected at any stage and referred back to the Commission. In 1974, for example, there was a 201-day time lag between the completion of the draft milk powder programme and its approval by the Council because the draft was rejected by the Ad Hoc Group; the following year when matters ran more smoothly the time lag was only 89 days. Only after the Council has approved the annual programme can negotiations commence with each proposed recipient, and only after all these complications are overcome are tenders published for the supply of food. At this stage, responsibility is transferred to the Directorate-General for Agriculture (DG6) which has to acquire and transport the food.

Table 2.8: Time Lag in Preparing EEC Food Aid Programme

Commodity	Year	Days elapsed between beginning of October and approval of programme by Council of Ministers
Cereals	1973	225
Cereals	1974	171
Cereals	1975	153
Milk powder	1973	79
Milk powder	1974	274
Milk powder	1975	237
Butteroil	1974	154
Butteroil	1975	258

Source: *Studie Voedselhulp Europese Gemeenschappen — Deel 1* (Instituut voor Sociaal-economische Studie van Minder Ontwikkelde Gebieden, Amsterdam, May 1977).

The delay on each phase can vary widely. Table 2.8, above, gives the time lag for the annual programme phase for the years 1973-5. The country agreement phase varies between recipients and years, but it takes on average 39 days for the Commission to draft an agreement, and 63 days for the recipient to approve it.[19] Until 1975 each separate agreement had to be approved by the Council, but the Commission is now empowered to use a standard form. A further 73 days on average elapse between approval of the agreement by the recipient and publication of tenders for the food.

On average, it takes 12 months from the date on which a request is made for normal aid to the date on which tenders for delivery are sought, and on top of this comes the time needed for supply and delivery. This average figure conceals major variations. An analysis of the time taken from date of request to date of arrival of the food in a European port ready for shipment gives the figures shown in Table 2.9, page 38, for three recipient countries over three years (1972/3-1974/5).[20]

Table 2.9: Time Taken from Date of Request to Arrival Date at
European Port for Shipment to Three Recipient Countries, 1972/3–
1974/5

| | Days | | |
	Average period	Shortest period	Longest period
Sri Lanka	503	420	634
Bangladesh	479	198	856
Egypt	431	300	515

Emergency aid procedures are more rapid because requests can be
met from the reserve stock of food aid and do not have to wait upon
Council approval of an overall annual programme. Nevertheless, it
still takes an average of six months from the date a request is made until
the approval of an agreement by both donor and recipient. As a result
emergency food aid does not always arrive until after the emergency
has passed. This not only undermines its *raison d'être,* but may actually
be dysfunctional for the recipient if the food aid competes with a good
post-emergency harvest. Emergency aid is designed to alleviate
temporary falls in food production as, for example, would follow a
drought. It is supplemented by a third category of relief, disaster aid,
which supplies food when there is an acute shortage following an earthquake or the like. The EEC is able to respond very rapidly to requests
for disaster aid, but this is not given more prominence in this book
because none of the four countries studied has received it.

The World Food Programme

The World Food Programme (WFP) was founded in 1963 under the
umbrella of the UN and FAO partly as a device by the USA to encourage
'burden sharing'. The bulk of its food aid is tied to well defined projects
in the recipient country, and WFP has become something of a champion
for the cause of project food aid. Although small in comparison with
PL 480, WFP is growing fast, has acquired a justifiable reputation as
a relatively effective operator, and is increasingly influential in
determining food aid policy. Following the 1974 World Food
Conference, the WFP's governing body, hitherto the Intergovernmental
Committee (IGC), was reconstituted as the Committee on Food Aid
Policies and Programmes (CFA) with a broader remit to 'evolve and
co-ordinate short-term and longer-term food aid policies . . .'[21]

The World Food Programme's emphasis on projects requires a heavy staff input. It currently employs over 800 people, of whom 251 are based in its Rome headquarters while the remainder, comprising 147 professional officers and 412 local staff, are to be found in almost every ldc in the world. There is an important project management division in Rome, split into six regional branches,[22] an emergency unit and an evaluation service which regularly monitors projects; the scope of the evaluations may not be as broad or deep as academics might wish, but at least they occur.[23]

Requests for food aid can be submitted at any time, and are processed in one of three ways. If the food value, based on current international prices, does not exceed $1 million the Executive Director may take responsibility for approval,[24] otherwise it is considered by the Committee on Food Aid Policies and Programmes at one of its biannual sessions, unless there is a need for urgency, when the Committee can take its decision by correspondence. All projects are appraised in co-operation with the relevant UN agencies and in addition, with more complex projects, WFP may commission an economic appraisal by a consultant or a team representing interested parties before the preparation of a report for approval. If the project is approved, a plan of operations is drafted incorporating a formal agreement between WFP and the recipient, a description of the project, the inputs to be provided by the host, the commodities to be supplied by WFP and details of the information to be supplied during the life time of the project to facilitate evaluation. When WFP is satisfied that any preliminary preparations required of the recipient have been accomplished and that the project is operational, it issues a Letter of Readiness and distribution of commodities can begin.

These hoops that have to be passed through can be time consuming. The Committee on Food Aid Policies and Programmes meets only twice a year, and the recipient may be slow to produce the information required by WFP. An analysis of 159 projects from sub-Saharan Africa shows that the time lapse between the submission of a request and the start of food distribution ranges between 0 and 59 months, with a mean time lag of 20 months and a mode of 12 months.[25] The response to emergency operations tends to be quicker than for development projects, since a special rapid approval system exists. Although the time lags can be as great as or greater than those experienced with EEC food aid, they tend to cause the recipient fewer administrative headaches. Unlike the EEC, the WFP can make commitments over several years (up to a maximum of five at a time) and it is therefore unnecessary and unusual to pass through the hoops every single year. Furthermore, while there are delays, these normally result from difficulties that arise with specific countries or projects, and the whole programme is not held up as it is when the EEC Commission and Council cannot agree.

The World Food Programme's food aid, like that of the EEC, is all supplied as a grant; but unlike the EEC, it is also all paid c.i.f. Until 1972, WFP covered only transport costs to the recipient's frontier, but since then it has been able to pay a proportion of internal transport costs for the least developed countries. The proportion was initially 30 per cent but has since been raised to 50 per cent.

The Programme raises assistance mainly through the mechanism of the biennial pledging period. Every two years a pledging conference is convened and donors are requested to commit themselves to provide over the biennium, which starts 11 months after the conference, certain quantities or values of aid in any combination of commodities and cash. Because the programme raises the bulk of its resources in this way it is only able to commit itself to supply recipients with food up to the end of the following biennium. When, as is often the case, projects are planned for a longer period of, say, five years, WFP is able to give only advisory figures for the probable level of its support after the first two years or so. These pledges have been supplemented since 1969 by contributions made under the Food Aid Convention (FAC). Separate agreements are signed with each country making contributions to the Programme under FAC. Sharp fluctuations in the size of a donor's pledges or contribution from one year to the next can embarrass the Programme. So, too, can variations in the proportions of different commodities supplied. Dried skim milk (DSM) has been the subject of particularly violent fluctuations in recent years, and as a result of shortfalls in its supply in the early 1970s, a number of substitute foods such as corn soya milk (CSM) were introduced since they used other commodities to supplement the DSM.

Table 2.10, page 41, shows the increase in WFP's resources since its inception, while Table 2.11, page 42, gives the geographic distribution of expenditure. As with the other donors, Black Africa is a relatively small recipient, but unlike the others the largest share of WFP aid has gone not to Asia but to North Africa and the Near East. If commitments to development projects alone are considered, the biggest recipient (up to 1977) has been India, with $405.2m, followed by Egypt with $270.1m; then comes Syria with only $139.9m.

The main contributor to WFP's coffers is the USA. Between 1963 and 1976 it accounted for 36 per cent of total pledges. The next largest contributor was Canada, with 18 per cent of total pledges,

Table 2.10: Resources of the World Food Programme: Pledges,
Contributions and Miscellaneous Income Available

	1963/5	1966/8	Pledging period 1969/70 (US $ million)	1971/2	1973/4	1975/6
Commodities						
Pledges	59.2	127.6	221.1	178.8	267.1	365.5
FAC	−	3.4	24.7	29.4	26.1[a]	n.a.
Total commodities	59.2	131.0	245.8	208.2	293.2	365.5
Cash						
Pledges	19.0	35.1	35.2	34.0	51.7	136.7
FAC	−	0.7	4.8	6.4	10.4[a]	n.a.
Miscellaneous income[b]	10.8	3.1	4.8	5.3	4.0[d]	n.a.
Total cash	19.8	38.9	44.8	45.7	66.1[d]	136.7
Services						
Pledges	6.4	26.8	27.0	37.0	41.2	40.0
Total services	6.4	26.8	27.0	37.0	41.2	40.0
Total resources	85.4	196.7	317.6	290.9	400.5	542.2
Total pledged resources	84.6	189.5	283.3	249.8	360.0	542.2
Percentages of total pledged resources[c]						
Commodities	70	67	78	72	74	67
Cash and services	30	33	22	28	26	33
	100	100	100	100	100	100

a = total of contributions for 1973/4 and 1974/5.
b = interest on liquid holdings and refunds from underwriters and insurance
    companies in respect of claims for losses and damage to foodstuffs.
c = excluding FAC contributions and miscellaneous income.
d = estimated.

Sources: *Ten Years of World Food Programme Development Aid 1963–72* (Rome,
1973); *Resources of the Programme: Report by the Executive Director,* Doc
WFP/IGC. 28/4 Add 1 (September 1975); *Resources of the Programme and
Recommendations for the Pledging Target for the Period 1977–78: Report by the
Executive Director,* Doc WFP/IGC: 28/4 (June 1975).

followed by the EEC with 12 per cent.[26] During the 1977/8 pledging
period the proportion of total pledges made by the main donors was
30 per cent for the USA, 22 per cent for Canada and 8 per cent for
Saudi Arabia.

Table 2.11: Geographic Distribution of WFP Development Commitments, Cumulative Data, 1963–1977[a]

	1963		1965		1968		1971		1974		1977	
	$m	%	$m	%	$m	%	$m	%	$m	%	$m	%
Sub-Saharan Africa	4	17	14	21	67	15	153	14	291	16	580	19
Asia and Pacific	2	10	13	20	106	24	290	27	530	29	1,032	34
Europe	2	7	2	3	9	2	16	1	22	1	38	1
Latin America	7	31	13	20	42	10	149	14	270	14	354	12
North Africa and Near East	7	35	23	36	212	49	473	44	744	40	1,051	34
Cumulative total	22		65		436		1,081		1,857		3,055	

a = position as at 31 December.

Source: *Ten Years of World Food Programme Development Aid 1963–72* (Rome, 1973), Table 7; updated to end December 1977 by WFP.

Canada and France

Although Canada is one of the main donors, it is not considered at
great length here because, out of the four recipients studied, only
Tunisia has received Canadian development food aid. Similarly, only
Tunisia and Upper Volta have received French food aid. In the case of
both donors, the transfers have been very straightforward and they
accord the recipient a maximum discretion in deciding how to use the
food aid, which is generally supplied in bulk.

Canada is the second largest bilateral food aid donor, although its
efforts fall far short of those of the USA. Like the USA, its food aid
policy has its origins in surplus disposal, particularly of cereals, although
there has since been increasing emphasis on development considerations.
Canada began to give food aid in the 1950s, but not until the 1960s
did flows reach substantial levels. The value of aid in recent years is
indicated by Table 2.12, below, and its geographic distribution by
Table 2.13, page 44. Over the period 1970-3, the budgetary allocation
for food aid remained fairly steady, so the quantities shipped fell
drastically as unit costs rose. However, since then there has been a
doubling of the money value of aid which has partly redressed the
balance.

Table 2.12: Value of Canadian Food Aid ($ million)

	1965/7 (average)	1970	1971	1972	1973	1974	1975	1976
Bilateral	71.2	80.6	71.8	73.4	75.1	124.4	171.6	128.8
Multilateral	n.a.	18.6	16.7	14.4	20.8	14.8	91.7	60.8
Total	—	99.2	88.5	87.8	95.9	139.2	263.3	189.6

Source: *Development Co-operation: 1977 Review,* Table A.12; *Development
Co-operation: 1975 Review,* Table 12 (Organisation for Economic Co-operation
and Development, Paris).

The food aid of Canada is more geographically concentrated than
that of the other donors considered above. Asia is the most favoured
region, with Africa a poor but improving second. As usual, India has
received the lion's share, with 60 per cent by value over the period
1966-72. In line with the shift in philosophy away from surplus disposal,
commodities other than cereals have been included in food aid shipments. Wheat and flour still form the bulk of aid (71 per cent by value
in 1973/4) but dairy products, fish concentrates and vegetable oil are
growing in importance. Almost all Canadian food aid is supplied as a

grant c.i.f. The provision of transport costs is fairly generous since Canada has a small merchant fleet and therefore most of the food is shipped by foreign carriers. Aid is allocated annually in a fairly tight schedule defined at one end by the date that the government fixes the financial ceiling for the year (normally February–March), and at the other by the freezing of the St Lawrence river in November–December.

Table 2.13: Geographic Distribution of Canadian Food Aid Disbursements, 1966-72*

	Europe	Africa	Asia
1966			
$m	—	1.8	83.1
%	—	2	98
1967			
$m	—	4.7	69.4
%	—	6	94
1968			
$m	—	8.72	44.36
%		16	83
1969			
$m	—	7.95	43.86
%		15	85
1970			
$m	2.32	11.8	64.12
%	3	15	82
1971			
$m	4.53	8.86	55.03
%	7	13	80
1972			
$m	—	12.8	56.37
%		19	81

* Percentages may not add up due to rounding.

Source: *Food Aid* (Organisation for Economic Co-operation and Development, Paris, 1974), Table 31.

Until 1968, France's only contribution to food aid was through a $1m annual contribution to WFP. However, following signature of the Food Aid Convention it began to supply cereal food aid on a bilateral basis. Since its dairy products aid is channelled through the EEC, France's bilateral food aid is confined to cereals, and overwhelmingly to wheat and flour. The value of its aid since 1970 is shown in Table 2.14,

below. Geographic coverage is concentrated on a few countries.
Tunisia, Egypt, Indonesia, Pakistan, Sri Lanka and Bangladesh have
been among the chief recipients since 1969, and in addition since 1972,
special emphasis has been given to sub-Saharan Africa and in particular
the states of the Sahel.[27] French bilateral food aid is supplied as a
grant, but except for food shipped to the Sahel it does not cover
transport costs.

Table 2.14: Value of French Food Aid ($ million)

	1970	1971	1972	1973	1974	1975	1976
Bilateral	13.7	13.7	5.2	30.3	41.5	32.2	20.8
Multilateral	0.9	0.1	27.3	37.2	63.7	51.5	29.4
Total	14.6	13.8	32.5	67.5	105.2	83.7	50.2

Source: *Development Co-operation: 1977 Review,* Table A.13; *Development
Co-operation: 1975 Review,* Table 13 (Organisation for Economic Co-operation
and Development, Paris).

The Regulatory Framework

In the arcane language of the food aid fraternity, the system is policed
by the CSD with its main instrument the UMR. The initials CSD stand
for a body that is, in theory at least, very powerful but of which little is
known outside the food trade: the Consultative Subcommittee on
Surplus Disposal. The CSD includes representatives of the main food
exporting and importing nations, and it meets about ten times a year in
Washington to keep under review the disposal of agricultural surpluses,
and in particular proposed shipments of food aid. It was founded in
1954 following an FAO resolution which recommended that food donor
governments should 'dispose of such products in an orderly manner so
as to avoid any undue pressure resulting in sharp falls in prices on world
markets', and that 'there should be an undertaking from both importing
and exporting countries that such arrangements will be made without
harmful interference with normal patterns of production and
international trade'.[28] In short, the CSD was established to ensure that
food aid did not disrupt commercial trade, and it retains this function
still. All members are required to report on any transaction classified
as food aid, and if any other member is unhappy about it there is a
debate, although the CSD itself can not apply sanctions to enforce its
views. In deciding whether or not to approve of such a transaction, it
is in theory guided by the FAO principles of surplus disposal which

inter alia frown on aid that substitutes for commercial imports, although there are let-out clauses which provide, for example, that the danger of displacement 'will have to be weighed against the character and extent of the benefits resulting from the contribution to the [recipient's] welfare programme.'[29]

The main instrument of the CSD for deciding whether or not a proposed food aid transaction displaces commercial imports is the UMR, or Usual Marketing Requirement. A UMR is determined for each recipient country each year, and is supposed to indicate its 'normal' level of commercial imports: food aid must not be supplied on such a scale that the recipient fails to purchase commercially food equal to its UMR. The level of the UMR is based on past import figures, with allowances for balance of payments problems and changes in domestic production. In practice, of course, the determination of a UMR is a fairly haphazard undertaking for countries with wide annual fluctuations in food imports, and there is ample evidence that the CSD's precepts, notably that food aid should not displace commercial sales, are evaded.

Notes

1. The basis on which food aid should be valued has been a source of some controversy, and is dealt with in Chapter 3. Throughout Chapter 2 the value figures given will be those of the donor.

2. See Bibliography: OECD (1976a), pp. 148–9.

3. See Bibliography: Singer and Maxwell (1978), p. 2.

4. See Bibliography: OECD (1974a), p. 88.

5. See Bibliography: Mettrick (1969), p. 32.

6. See Bibliography: USDA (1977a), Table 2.

7. Ibid., Table 6.

8. USDA (1977a), p. 4.

9. Public Law 95–88, August 3 1977.

10. USDA (1977a), Table 10.

11. Ibid., Table 17.

12. Ibid., Table 12.

13. See Bibliography: Jones (1976a) provides an excellent analysis of European food policies including the role of food aid.

14. Commission of the European Communities, Information Directorate-General, *Information: Development and Co-operation* (November 1974, Brussels), p. 2.

15. See Bibliography: Klaasse Bos (1978); and ISMOG (1977).

16. The proportions refer to the years 1973–5; ISMOG (1977).

17. Klaasse Bos (1978).

18. These have been studied in detail, with special reference to Niger, Upper Volta, Sri Lanka, Bangladesh and Egypt in ISMOG (1977); an English summary is incorporated in Klaasse Bos (1978).

19. Average for 1973–5; ISMOG (1977).

20. ISMOG (1977).

21. Resolution XXII, *Report of the World Food Conference 1974* (New York, 1975), p. 18, para. 6.

22. Latin America and Caribbean, North Africa and the Near East, West Africa, East Africa, the Mediterranean and Europe, Asia and the Far East.

23. For further details of WFP's organisation see Bibliography: Shaw (1970).

24. Aid in emergencies, up to any limit within the global earmarking for the year, is approved by the Director-General of FAO on the recommendation of the WFP's Executive Director, case by case in accordance with needs and aid received from other sources.

25. Calculated from WFP figures.

26. See Bibliography: WFP (1973a), WFP (1975e).

27. See Bibliography: OECD (1974b), p. 48.

28. Resolution No. 14 (53), FAO 7th Session: Bibliography, FAO (1972a) p. 2.

29. FAO (1972a), pp. 6–7.

3 THE RECIPIENTS

No four countries can be typical of a continent. Indeed the four countries studied in this book — Tunisia, Botswana, Lesotho and Upper Volta — are in a sense untypical since, as explained in Chapter 1, they were selected as being 'good of their kind'. However, while they are obviously not typical or representative, between them they do illustrate many facets of contemporary Africa, and most of the ways in which food aid can be supplied and used. Table 3.1, below, sets out a few comparative economic indices for the four countries, from which it is clear that they vary widely in terms of size, wealth and growth rates. They also differ in historical and cultural backgrounds, and importantly, in their prospects for economic growth. Tunisia's GNP is 21 times the size of Lesotho's, and even in per capita terms it is over four times as great. Botswana's per capita GNP growth rate during the period 1960-75 was over eight times more rapid than Upper Volta's. Population densities range from 40 persons/sq km in Lesotho to 1 person/sq km in Botswana. Tunisia and Upper Volta are French speaking and have administrative traditions inherited from French colonialism; Botswana and Lesotho are English speaking and their administration has been influenced by British practice. Tunisia is also Arabic and wholly Muslim, Upper Volta is partly Muslim, while Botswana and Lesotho are both firmly Christian.

Table 3.1: Comparative Economic Indicators for Tunisia, Botswana, Lesotho and Upper Volta

	Population (000)	GNP[a] ($m)	GNP[a] (per capita, $)	Growth rates, 1960–75 (%) Population	Real GNP (per capita)
Tunisia	5,594	4,090	730	2.2	4.1[b]
Botswana[c]	666	230	350	1.9	6.0
Lesotho[c]	1,217	190	160	2.2	4.6
Upper Volta	6,032	640	110	2.1	0.7

a. GNP at 1975 market prices.
b. GNP per capita growth rate relates to 1961–75.
c. Estimates of GNP per capita and its growth rate are tentative.
Source: *World Bank Atlas: Population, Per Capita Product, and Growth Rates* (World Bank Washington, 1977), p. 14.

Table 3.2: FAO Indices of Per Capita Food Production*

	Tunisia	Botswana	Lesotho	Upper Volta
1964	108	99	94	103
1965	108	106	98	106
1966	97	113	92	105
1967	99	131	95	107
1968	99	130	95	106
1969	89	128	94	103
1970	105	121	92	102
1971	126	133	92	93
1972	120	117	69	86
1973	126	131	107	77
1974	128	139	97	82
1975	147	143	97	84

* 1961–5 = 100.
Source: FAO, *Production Yearbook 1975* (Rome), Table 9.

Table 3.3: Cereals Trade of Tunisia, Botswana, Lesotho and Upper Volta (\$ thousands)

	1968	1969	1970	1971	1972	1973	1974	1975
Tunisia								
Imports	24,080	40,318	36,330	19,670	23,910	36,670	53,370	56,520
Exports	128	220	1,160	1,560	950	2,760	460	460
Botswana								
Imports	4,720	3,280	5,430	5,400	6,900	10,400	7,560	8,100
Exports	2	140	–	150	–	–	–	–
Lesotho								
Imports	7,346	9,710	10,900	12,640	16,600	16,800	21,000	22,300
Exports	251	596	200	200	190	120	240	250
Upper Volta								
Imports	1,838	1,739	2,390	1,600	3,670	4,300	11,400	15,400
Exports	81	48	20	40	–	–	–	–

Source: FAO, *Trade Yearbook* (Rome).

Despite these differences, there are some similarities. All are net importers of food, and although Tunisia has the potential to be self-sufficient in the middle term, there is no such prospect for the other three. All are generally dry countries which are subject to periodic droughts that can persist for several years and play havoc with domestic agriculture. Some aggregate figures on food production and cereal trade are given in Tables 3.2 and 3.3, page 49. Furthermore, all four export labour: Batswana and Basotho migrants go most frequently to South Africa, Voltaiques to Ivory Coast and Tunisians to France and Libya. Such migration has had a generally adverse effect on agricultural production by robbing the rural economy of its most able-bodied members. They have all received food aid, both on a continuing basis for development purposes and as emergency relief. Between them they have experience of the USA, Canada, the EEC, France and the World Food Programme (WFP) as development food aid donors, and of a wide variety of types and forms of food aid. Taken together, they show that the impact of food aid can vary according to the wealth of the receiving country, its growth rate and its prospects, and that methods of utilising food aid that may be feasible in the circumstances of one country may not be feasible in those of another.

Tunisia

Tunisia is the richest of the four countries. It has the best physical and administrative infrastructure and it has received development food aid over a longer period from more donors and in more ways than have the others. It has also been independent the longest.

It can date its history back to pre-Christian times and the ascendancy of Carthage. A French Protectorate was forced upon the *Bey* of Tunis in 1883, and heralded 73 years of French rule which ended in 1956. The first decade of independence was characterised by rapid and dramatic changes in relations between the new state and France which have influenced the use of food aid. Relations were marred in the early years by France's refusal to evacuate its troops, and eight months after independence Tunisia temporarily severed diplomatic relations. In 1957 France suspended economic aid, and in 1958 diplomatic ties were again broken off. Relations between the two countries began to mend after 1958 and the accession to power of General de Gaulle, and survived the announcement in 1960 of a Tunisian decision to purchase all agricultural land in the country owned by French citizens for distribution to indigenous farmers. French refusal to abandon control of Bizerta led to a further cooling and a suspension of diplomatic relations in 1961 after 800 Tunisians had been killed in an attempt to sieze the town and base, but this thorny problem was finally resolved the following year. In 1963 agreement was reached for the transfer of 370,000 acres of foreign-owned farm land to the Tunisian Government, and the two countries established trade and finance agreements to help reduce Tunisia's balance of payments deficit with France. However, this cordiality was soon upset when, in 1964, the Tunisians negated the 1963 agreement on the transfer of French land by enacting leglislation which permitted the expropriation of all foreign-owned land; in response, French financial aid was immediately suspended and then cancelled.

The nationalisation of foreign-owned land was part of a trend towards a more socialist agricultural policy, associated with the powerful Minister of Finance and Planning, Ahmed Ben Salah. Between 1964 and 1969, Ben Salah introduced a programme for the progressive collectivisation of agriculture, which was reversed sharply in September 1969, and followed the next year by Ben Salah's own trial and imprisonment. The main feature of ministerial politics since then has been the emergence and subsequent fall of a string of possible successors to the aging President Bourguiba. Following Ben Salah's downfall farmers were given the option to leave the state system, which was soon dismantled, so that by mid 1970 approximately 50 per cent of the cultivated land was in private hands, while 30 per cent was worked by co-operatives and the rest was in large estates or under forest. The government has expressed its intention to break up large estates. Nevertheless, the distribution of land holdings is still skewed, and in 1972 41 per cent of holdings were of less than 5 hectares, and between them covered over 7 per cent of the total cultivable area, while at the other end of the scale the 1.4 per cent of holdings over 200 hectares covered 22 per cent of the total area.[1]

Agriculture is still the mainstay of the economy, and during the decade 1962-71 it absorbed over 20 per cent of the country's investment. The major crops are wheat, barley, olives, grapes, citrus fruits and dates, with wheat predominantly in the north and centre, and olives in the centre. The country is subject to periodic droughts, and in 1969 production was severely disrupted by floods following three years of drought. In addition to agriculture, there are exploited deposits of minerals, notably petroleum and phosphates, and a small industrial sector. The government's current economic strategy is to encourage both public and private sectors, and to attract foreign private investment in export-oriented industries. Tunisia usually runs a balance of trade deficit, which is offset by receipts from tourism, foreign aid, and also by remittances from migrant workers. In 1973 an estimated 200,000 Tunisians were living abroad, and net emigration of workers was 19,000, although in 1974 this figure fell to 9,000. The growth in emigration has occurred largely since 1960.

Botswana

In the 12 years since it became independent, Botswana has seen its economic prospects transformed. It came to independence in 1966 in the middle of a particularly severe drought with over 100,000 people (one-sixth of the population) dependent on food aid handouts, and it needed British aid just to balance the recurrent budget. Since then diamond, copper/nickel and coal mines have been developed, although only the first is notably lucrative, and the agreement covering the division of revenue accruing to the Southern African Customs Union (to which Botswana, Lesotho, Swaziland and South Africa belong) has been revised in favour of the three black states. As a result the capacity of the government to invest has changed dramatically.

However, this improvement in public finance and impressive increases in macroeconomic aggregates are best seen not as signs that the economy as a whole is developing, but as providing the possibility that it will be able to do so in the future. Six out of seven Batswana still live in the rural areas, and 80 per cent of rural households are directly involved in agriculture, which contributes 35 per cent of total rural incomes. In aggregate terms, rearing livestock is the dominant agricultural activity, which contributes 80 per cent of total agricultural production.[2] However, since the distribution of livestock ownership is highly skewed, arable farming is of more importance to the poorest households than this overall figure suggests. In consequence the economy is still vulnerable to the periodic droughts which often recur over a number of years, and it is estimated that one of moderate intensity would halve production in the subsistence sector.[3] Although the very low average population density of one person/sq km is not typical because the majority of the populace live in the east of the country, Botswana is still a sparsely peopled land with great distances between settlements. As a result of this and of past poverty, the physical infrastructure of the country is very poor. The settlement pattern itself is unusual: most Batswana owe allegiance to one of a small number of major villages where they maintain a dwelling even though they often have other houses at their arable smallholding, cattle post or in one of the four towns, where they may spend most of the year. As a result, the very low average density of population is combined with some of the largest villages in Africa. Traditional land tenure practice is, in theory, highly equitable because every Motswana is entitled to as much land as he can utilise efficiently. However, utilisation capacity is dependent on access to water and draught power, both of which favour the rich, and also on the availability of human labour: households headed by a single woman or by the elderly are particularly vulnerable. As a result of the skewed distribution of draught power poor farmers are not only more vulnerable to drought but also to late rainfall than are rich ones. Normal practice is for farmers without cattle to borrow or hire draught power from their richer neighbours. Naturally those with cattle tend to plough their own lands before helping others, so that if the rains are late and the ploughing season shortened there may simply be no time for poor farmers to plough.

Table 3.4: Net Aid Receipts Per Head of Five African Countries, 1972–4 ($)

| Country | Annual average aid receipts per head 1972–4 from[a] | | |
	UK	Other DAC[b]	Total
Swaziland	10.2	8.9	19.1
Botswana	11.1	57.6	68.7
Kenya	1.8	8.2	10.0
Malawi	3.5	4.0	7.5
Lesotho	4.7	9.7	14.4

a. The figures are for official development assistance only and exclude the operations of the Commonwealth Development Corporation (CDC). They are net of amortisation but not of interest.
b. DAC = Development Assistance Committee, OECD.
Source: Robert Wood and Kathryn Morton, 'Has British Aid Helped Poor Countries?' *ODI Review,* no. 1, 1977, p. 53.

Party politics are a low-key affair.[4] Cleavages within society have been fairly shallow and cross-cutting in the past, and the unprecedented change in the country's fortunes has enabled the government to spend its way out of trouble so far, although this happy state of affairs cannot be expected to last since economic change creates its own divisions. The dominant feature of the polity over the past 12 years has been the powerful position of the civil service and, within the bureaucracy, of the finance ministry. One corollary of this has been that Botswana has been extraordinarily successful in attracting foreign aid, even allowing for small-country bias, as may be seen from Table 3.4, page 53, which compares the annual average per capita aid receipts of five African countries.[5]

Until 1976 Botswana belonged to the Southern African Monetary Area and used the Rand as legal tender. However, it then withdrew and issued its own currency, the Pula. Since the events covered in this book mainly predate this change, most of the values referred to are denominated in Rand. However, figures for the period since 1976 are also sometimes given in Pula. (See the Appendix, page 210, for conversion rates for all the currencies used in the book.)

Lesotho

Lesotho is small, overpopulated, poor and vulnerable. Like Botswana, its economy is dominated by South Africa which surrounds it and to which it is joined in a customs and a monetary union. Only 13 per cent of the country is suitable for arable cultivation, and this factor together with rapid population growth, serious erosion problems and declining agricultural yields has been partly responsible for a situation in which only 80 per cent of the country's food requirements can be produced locally. Undoubtedly Lesotho's rural economy has also been under-mined by its position in the periphery of the Southern African economic system, and it can be argued that the more obvious causes of its present predicament -- population outstripping production, erosion, and falling yields -- are merely the outward signs of this more fundamental problem. Traditional rural activities still provide an important source of income for about 85 per cent of the population and contribute some 45 per cent of GDP; the land tenure system is similar to that in Botswana. However, the most important source of income for many families comes from migratory labour in the South African mines. At present, a substantial proportion of the male labour force (up to 60 per cent according to some accounts) is absent from Lesotho while working as miners in South Africa, and it has been calculated that their total earnings may amount to over R60m a year, or more than Lesotho's own GDP.[6]

Two political events of recent years should be mentioned for their effects on the country's economic policy. The first is the constitutional crisis of 1970. The first elections after independence were held in January 1970. It became clear during the counting of votes that the governing Basutoland National Party (BNP) had been defeated by the opposition Basutoland Congress Party (BCP), but the government then halted the count and suspended the constitution while alleging that the opposition had used force and fraud. Following the crisis, Britain suspended aid to Lesotho, but this was resumed after a change in government at Westminster in June 1970. The aftermath of the crisis also saw a shake-out of the civil service which was associated to some extent with the opposition. Although neither event has had long-term effects on economic policy, they produced a certain hiatus in some development projects and may have contributed to a continuation of the extreme frugality that has characterised Lesotho's recurrent expenditure practices over the years but for which some of the justification has disappeared since the renegotiation of the Southern African Customs Union Agreement in 1969.

The second political event to be noted was the eruption of wide-spread violence at a number of South African mines in 1974 which prompted some 10,000-15,000 Basotho migrant workers to return to Lesotho. Although most of them later went back to South Africa, this crisis underlined the unstable nature of Lesotho's main source of employment and the government sought UNDP (UN Development Programme) and World Bank advice on how to cope with the unemployment problems that could be expected to follow a repetition of the exodus. As a result of this advice it was decided to create a labour intensive construction industry. These plans are still at an early stage, but it is the government's intention to develop a pilot Labour Intensive Construction Unit during the current plan period. Until now, the only widespread form of labour intensive construction has been food for work. Under the new plan, food for work is to be continued but it is not to be expanded and, in theory at least, the bulk of labour intensive activities will be wage earning.

Upper Volta

Upper Volta is small, populous and poor with a stagnant economy. The country suffers from overpopulation in some areas, even though other areas are underutilised. The average density is 22 persons/sq km but in a central belt running from Ouahigouya south east towards Zabré and including the capital, Ouagadougou, the density rises to 50 persons/sq km, and even up to 70 persons/sq km (and not just in the capital city). In other parts the density is 10 persons/sq km or less, notably around Bobo-Dioulasso in the west, Fada N'Gourma in the east, and Dori in the north. One reason for the low population density in some parts is the dryness of the climate and poor soils, although only the north (13 per cent of the country) is classified as Sahelian. In the west, however, it is not the absence but the overabundance of water, or rather a corollary of it, that has hindered settlement. The valleys of the Volta rivers (White, Black and Red) are infested with flies carrying river blindness (onchocerciasis). With assistance from the World Health Organisation (WHO) and other agencies, areas of potentially valuable agricultural land are being cleared of river blindness, and a major government policy with which food aid has been associated involves resettling farmers from the overcrowded areas on these new lands. An important response to the overpopulation and stagnant economy is migration, notably to neighbouring Ivory Coast. According to the government's estimates, there were in 1970 some 535,000 migrants, of whom 155,000 could be counted as temporary.[7] Remittances from temporary migrants play an important part in the Voltaique balance of payments. It is estimated that in 1972, for example, total remittances by Voltaique workers in Ivory Coast totalled CFA (West African franc) 5,500 million,[8] or 5 per cent of the GNP that year as estimated by the World Bank.

The remittances from abroad are important because ever since independence Upper Volta has run a trade deficit, which is both large (less than half of imports are paid for by exports) and growing in money terms. The country's major exports by value in 1974 were live animals (35 per cent), cotton (21 per cent), and groundnuts (20 per cent). Some 96 per cent of the resident population is located in the rural areas, and 90 per cent of arable production involves subsistence crops of which the most important in volume terms are millet and sorghum, although rice and groundnuts are also grown, with the demand for rice increasing among higher income urban families for whom it is replacing sorghum and millet. Upper Volta belongs to the West African Monetary Area served by the Banque Centrale des Etats de l'Afrique de l'Ouest (BCEAO) and uses as currency the convertible West African franc (abbreviated as CFA).

The country became independent in 1960. By 1966 the government had accumulated budget deficits amounting to more than half a year's revenue, and a new military government which assumed power that year imposed severe budgetary restraint, cutting civil servants' salaries by 10 per cent and reducing total government expenditure by 12 per cent between 1966 and 1967. The tax system was reformed in 1969, resulting in an increase in tax revenue, although since the onset of the drought this may have begun to fall again. As a result, a growing budget surplus has been recorded since 1966. Alongside this restraint, the government has pursued a policy of keeping urban grain prices low. In

1965 a system of development administration was adopted based on
the creation of independent and self-accounting Organismes Régionaux
de Développement (ORDs), of which there are now eleven. Responsibility for planning and implementing development programmes is
shared between the central government (which has local representation
in the départements and cercles) and the ORDs.

Despite the accession to power of a military government in 1966,
party politics have been in evidence for much of the past ten years,
although parties were banned in 1974, and the country has now
returned to civilian rule. In January 1976, there was a trade union
strike of major political importance, and the following March the
Ministère du Plan, du Développement Rural, de l'Environment et du
Tourisme was split up, and a separate rural development ministry
created.

How Much is Their Aid Worth?

Chapter 2 supplied many figures on the value of food aid — all of them
notional figures used by the donors. However, since bilateral food aid
is double tied, these figures may not correspond to the value of the
aid to the recipient. It is tied firstly to a specific source of supply, what
may be called procurement tying, and secondly to specific foods, or
commodity tying. It is possible to obtain a general idea of the untied
value of the aid by calculating what the recipient would have paid for
the same commodities on the world market, and by considering
whether, in the absence of food aid, it would have purchased other
commodities in place of those actually supplied. An attempt is made
to adjust for procurement tying in Table 3.5, pages 58/9. The table takes
one example for each of the main donors — the Catholic Relief Services
(CRS), EEC, France, USA and WFP — and compares the donor's
notional valuation with a figure that shows roughly what the recipient
would have had to pay for the food had it been imported on a
commercial basis. The first column of figures gives the unit value of the
food on the donor's valuation, and the second column provides a figure
for the untied value of the aid; the third column shows this untied
value as a percentage of the donor's value. In most of the examples, the
figure for the untied value has been derived by calculating the unit value
of the recipient's commercial imports of the commodity in question.
However, in the case of the CRS and WFP examples, which are based on
Lesotho data, the untied value has been derived from local market
prices because trade data for the country are very inaccurate and because
prices are largely determined by South African levels and are little

affected by Lesotho's trade outside the Customs Union. It can be seen
that the relationship between the notional and untied values varies
widely. In general the untied value is much lower, often between

Table 3.5 (A, B, C, D, E): Comparison of Donor and Untied Values of
Food Aid Commodities

A. Catholic Relief Services (CRS)
(comparison based on Lesotho data: in Rand)

Commodity	(1) CRS value[a]	(2) Untied value[b]	(3) (2) as % of (1)
Cornmeal (per kg)	0.28	0.10	36
Milk (per kg)	1.32	1.43	108
Oil (per litre)	1.10	0.90	82
Wheat flour (per kg)	0.30	0.15	50

a. For period 1 July 1975 – 30 June 1976.
b. Figure calculated by WFP Maseru for local replacement cost at August 1975.

B. EEC
(comparison based on Upper Volta data: in $)

Commodity	EEC value[c]	Untied value[d]	(2) as % of (1)
Maize (per tonne)	211	96	46

c. Average of EEC unit values 1971–4.
d. Average of unit value of all imports 1971–4.

C. France
(comparison based on Upper Volta data: in $)

Commodity	Donor value[e]	Untied value[f]	(2) as % of (1)
Wheat[g] (per tonne)	275	141	51
Maize[h] (per tonne)	284	99	35

e. Average French unit value over serveral years.
f. Average unit value of all imports of the same commodities over several years.
g. 1973 and 1975.
h. 1971–4.

Table 3.5 (A, B, C, D, E) continued

D. USA
(comparison based on Tunisian data: in $)

Commodity	Donor value[i]	Untied value[j]	(2) as % of (1)
Soft wheat (per tonne)	145	136	94

---

i. US unit value for 1976 Title I wheat agreement.
j. Unit value of all imports in first five months 1976.

E. World Food Programme
(comparison based on Lesotho data: in Rand)

Commodity (per tonne)	Donor value[k]	Untied value[l]	(2) as % of (1)
Vegetable oil	545	970	178
Pulses	340	310	91
Dried fruit	545	640	117
Wheat flour	150	150	100
Canned fish	885	700	79
Soluble coffee	6,809	5,720	84
Dried skim milk	654	1,430	219

---

k. WFP f.o.b. notional values for June 1975 plus 23% to cover transport, etc.
l. Figure calculated by WFP Maseru for local replacement cost at August 1975.
Sources: CRS/Lesotho *Annual Summary of Operations 1 July 1975 – 30 June 1976* (Maseru); WFP, Maseru and Rome; EEC Commission, Brussels; French Embassy, Ouagadougou; FAO, *Trade Yearbook;* USA Embassy, Tunis; *Bulletin Mensuel de Statistique* (Tunis), no. 261–4, September-December (1976).

one-third and one-half of the donor's value. The major exceptions are some WFP foods and very importantly PL 480 Title I soft wheat to Tunisia where the two prices are close; important because this is also the only case in which the food aid has been supplied as a loan.

The figures in Table 3.5 indicate in very broad terms what it would have cost the recipient to have bought commercially the commodities supplied as food aid. There remains the possibility that in the absence of food aid, the recipient would not have bought the same commodities but would have substituted cheaper ones. Obviously, any attempt to take account of this must be speculative. However, a general idea of the magnitudes involved in untying by commodity can be obtained by considering the case of blended foods supplied to nutrition programmes. In recent years the USA has been supplying directly and via WFP a number of blended foods such as corn soya milk (CSM) and wheat soya blend (WSB). These concoctions are high in protein, and are designed to make full use of foods in surplus supply. Their utilisation received a boost in the early 1970s when dried skim milk was in short supply. Since blended foods are not available outside the realm of food aid, recipient governments running school lunch and vulnerable-group feeding programmes would have to substitute other foods in the event of food aid being terminated. What they would or should supply is the subject of hot debate: as is explained in Chapter 7, there is controversy over whether nutrition feeding programmes should boost the protein intake of the recipients, or whether they need only supply calories, which are generally cheaper. In Botswana, the primary school lunch ration is 150 grammes CSM/CSB (corn soya blend) and 15 grammes of vegetable oil per child per day. It has been calculated that the corn soya milk could be replaced by a mixture of maize (65 per cent) and cowpeas (35 per cent) which would have almost identical nutritional properties.[9] The notional WFP value of this ration is some R11.38 per year; the local replacement cost of the proxy ration is only R5.58. Although maize is an acceptable nutritional substitute, it requires more processing than CSM, and the cost of this has to be taken into account. If higher priced maize meal is substituted, the ration becomes 97.5 grammes of maize meal, 52.5 grammes of cowpeas, and 15 grammes of vegetable oil, with a local value of R6.25 per year, or 55 per cent of the notional value.[10] The relationship between the notional value used by WFP and the proxy value will vary between commodities and, therefore, between projects. Thus the Botswana mother and child feeding scheme uses the same commodities as the primary school lunch, but in different proportions, and here a ration using maize meal and cowpeas in place of CSM has a value of some 66 per cent of the notional WFP figure.

These untying exercises serve a twofold function, even though the percentages quoted are at best only rough guides. First, they indicate that donor figures for the value of food aid flows are really useful only for comparing aspects and trends within donor programmes; they are of little help in comparing the performances of different donors or in indicating how much the aid is 'worth' to the recipient. The donor's notional valuation may not even be very helpful for calculating the proportion of food aid in total aid. In the case of EEC food aid, for example, the figures cited in Table 3.5 are based on the price of the food under the Common Agricultural Policy (CAP), but the development budget is debited only with what is calculated to be the world market price, with the difference between the two being met from the agriculture budget. Second, they can be used when calculating the financial terms on which food aid is offered, so that it may be compared with the financial terms of cash aid. There is widespread agreement that if both cash aid and food aid are offered on similar terms, the former is preferable because, except sometimes in emergencies, it can do everything food aid does and more besides. However, this preference for cash need not apply if the two forms of aid are offered on different terms: if food aid is 'softer' than cash aid it may be preferable. A distinction can be drawn between the various costs of aid. First there are the costs associated with the financial terms on which it is given: interest rate, period of amortisation, etc. Second, there are the costs of tying (of both the procurement and commodity varieties) which will tend to lower the real value of the transfer to the recipient and hence harden the effective financial terms. Third, there are utilisation costs which cover ancillary expenses necessarily incurred by the recipient if it is to use the aid. In addition to all these, of course, it is necessary to take account of the versatility and wider implications of different modes of aid: apart from bulk supplies, food aid can be used only for certain types of project and may have adverse effects, for example on agricultural production, in the recipient. These broader considerations are dealt with in Section Three; in this chapter only the three more narrowly defined costs are considered.

A comparison of the costs associated with cash aid and food aid is complicated because they do not fall into the three categories in the same proportions. With the exception of Tunisia in respect of PL 480 Title I loans, the four countries have not encountered any financial costs for food aid because it has all been supplied as a grant. However, they have incurred utilisation costs that might not have arisen with cash aid.

Tunisia is the only one of the case studies to have received food aid as a loan. The terms of PL 480 Title I loans have varied over the years. Until 1969, Tunisia was able to repay 70 per cent of the loans in dinars, but since then only dollar repayment has been acceptable. The repayment terms of Title I can change from year to year, since each consignment of food is the subject of a separate agreement. However, the agreement signed on 21 January 1977 for 40,000 tonnes of wheat valued at $4.8 million may serve as an illustration.[11] This loan carries a two-year grace period, and then requires an initial repayment of 20 per cent with the balance repayable over 19 years; the rate of interest is 3 per cent. Since food aid under PL 480 Title I has largely substituted for commercial imports and has been distributed through the state importing monopolies (see Chapters 4, 8 and 9) it is valid to argue that it has not involved the government in any special utilisation costs, and that commodity tying has not resulted in overvaluation. An indication of the influence of procurement tying is given in Table 3.5 which suggests that the notional valuation given to the Title I wheat is reasonably competitive. There are perhaps more grounds for concern over the quality of the foods than over their price. Complaints have been voiced, although not specifically with respect to Tunisia, that PL 480 grains are sometimes of poor quality.[12] Indeed, the problem is not restricted to the USA, and most donors have been accused of supplying poor quality food at some time or another.

It has been possible to calculate the utilisation costs of grant food aid only in the cases of Botswana and Lesotho, since the administrative system in Tunisia and Upper Volta splits costs between many different organisations. In both Botswana and Lesotho, by contrast, there are central units with responsibility for the bulk of food aid logistics. For the purpose of this exercise it is assumed that the difference between the utilisation costs of food and cash aid is equal to the expenses of these central units. This is a bold assumption. As noted below, the units' expenditure may not accurately reflect the utilisation costs of food aid, and furthermore there may well be other utilisation costs which are associated with cash aid but which do not apply to food aid. Both of these factors would tend to overestimate the costs of food aid relative to cash aid, so this exercise is likely to underestimate the 'softness' of food aid. In Botswana, food aid logistics are the responsibility of the Institutional Food Programme (IFP), a body which handled 32,467 tonnes of WFP food between 1971 and 1975. Valued at WFP prices this food was worth approximately R3.9 million. The calculations above suggest that the local value might be 89 per cent of the notional value when procurement-untied and 60 per cent when untied by commodity as well. During the financial years 1971/2-1975/6, IFP spent R854,589 which represents 25 per cent or 37 per cent of the value of aid received, depending on whether account is taken of procurement tying alone or of commodity tying as well. However, IFP expenditure may not fully reflect the costs of handling food aid. On the one hand, it is doubtful whether its accounting practices make sufficient allowance for transport and storage capital costs. On the other side of the coin, replacing food aid by cash would not necessarily result in government savings equal to IFP's costs, and still less in savings of this magnitude to the economy as a whole. The distribution trade in Botswana is fairly weak. Even educational institutes in Serowe, which is an important administrative centre and only a few miles from the line of rail, are experiencing difficulty in obtaining tenders from private shops to supply their food needs now that one of the food aided programmes has been terminated. It is most improbable that the private sector could meet the requirements of the continuing food aided projects. In other words, even if the government received cash aid to support these projects it might still need to keep part of IFP operating in order to purchase food centrally and transport it to all distribution points. Furthermore, Botswana is a large country with a small population and poor infrastructure; transport costs are therefore high. In Lesotho, using the same methodology, the costs of the food aid office during 1968/9-1972/3 represent only 10 per cent of the value of food untied by commodity. These figures, even the higher one for Botswana of 37 per cent, suggest that food aid is a fairly soft form of aid, particularly in light of the fact that they probably understate its attraction vis à vis cash aid.

Notes

1. Yusif A. Sayigh, *The Economies of the Arab World* (London, Croom Helm, 1978), p. 487, Table 11.5.
2. See Bibliography: Botswana (1976b), p. 135.
3. Ibid., p. 44.
4. See Bibliography: Stevens and Speed (1977) for further details.
5. For further details of the Botswana economy and aid performance see Bibliography: Jones (1977).
6. See Bibliography: World Bank (1975a), p. xvii; see Jones (1977) for further details of the economy.
7. See Bibliography: Upper Volta (1972a), Table 1.
8. See Bibliography: USA (1975a), p. D–4.
9. I am indebted to Mark Bowden, Department of Nutrition, Queen Elizabeth College, University of London for calculating this proxy ration.
10. The WFP notional figure of R11.38 is based on 1976 prices of R7.10 per 50 lb c.i.f. of CSM, and R0.76 per kg c.i.f. for vegetable oil. The school year is assumed to be 195 days. The values of maize (R6.80/90 kg) and cowpeas (R11.45/90 kg) are based on the 1976 selling price of the Botswana Agricultural Marketing Board (BAMB). The figure for oil (R0.97/kg) is based on an estimate made in August 1975 for Maseru, Lesotho by WFP. The value for maize meal is based on an average purchase price paid by rural households over the period 1 May 1974 to 30 April 1975 (Bibliography: Hamilton, 1975, Table 5.1, p. 42), (10 cents/kg) plus 11 per cent to bring it up to 1976 price levels.
11. *Agreement between the Government of the United States of America and the Government of Tunisia for the Sale of Agricultural Commodities under P.L. 480 Title I Program* (21 January 1977).
12. See, for example, USAID, *Report on Examination of Transportation of PL 480 commodities to the Sahel Area,* Audit Report No. 3–625–76–33 (30 April 1976).

SECTION TWO: THE USES OF FOOD AID

4 FOOD FOR CASH

The purpose of Section Two is to describe the ways in which food aid
has been used in Botswana, Lesotho, Upper Volta and Tunisia. This
is certainly not easy. Food aid has been used in a host of different ways
and many of the projects with which it has been associated have
multiple and, sometimes, conflicting objectives. The list of achievements
worldwide claimed by food aid is endless: improvement of animal
husbandry, crop diversification, settlement of new lands, rehabilitation
and regeneration of natural pastures, reduction of unemployment
and underemployment, community development, vaccination,
improvement of health, alertness and proficiency of school children,
control of cholera and typhoid, educational reform including improvement of the urban/rural balance, slum clearance, promoting fairer
income distribution, increasing labour productivity, and even training
in carpet making![1]

Some kind of categorisation is needed to identify broad types of
food aided activity and to distinguish between first and second order
goals. The classification system used here cuts across the traditional
division between programme (or bulk supply) aid and project aid, and
concentrates on the primary goal of each development food aid transfer,
which is distinguished as food for cash, food for nutrition or food for
wages. With food for cash, the primary aim is to realise the money
value of the food aid so that, in theory at least, it can be channelled
into development projects that perhaps cannot utilise food aid directly.
Bulk supply of food aid for open-market sales clearly falls into this
category, but institutional feeding schemes whereby food aid is sent to
secondary schools, hospitals, etc. is also included. In food for nutrition
schemes the food is distributed for its nutritional value to people
assumed to be especially vulnerable or deserving. Mother and preschool
child feeding projects and the supply of food aid to primary schools
both come within this category. Food for wages projects are those in
which people are given a ration of food aid as full or part payment for
work they have performed; this often involves unskilled or semi-skilled
labour in food for work projects but also includes various incentive
schemes whereby farmers are given food to encourage them to
introduce new or extended farming practices.

There are, of course, dangers in any such taxonomy. Bad

67

classification may result in projects being assessed for success, or lack
of it, in achieving something they were never really designed to achieve.
Also, with such a complex set of goals as are applied to food aid an over-
concentration on the primary objective of each activity may lead us to
neglect the others. It is certainly true that there is much overlapping
between different categories: institutional feeding, for example, would
be classified as food for nutrition by many observers instead of food
for cash. However, it is precisely because there is such overlapping that
some degree of sorting is needed. It is hoped that the final chapters
in which the threads of different types of project are brought together
will overcome the problem of neglecting secondary objectives.

The balance between the three types of food aid varies between the
countries studied. In Botswana the bulk of food aid currently goes to
food for nutrition projects, while in Lesotho it is absorbed by food for
wages. Neither country has received substantial amounts of food for
cash, which is in strong contrast to the experience of Upper Volta and
Tunisia where that is the most important form of food aid. Because of
this difference of emphasis it is possible to observe each type of food
aid both in situations where it is important and in those where it is
unimportant relative to other food aid uses.

Bulk Supply

The most common form of food for cash is where food aid is provided
in bulk. It may be added to the general supply available to the consumer,
or sold through a differentiated market, or put into specific uses such as
the creation of a commodity price stabilisation reserve; in some cases
the donor tries to set the resale price, while in others it is left to the
discretion of the receiving government. Only Tunisia and Upper Volta
have received bulk supplies; Botswana and Lesotho have received
development food aid only for projects.[2] In value terms, bulk food for
cash has been the most important form of food aid received by
Tunisia. The quantities committed between 1965 and 1976 which
were valued by the donors at $161 million, are shown in Table 4.1,
page 69, for each of the main donors: the USA, Canada, France and the
EEC, and the total annual commitments for cereals and oil are shown
graphically in Figure 4.1, page 70. The table and figure reveal a peak
in the quantities committed between 1967 and 1971, and in the number
of donors between 1969 and 1974. In recent years only relatively
small amounts have been supplied. The most important commodities
(by volume) have been cereals and soyabean oil.

Table 4.1: Bulk Food for Cash Committed to Tunisia by the USA, Canada, France and the EEC, 1965–76 (in tonnes unless otherwise specified)

Year	Donor	Cereals	Soyabean oil	Other	
1965	USA	130,636	17,881	—	
1966	USA	91,270	—	—	
1967	USA	181,225	37,144	(Cotton)	2,850 bales
	Canada	12,365	—	—	
1968	USA	139,690	30,535	(Cotton)	863 bales
	Canada	18,835	—	—	
1969	USA	168,289	32,720	(Tobacco)	669
	Canada	39,168	—	—	
	EEC	20,000	—	—	
1970	USA	51,390	24,406	(Cotton)	6,250 bales
				(Cattle hides)	15,086 bales
	Canada	41,800	—	—	
	France	30,000	—	—	
	EEC	35,000	—	—	
1971	USA	65,081	31,343	—	
	Canada	59,000	—	—	
	France	30,000	—	—	
	EEC	25,000	—	—	
1972	USA	60,080	58,104	—	
	Canada	32,500	—	—	
	France	25,000	—	—	
	EEC	25,000	—	—	
1973	USA	—	20,489	—	
	Canada	16,100	—	—	
	France	25,000	—	—	
	EEC	10,000	—	—	
1974	Canada	11,000	—	—	
	France	25,000	—	—	
	EEC	7,500	—	(DSM)	100
1975	France	20,000	—	—	
1976	USA	21,300	—	—	
Totals		1,417,229	252,622	—	

Source: various donors.

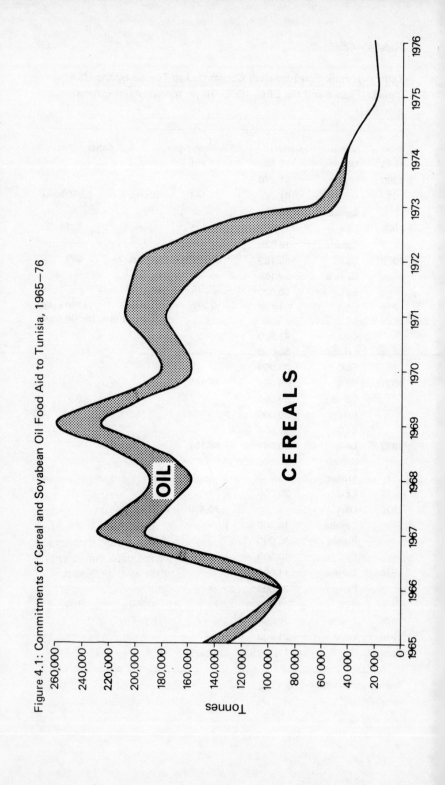

Figure 4.1: Commitments of Cereal and Soyabean Oil Food Aid to Tunisia, 1965–76

Table 4.2: Tunisian Imports of Cereals and Food Aid Cereal
Commitments: Three-Year Averages, 1965—75 (thousand tonnes)

Year	(1) Average annual Imports	(2) Average annual Food aid	(3) (2) as % of (1)
1965/7	303.8	138.5	46
1968/70	471.6	181.5	38
1971/3	300.9	124.3	41
1974/7	342.1	28.3	8

Sources: Table 4.1; FAO, *Trade Yearbook* (Rome).

Table 4.3: Tunisian Soyabean Oil Imports and Food Aid Commitments:
Three-Year Averages, 1965/6—1973/4 (thousand tonnes)

Years	(1) Average annual Imports	(2) Average annual Food aid	(3) (2) as % of (1)
1965/6—1967/8	42.7	18.3	43
1968/9—1970/1	43.0	29.2	68
1971/2—1973/4	49.1	36.6	75

Sources: Table 4.1; Office National de l'Huile.

It would be desirable to compare flows of food aid and commercial
imports in Tunisia but this is not possible because data are available
only on aid commitments and not on deliveries. An attempt is made in
Tables 4.2 and 4.3, above, to indicate the relationship between the two
in general terms for cereals and soyabean oil by grouping the data into
three-year averages. Table 4.2 shows that cereal food aid commitments
represented around 40 per cent of imports until the mid 1970s, when
the proportion fell considerably to 8 per cent. The opposite trend is
discernible for soyabean oil from Table 4.3, with the proportion rising
from 43 per cent in the 1960s to 75 per cent in the early 1970s;
however no oil food aid has been committed since 1973. Thus, in both
cases there has been a major fall in food aid relative to imports since
1973/4.

Over 62 per cent[3] of all the cereal commitments listed in Table 4.1
have been in terms of soft wheat. The other cereals supplied have been
hard wheat (from Canada), barley, maize, sorghum and feedgrains.

Bulk food aid is imported by the Office des Céréales de Tunisie (OCT) and the Office National de l'Huile (ONH) both of which are national bodies of considerable importance. Tunisia has had a national cereals office operating under various guises since 1937. The OCT, which was created in 1962, has a monopoly of cereal imports and exports, and with two co-operatives (Co-opératif Centrale de Grandes Cultures, and Coopératif Central de Blé) it has an official monopoly of domestic grain trade. However, while private domestic trade in cereals is illegal, in practice this parallel market is tolerated. Since farmers must pay a tax on wheat sold through the official channels they may be able to obtain higher prices on the parallel market. One study of the Tunisian grain marketing system has produced figures suggesting that only 25 per cent of the cereal crop moves through the official channels: 50 per cent is consumed on the farm, and 25 per cent is sold on the parallel market.[4] However, the report itself finds it difficult to believe that such a low proportion moves through the relatively highly developed commercial marketing infrastructure, and suggests that the figure may partly reflect data inadequacies. As might be expected, the highest proportion of subsistence consumption is found in the smallest farms.[5]

Food aid cereals are added to the OCT's general stock of imported and domestically purchased grain which is sold at a fixed price. The situation with oil is similar since the ONH has a monopoly of all foreign and domestic trade in vegetable oils. The only complicating factor is that Tunisia is a major producer of olive oil, while food aid is in the form of soyabean oil. The ONH mixes the two types to produce a 'mixed oil' which is sold domestically at a price considerably below that of pure olive oil.

The ground rules under which food aid is given frown on aid that substitutes for commercial imports, and are even more critical of aid that releases for export the domestic production of the recipient. Nonetheless, it is clear that such principles have been applied only loosely to Tunisian food for cash (and as noted in Chapter 2, there exist let-out clauses). Not only has food aid substituted for commercial imports, it has also freed domestic production for export. Although Tunisia is a net importer of wheat it is an exporter, at least in good harvest years, of hard wheat and products which are highly regarded in Southern Europe for pasta, and an importer of soft wheat. It is clear enough that in years when hard wheat has both been exported and received as food aid, the aid has freed domestic production for export. Furthermore, it can be argued that even soft wheat and soyabean oil food aid have had

a similar effect. It can make sense for Tunisia to import lower value
soft wheat and soyabean oil in order to free higher value hard wheat
and olive oil for export. An 'exchange' policy of this kind will benefit
the balance of payments provided that the f.o.b. value of exports
exceeds the c.i.f. value of imports, and it will be feasible if the varieties
involved are substitutable in the Tunisian diet; in the case of wheat
the products to be substituted are bread for couscous. An 'exchange'
policy has been followed for both commodities, and is particularly clear
for oils (see Table 4.4, page 74). In cases where the price differential
between imports and exports is small or negative, food aid may actually
make 'exchange' viable when it would not otherwise have been. In cases
where the differential is large, food aid merely increases the balance
of payments gain from an 'exchange' that would have occurred anyway.
It is probable that cereals fit into the first category and oils into the
second. Possibly for this reason the wheat exchange policy appears to
have been pursued with more circumspection than has been necessary
with oils. On occasion a proposed Tunisian export sale of hard wheat
has been too close in time to a food aid shipment or has too obviously
substituted for it, and the sale has been cancelled. The same problems
do not appear to have arisen with oils, where the price differential is
wide. In 1974, for example, the unit values per tonne of soyabean oil
imports and olive oil exports were $581 and $1,740 respectively.[6]

The most important food for cash activity in Upper Volta, in
quantity terms, has been grain price stabilisation. Food has been
received from WFP, USAID, France and the EEC to help various price
stabilisation agencies build up reserves. The cash value of the aid is
released when the food is eventually sold. The quantities involved are
shown in Table 4.5, page 75. The price stabilisation exercise is dealt
with at length in Chapter 8. Suffice it to note here that none of the
schemes was very successful. One of the problems has been that the
stabilisation scheme of the 1970s, which centred on the national
cereals office (OFNACER), was overtaken by the Sahelian drought.
The cereals office has therefore handled emergency supplies as well
as food for cash and one corollary of this is that some discretion has
been required when deciding which shipments to include in Table 4.5
and which to omit since, as is explained in Chapter 8, not all the aid
channelled through OFNACER was intended for price stabilisation
and not all that was intended for this purpose was so used.

Table 4.4: Tunisian Production and Exports of Olive Oil and Imports of Soyabean Oil, 1965/6—1975/6 (in tonnes)

	(1) Production	(2) Exports[a]	(3) Imports[b]	(4) Net domestic supply
1965/6	52,500	40,772	33,321	45,049
1966/7	19,500	22,013	52,680	50,167
1967/8	51,000	33,346	42,070	59,724
1968/9	55,000	30,249	40,140	64,891
1969/70	25,000	24,994	40,642	40,648
1970/1	90,000	69,458	48,235	68,777
1971/2	167,000	130,956	61,277	97,321
1972/3	70,000	51,763	36,710	54,947
1973/4	130,000	92,961	49,319	86,358
1974/5	117,000	41,740	69,160	144,420
1975/6	180,000	70,109	18,894	128,785

a. Figures for exports are for calendar years, not crop years; the figure under 1965/6 is for the 1966 calendar year, etc.
b. 'Huiles de graine'.
Source: Columns (1) and (3): Office National de l'Huile; column (2) FAO, *Trade Yearbook*.

Since 1977, a new food for cash scheme has been in operation in Upper Volta. Although the country does not grow wheat, bread was introduced during the colonial period and has acquired a following particularly in the urban areas. Indeed, the popularity of bread is such that there exists a political demand for it. At present imported wheat is milled into flour by the Grands Moulins Voltaiques de Banfora (GMV), a joint venture between the government and a French-owned private company. Under agreements that came into force in 1977, both France and the EEC are to supply wheat as food aid to the mill. The foreign exchange savings made by this means are to be creamed off by the government and placed in a special development account for expenditure on projects to be agreed with the donors. Since the value of commercial wheat imports in 1974 was CFA 617 million[7] ($2,776,153), this would seem to be an important vehicle for food as cash, but as the scheme has only just begun it is not possible to assess its success. One potential argument against it is that in certain years since 1973 the flour produced by GMV has been a mixture of wheat and locally purchased sorghum. If the government does not cream off the full financial transfer implicit in the food aid, GMV could be discouraged from purchasing local sorghum by the fall in the relative price of wheat. However, this seems to be a surmountable problem, and in any case, the main impediments to the use of sorghum at present seem to be indeterminate supply and the government's pricing policy which prevents GMV spreading its variable production costs over its sorghum as well as its wheat throughput.[8] There is a further danger that if food aid is used as a means to reduce its price, bread will gain in popularity at the expense of locally produced staples. Again, this is a surmountable problem, although it is too soon to judge whether it will be surmounted.

Table 4.5: Food Aid Supplied to Upper Volta for Grain Price Stabilisation

Year	Donor	Quantities supplied by commodity (tonnes)
1966	WFP	650 maize, 100 sorghum
	USAID	15,000 coarse grains
1967	WFP	2,250 maize
1971	USAID	20,000 sorghum
	France	4,000 maize
1972	USAID	13,815 sorghum
	France	3,500 maize
1973	USAID	7,874 sorghum
	France	5,000 wheat, 5,000 maize
	EEC	5,000 mainly maize, some sorghum
1974	USAID	18,844 sorghum
	France	10,000 maize
1975	France	3,000 wheat

Note: figures for USAID from 1971 are for quantities actually accounted for by OFNACER.
Source: USAID, French Embassy, OFNACER, EEC.

Project Food for Cash

Although, taking a global view, bulk supply is probably the most important form of food for cash, it is not the only kind. In all the countries studied WFP operates food for cash projects which are known by the collective title of 'institutional feeding'. In Botswana, some inmates of teacher training colleges, the agricultural college, rural training centres and youth Brigades[9] together with nurses and health assistant trainees have received food aid commodities as part of their food rations. The scheme is no longer fully operative, but between 1971 and 1975 it reached 2,000-2,500 beneficiaries per year. In Lesotho, food aid has been supplied to secondary schools, hospitals, teacher training colleges, the university, technical schools, the youth service camp and farmer training centres, and in 1972 there were some 10,358 beneficiaries. In Upper Volta, alongside the bulk supply schemes, there have been food for cash projects which have channelled WFP commodities to secondary schools, centres for agricultural training and rural craftsmen, rural youth organisations and hospitals. Similarly in Tunisia, WFP aid has been received by agricultural, prevocational and vocational training centres, orphanages and boarding schools.

One claim commonly advanced for these schemes is that they improve the nutrition of the recipients. However, they are not classified here as food for nutrition partly because there is no reason to suppose, in most cases, that the recipients are especially vulnerable to malnutrition (on the contrary, secondary and university students are likely to be privileged), but largely because the over-riding goal has been to reduce the authorities' recurrent costs and enable them to accumulate savings. Although there are examples of secondary schools and even hospitals around the world in which meals are not provided, this is not the case in these four countries where a majority of institutions receiving food aid supplied rations before the WFP foods began to arrive, and have subsequently been able to reduce their expenditure on food. In some cases the WFP ration may be larger and/or more nutritious than the food that would have been supplied by the authorities but this is an additional attraction of the scheme, not a central objective. The point is underlined by the Upper Volta Government's initial accounting practice for the secondary school feeding project which assumed that there would be no additional consumption and that the WFP ration would wholly replace local purchases and imports. Further, WFP requires governments receiving institutional food aid to establish a counterpart fund into which the savings on recurrent expenditure are to be deposited.

The institutional feeding projects in all four countries have encountered difficulties. Some of the problems have arisen because the projects into which food aid was slotted have not run according to plan. Others arise from the logistics of supplying food to numerous small institutions, and from the degree of acceptability of some commodities.

An early food for cash project in Lesotho involved the supply of food aid to agricultural students and trainees at various agricultural training centres, and as animal feed to help promote the livestock industry. The project began in 1969 but was soon caught up in the events following the 1970 constitutional crisis. The financial stringency which followed the crisis meant that funds were not available to implement other parts of the overall project, while the administration of the scheme was hindered by the departure of key staff from the Livestock Division of the Ministry of Agriculture.[10] In Upper Volta, problems arose over the projects to be financed from food aid. Savings from secondary school feeding were earmarked for a novel classroom building programme. Concerned at the location of secondary schools predominantly in urban areas, the government planned to add blocks of two classrooms to existing rural primary schools and to use them to house the first two grades of the secondary school curriculum. However, government thinking subsequently shifted away from this idea towards the provision of additional classrooms at existing secondary schools. Partly for this reason and also because savings were lower and building costs higher than anticipated, food aid financed only four of the new blocks instead of the 22 envisaged.[11]

The problems of logistics and food acceptability stem from the existence of a small number of highly dispersed benefiting institutions, from the need to supply a wider range of foods than is required for, say, food for work or supplementary feeding, from the relatively high social status of the beneficiaries, and from an inherent danger of conflict of interest between the government and the recipient institutions. The first two of these are fairly obvious, but further explanation may be justified in the case of the others. Students at the recipient institutions, particularly the secondary schools and universities, consider themselves to be socially superior to the beneficiaries of food aid under other projects — primary school children, participants in food for work, etc. They therefore feel entitled to better food, and may be particularly upset if offered an exotic food that has acquired a social stigma through use in a low-status activity. It is noteworthy that the most severe problems of food acceptability encountered during the fieldwork for this book were linked to institutional feeding. In 1972 there was a riot at one Botswana secondary school during which WFP yellow maize-meal was pointedly strewn on the ground. In this instance the problem was exacerbated because secondary school feeding is in any case a sore point. Government training institutes have to cater on a shoestring budget and many private institutes must cope on even less. As a result, meals are inevitably rather dull and monotonous despite the ingenuity of catering staff. WFP aid simply provided a convenient focus for general student discontent about the standard of food. However, Lesotho's experience also tends to confirm that the acceptability of food aid is inversely related to the social status of the recipient. Of the institutions receiving food aid, the only one to experience vociferous complaints was the university, where yellow maize was particularly disliked, partly because of its association with food for work.[12]

The inherent danger of conflict between recipient institutions and the government derives from the fact that the receiving school or hospital has all the problems of additional administration and food acceptability but sees little profit for itself, at least so long as the government claws back the savings. Administrative difficulties cover not only the problem of multiple sources of food supply, but also accounting complications. In Botswana an accounting error in 1972 resulted in the claw back deduction from the government's food subvention to participant institutions being far in excess of the value of the food aid they had received. The system was therefore revised and the food aid commodities given an imputed price which was 10 per cent less than the corresponding wholesale rate. However, this wisdom was somewhere lost in the movement of staff, so that by 1974 full wholesale prices were being used. In Upper Volta, participating hospitals found at various times that budgetary funds were withheld before the food aid had actually arrived, thus causing temporary financial stringency. Voltaïque schools experienced similar problems to those in Botswana: the imputed value of the food aid was initially set too high, and in 1971 had to be reduced from CFA 35-40 to CFA 20 per ration.[13]

Conflicts of interest are a problem even if the savings are earmarked for expansion in the recipient's own sector (i.e. educational development in the case of secondary schools). As a result, the recipients try to keep any savings for themselves. In Upper Volta a misunderstanding arose on this score between the government and the private schools which believed that, unlike the public schools, they could use the savings in accordance with their own requirements. The government demurred, and in November 1969 decided that the private schools must transfer into a special account at the education ministry used for the public school funds 70 per cent of the savings that had accrued since the inception of the project the year before. This did not happen, and the government halted the supply of food aid for three months from June 1970.[14] In Botswana the feeding project was changed in the light of opposition from recipient institutions and following the 1972 riot. Under the amended scheme, instead of being forced to accept all the food aid on offer, institutes could order as much or as little as they required and had their government subventions reduced only in relation to the food aid actually consumed. Of the participating bodies, only the Brigades continued to make full use of food aid and they did so because, unlike the other institutions, they were allowed to treat the free food as general financial support. This episode not only underlines the problem of providing incentives for the recipient institutes but also indicates the extent to which they may be prepared to participate in the absence of such incentives. If consumption of WFP food by the Brigades is taken to represent the realistic maximum rate of utilisation of food aid, a comparison with consumption levels in other recipient institutions will illustrate the degree of their underutilisation. This comparison is undertaken in Table 4.6, below, which shows that, depending on the commodity, recipients other than the Brigades consumed between 11 per cent and 40 per cent of the food aid available.

As a result of the freedom of choice given to participants in the Botswana institutional feeding project, the savings accruing to the

Table 4.6: Botswana — Actual Per Capita Daily Rations of WFP Food for the Brigades and for all Other Beneficiaries of Project 610 in 1975

	(1) Brigades (grammes)	(2) Others	(3) (2) as % of (1)
Maize meal (plus rolled oats)	371	72	19
Dried skim milk	41	11	27
Vegetable oil	46	9	20
Canned fish	32	7	22
Sugar[a]	5	2	40
Dried beans[a]	9	1	11

a. Commodity in short supply during the year.
Source: World Food Programme.

government were much smaller than had been anticipated. The initial plan was to produce savings of R1 million, but in the event only R400,000 was transferred to the specially created development account over the five years 1971-5. Similar problems have been experienced elsewhere. In Lesotho it was calculated that savings accruing from the start of the institutional feeding project for hospitals, schools, youth service trainees and the university in 1971 up to the end of 1972 totalled R258,516, but of this only R69,370 was remitted to the counterpart fund.[15] In Upper Volta the secondary school feeding project produced savings of only $1.2 million over six years instead of a predicted $1.5 million over four years.[16]

None of the problems associated with institutional feeding are insurmountable. In some cases, they have been surmounted perfectly well. The main criticism of institutional feeding is that it involves numerous headaches for only low returns. The potential benefits are limited by the size of the recipient institutions. The R258,516 savings achieved in Lesotho between 1971 and 1972 were equivalent to only 1 per cent of the country's total ordinary general revenue for the years 1970/1 and 1971/2. The scope for institutional feeding will often be smaller than the capacity of a country to absorb bulk food for cash. The value of the food aid supplied to Upper Volta's hospital project (using WFP value figures) by end 1974 was $546,100, while the commodities sent to the secondary school project by mid 1974 were worth $1,078,300.[17] Since the projects commenced in 1970 and 1968 respectively, this represents a combined average annual flow of $316,242. This figure may be compared to the annual average bulk food for cash shipments by USAID, the EEC, and France to OFNACER. Using the donors' valuation, these averaged $1.9 million during 1971-4. The difference in scale between the two types of food for cash is equally marked in the case of Tunisia. The total value of institutional food aid (on WFP's valuation) supplied up to end 1975 was $5,330,700,[18] or $592,300 p.a. over the nine full years since the first projects began. This may be compared with the 1976 PL 480 Title I agreement for 20,000 tonnes of wheat, valued by the USA at $2.9 million.

It cannot even be said in favour of institutional feeding that although it is smaller in scale than bulk supply it is also less liable to produce adverse effects on the recipient's economy. Such a claim is sometimes made, but there seems little justification for it, except to the extent that since institutional feeding is smallscale all its effects, both positive and negative, will be correspondingly small. The most frequent criticism of bulk food aid is that it may depress local agricultural production. This criticism is considered in Chapters 8 and 9 and found to be not wholly valid. However, to the extent that it is valid, it applies equally to institutional feeding in which the primary goal is not to increase consumption levels but to shift supply from one source to another. Some of the food aid commodities undoubtedly substitute for commercial imports, but others may displace local production. In Botswana, for example, it was found that in 1972 a secondary school, a hospital and a teacher training college in Serowe cut their purchases of milk from the Serowe Farmers' Brigade after receiving dried skim milk under the institutional feeding project. This minor example of market disruption was cleared up (at least in financial terms) fairly easily after the brigade protested to the government which eventually provided compensation for loss of earnings. Nevertheless, it illustrates the problem potential of institutional feeding. In 1975, Lesotho had a surplus of some 2,700 tonnes of locally grown beans, yet pulses were also being supplied by WFP. Again, the problem was kept to minor proportions by WFP suspending further shipments of pulses. However, the authorities were less well able to cope with a local surplus of 20,000 dozen eggs which the Lesotho authorities wanted to sell to the institutional food project, but which were not price competitive with WFP's other sources of supply.[19]

Counterpart Funds

Much of the food for cash supplied to Tunisia, Upper Volta, Botswana, and Lesotho has effectively substituted for commercial imports. As such, it has represented a transfer of free foreign exchange to the recipient. Looked at entirely from the viewpoint of the recipient, there are major advantages in food aid which substitutes for commercial imports if only because it gives them the maximum flexibility. In addition, it may be very simple to administer if the recipient already has a state importing agency, and it is easier to spot when things are going wrong than with other types of food aid. In the medium term there can be problems if food aid induces changes in consumer tastes or if the recipient's price policy encourages an increase in imports at the expense of domestic production[20] but these are dangers that can be recognised when they occur.

Precisely because food for cash often represents free foreign exchange, donors frequently make some attempt to control the use to which these resources are put by monitoring a counterpart fund into which the recipient is required to deposit the proceeds. It is clear from the four studies that the counterpart fund principle does not work in practice: recipients sometimes adhere to the letter of the fund but disregard its spirit, while in other cases they disregard both. What is still unresolved is whether or not this is desirable.

All food for cash donors to Tunisia require the government to establish a separate counterpart fund into which the proceeds are deposited. The USA specifies certain broadly defined projects for which the funds should be used, e.g. to 'increase the funds allocated for loans and other services to individual farmers and agricultural co-operatives'; to 'promote expanded cereals production'; to 'improve delivery of integrated health and family planning services which benefit the rural poor'. It is widely held that these categories are so broadly defined that they do not, in practice, influence government investment plans. The Canadians require to be given details of specific 'social and economic development' projects for which the counterpart funds have been used, but the Tunisian authorities do not have to report until after the money has been spent, nor do they have to earmark project funds as being derived from food aid. Thus the Tunisian government is free to treat the linking of food aid funds and specific development projects as a purely notional, ex-post accounting exercise. Under French regulations, the counterpart funds are intended to cover the local costs of French-aided capital projects over the succeeding three years; in practice, however, these regulations are not rigorously applied. The EEC asks to be informed of the development projects for which counterpart funds are used, but it does not seek to approve the projects selected. In practice, none of the donors influences effectively the way in which counterpart funds are used. The main difference between them is that some admit this fact ruefully, others proudly.

Counterpart funds are also required for the WFP assisted institutional feeding projects. In Botswana an account was kept and projects duly approved with the donor before funds were disbursed, but because of the small sums involved it is better seen as an accounting exercise than as a means of influencing government investment plans. In Lesotho, even this accounting exercise has not always been followed. In the case of hospitals, the government pre-empted the use of savings for special development projects by reducing the food provisions budget of government hospitals and the grant-in-aid to mission hospitals by some 50 per cent.[21] This occurred during the financial stringency following the 1970 constitutional crisis, and the cuts have recently been reinstated. However, although a health development fund has been established, by mid 1976 no funds had been paid into it. The conclusion that counterpart funds do not work is supported by evidence from other countries. A study of EEC food aid to Sri Lanka and Bangladesh found that the counterpart fund provisions were merely an accounting device.[22] Indeed, it can be argued that where food aid represents free foreign exchange, a recipient can always circumvent any fund provisions so long as it wants to and the donor is unable or unwilling to use leverage to force the issue.

The question thus remains whether it is worthwhile attempting to improve the effectiveness of counterpart funds either by exerting leverage on recalcitrant recipients or badgering more amenable governments. The argument in favour is that it helps the donor to ensure that its aid is well spent, though the premises for this need examination. The arguments against are that at the very least it wastes the administrative resources of the recipient (particularly for very small food for cash transfers), and that donor interference in the recipient's expenditure plans is undesirable and also to an extent illogical because it is only attempted with gains from aid and not with gains from trade. The issue remains unresolved, and most readers will probably form a judgement on the basis of their wider views about whether or not aid should be project tied.

Notes

1. See Bibliography: WFP (1973a); WFP (1975b); WFP (1976b); WFP (1976c).
2. Although both have received bulk supplies for emergency relief.
3. We say 'over 62 per cent' because the precise nature of EEC cereal aid is not known.
4. See Bibliography: Kansas State University (1974), pp. 24—6.
5. Ibid., p. 4.
6. FAO, *Trade Yearbook* (Rome).
7. See Bibliography: BCEAO (1976).
8. See Bibliography: SPEAF (1976).
9. The Brigades are training and production units. The aim is to train primary school leavers in various vocational and technical skills and at the same time to cover costs from production income. They are private bodies but receive financial and other assistance from the government.
10. See Bibliography: WFP (1974b).
11. See Bibliography: WFP (1975c), paras. 7 and 9.
12. WFP (1973c), para. 19.
13. WFP (1971b), para. 33.
14. WFP (1971b), paras. 7—8.
15. WFP (1973c), para. 22. There were other, additional reasons for this low level of remittances to the development account, but underutilisation and a desire of recipients to keep savings for themselves were important causes.

16. WFP (1975c), paras. 7 and 9.
17. WFP (1975d): WFP (1975c).
18. Excluding the small food for cash component of Project 374.
19. WFP (1976a), Annex II, para. 26.
20. See Bibliography: Dudley and Sandilands (1975).
21. WFP (1973c), para. 15.
22. A Klaasse Bos, 'Food Aid by the European Communities: Policy and Practice', *ODI Review,* no. 1, 1978.

5 FOOD FOR NUTRITION

'Food for cash' described in Chapter 4 may be supplied either in bulk or to specific projects. By contrast, 'food for nutrition' described here, and 'food for wages' which is dealt with in Chapter 6, can be provided only to projects. The term 'food for nutrition' has been coined to describe food aid that is channelled into projects which have as an over-riding stated objective the improvement of nutritional standards among a selected target group. In all four countries studied there are or have been schemes to provide food aid rations to pregnant and lactating women and their preschool children, as well as to primary school children. These schemes are known collectively as supplementary or vulnerable group feeding. Food aid has also been supplied to TB outpatients in Botswana and Lesotho, while in Tunisia, the Catholic Relief Services (CRS) have used food aid in various, mainly smallscale, welfare activities that fall under the rubric of food for nutrition. Of these schemes, by far the most important in terms of numbers of beneficiaries and quantities of food are the mother/pre-school child (MCH) and primary school lunch projects. A common link between both of these and with the TB outpatients' project is that the target groups are assumed to be not only vulnerable but also economically significant. These schemes do not cover vulnerable groups that are not economically significant, such as the elderly destitute. Pre-school and primary school children are the labour force of tomorrow, and it is assumed that their future contribution to economic development will be affected significantly by any malnutrition in their early years. Young mothers must stay healthy if they are to feed their babies well and produce strong children in the future. In societies where the bulk of arable farm labour falls on women, they also have productive years ahead. Rather different considerations apply to TB outpatients. The disease is widespread and the fight against it has a direct effect on the size of the labour force. In Botswana, for example, sufferers, of whom a majority were under 44 years old, formed the second largest group of hospital inpatients in 1974.[1] However, the reason for singling out TB patients for free food is not just the severity of the disease but also the fact that outpatient treatment requires attendance at a clinic over a long period of time; the food ration is intended as an incentive to encourage regular attendance.

Organising the Programmes

Although there are important similarities between the administration of food for nutrition projects in all four countries, the complexity of the operation varies widely between Botswana, which is the simplest, and Upper Volta, the most complex. In Botswana there is only one donor, the World Food Programme (WFP), and this undoubtedly simplifies matters. However, the government organisation of food for nutrition and the projects it supports is also well organised. Responsibility is split between a 'distributive' function performed by the Institutional Food Programme (IFP) which is in charge of logistics for all food aid, and a 'professional' function undertaken by the Ministries of Health, Education and Local Government and Lands which with the district councils run the MCH clinics and primary schools at which food aid is distributed. A number of non-governmental organisations such as the Botswana Council of Women and YWCA are also involved because they run voluntary feeding centres which supplement the clinics as distribution points for MCH rations. This split between the handling of food aid and running the programmes into which it is incorporated has been an operational success. Food aid control is a fairly selfcontained exercise, and the IFP has developed a reasonable degree of expertise. Delivery delays certainly do occur, and might sometimes have been avoided if the recipient institutions were responsible for collecting their own supplies: it is not unknown for an institution to be short of food even though the IFP depot in the same town has adequate supplies, because of a shortage of IFP transport. However, the institutions that would benefit most from such a switch would probably be those close to the regional IFP depots, while those in remote areas would probably be worse off. Possibly the most important organisational danger for the IFP arises precisely because it does perform a fairly selfcontained activity and therefore does not come into frequent contact with other ministries. It has responsibility for all food aid, but it is its role in emergency relief that attracts the highest level of attention. During the lulls between the periodic droughts that Botswana experiences, it is easy for the government, preoccupied by more pressing affairs, to neglect the IFP apparatus.

At a policy as opposed to an operational level, a disadvantage of the split in responsibility is that the 'professional' ministries which are, in any case, primarily interested in something other than food aid (education or health) have little contact with and show a certain lack of interest in the food aid they are using. Thus, the Ministry of Health's section in the current development plan devotes several paragraphs to MCH and nutrition projects without ever mentioning food aid; similarly, the only reference to primary school lunches comes not in the Ministry of Education's chapter but in that of the Ministry of Local Government and Lands, which has portfolio responsibility for the IFP.[2]

Lesotho also has a centralised 'distributive' office for handling food aid while the projects into which it is injected are organised by 'professional' ministries. There has always been an administrative unit somewhere in the government responsible for the receipt and distribution of food aid, although it has not always been known by the same name or located in the same ministry. It has recently been transferred to the Prime Minister's Office. However, before that it was in the Department of Community and Rural Development and then in the Ministry of Rural Development (Minrudev). Most of the references in this book are to Minrudev. Two food aid donors are involved, WFP and CRS, but co-ordination between them is good: with government encouragement they have moved their offices into a single compound, along with CARE (Co-operative for American Relief Everywhere) which has at various times supplied ancillary equipment for food aided projects, but which is not directly involved with food aid in Lesotho. Co-operation between CRS and WFP is so good that in 1974 they reorganised their activities to ensure a more rational distribution of responsibilities. The World Food Programme's position in Lesotho is similar to that in Botswana: it supplies food aid to the government which is then responsible for distribution. The role of CRS is rather different. It is not an original donor but rather a channel for American food aid sent under PL 480 Title II. In addition it provides technical assistance to a number of MCH clinics. It thus provides an integrated service of education and supplementary feeding from the clinics with which it is involved. CRS is involved only with the mother/pre-school child projects, but a similar technical assistance role for primary school feeding is provided by the Save the Children Fund (SCF) which is supplied with WFP food via the government.

In Tunisia there is no single government institution with responsibility for distributing food aid, as the procedure varies with the activity. Instead of the two-way split found in Botswana and Lesotho, there are three important food for nutrition schemes, since the MCH project caters only for children under three years of age, while those between three and six years old are provided for by a separate pre-school project. The MCH scheme does not use food aid at present, but in the past the 'distributive' function has been performed variously by

CRS/CARE and the health ministry (Ministère de la Santé Publique)
itself. Distribution in the case of the pre-school and primary school projects is undertaken by the Comité National de Solidarité Social (CNSS)
of the social affairs ministry. The main donor is the USA which has
supplied food aid under PL 480 Title II both directly on a government
to government basis and indirectly through CRS and CARE. In
Botswana and Lesotho the government or a voluntary agency is responsible for distributing the food all the way to the receiving clinic or
school. In Tunisia this does not happen: the government agencies
involves distribute only to a set of local depots from which each
institution must collect its own supplies.

This feature is shared by Upper Volta. It is not possible to compare
the efficiency of these full and partial distribution systems because one
corollary of the partial system used in the two francophone countries
is that systematic records of deliveries to individual institutions are not
kept. In Upper Volta it is difficult to obtain any useful data on the
distribution of food for nutrition, and this must be partly owing to the
complex administrative arrangements. There are two main donors:
USAID via CRS and the EEC. The primary school lunch project is
split between ordinary primary schools which are the responsibility of
the Ministère de l'Education Nationale et de la Culture, and rural
schools which come under the Ministère du Développement Rurale.
Some MCH programmes are run by the health ministry proper, others
by its social affairs department, while a third group are the initiative
of non-governmental organisations. CRS provides technical assistance
to the clinics and primary schools with which it collaborates. It is the
sole channel for PL 480 aid to such nutrition projects and it also
distributes some of the EEC's food, but it is not the only channel for
European food aid and it does not normally have contractual control
of the food in the same way that it does with PL 480. Normally EEC
food aid is a transfer to the Upper Volta government which has
contractual responsibility for it. Since 1973, a part of the transfer has
been distributed via CRS while the remainder is utilised directly by
the government. It appears that in future the EEC may supply some
food aid direct to CRS. This rather complicated distribution system
is illustrated in Figure 5.1, page 89. The decision by CRS to accept
food from two donors, with all the administrative complications that
this entails, was taken when the USA introduced blended foods to
replace dried skim milk which was in short supply. CRS calculated
that the problems of dual donors would be less than the difficulty
of explaining to MCH participants the correct use of corn soya milk

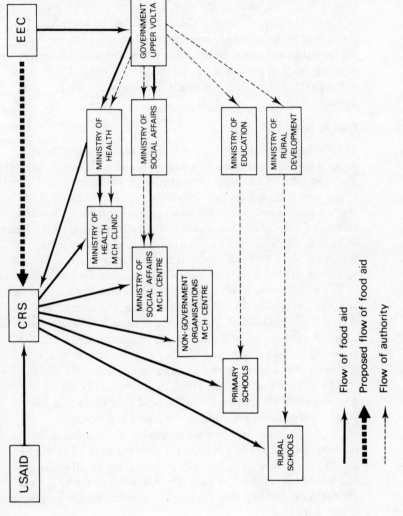

Figure 5.1: Distribution of Food for Nutrition Aid in Upper Volta

EEC

GOVERNMENT UPPER VOLTA

USAID

CRS

MINISTRY OF HEALTH

MINISTRY OF SOCIAL AFFAIRS

MINISTRY OF EDUCATION

MINISTRY OF RURAL DEVELOPMENT

MINISTRY OF HEALTH MCH CLINIC

MINISTRY OF SOCIAL AFFAIRS MCH CENTRE

NON-GOVERNMENT ORGANISATIONS MCH CENTRE

PRIMARY SCHOOLS

RURAL SCHOOLS

Flow of food aid

Proposed flow of food aid

Flow of authority

(CSM) which looks rather like corn meal.

The choice of which foods to supply to nutrition projects is an area of controversy, as is explained in Chapter 7. In particular, there is disagreement over whether the beneficiaries need calories and proteins, or whether calories alone are sufficient. It is helpful when describing the various projects that are operating to express the rations in nutritional as well as weight and value terms. The most convenient way of doing this is to give the approximate calorific value of each ration, although this procedure is not meant to prejudge the calorie versus protein debate.

Primary School Lunches

The numbers of beneficiaries served by the primary school lunch projects in the four countries studied are shown in Table 5.1, page 91. The table must be used with some caution as the figures do not all refer to the same year, and because the number of beneficiaries in Botswana assumes perfect coverage of the target group; in practice, the actual number of beneficiaries is unlikely to exceed 85 per cent of this figure, or 94,086, which equals 81 per cent of the total primary school enrolment. Even with this caveat, it is clear that coverage of primary schools by the lunch project varies widely between the four countries.

The best coverage is achieved in Botswana, where primary schools began receiving food aid before independence. The current WFP project is an expansion of one approved in April 1966 which was itself a natural continuation of the emergency assistance provided during the severe drought of the early 1960s. Under the scheme as operated at present, the children receive a mid morning meal of blended food (CSM/CSB) and vegetable oil. The daily allowance of oil is 15 grammes while the actual ration of blended food varies between 90 and 200 grammes according to the school and the child, although 150 grammes is now recommended (the recommended ratio supplies roughly 675 calories per child per day).[3] The children do not pay for their food, but they do contribute P0.30-0.60 a year into a fund administered by each school which is used mainly to pay the cooks and buy fuel; any surplus tends to be spent on general school amenities.

There are four categories of primary school in Botswana, only two of which receive food aid. In the *English medium schools*, which are administered by the Ministry of Education, the language of instruction is English and standards are high, as are fees.[4] They do not receive food aid, and neither do an unknown number of *unregistered private schools,* in which standards are often very low and which are not taken into account when compiling enrolment statistics. The largest group of schools which do receive food aid are the *Setswana-medium schools* which are administered by the local councils with the Ministry of Education providing professional advice and supervision, and in which fees are currently P3 annually. A fourth group which also receives food aid consists of *government registered private schools* many of which are administered by missions, and some of which receive government financial assistance. The schools which receive food aid provide the bulk of Botswana's primary education.

Table 5.1: Number of Beneficiaries of Primary School Lunch Projects in Botswana, Lesotho, Upper Volta and Tunisia

(1) Country	(2) Donor	(3) Estimated number of beneficiaries	(4) Total primary school enrollment	(5) (3) as % of (4)
Lesotho[a]	WFP	109,950	175,355	63
Tunisia	CRS, CARE	271,365[b]	865,768[c]	31
Upper Volta	CRS	45,000[d]	111,135[e]	41
Botswana[f]	WFP	110,689	116,293	95

Letters indicate year of data:
a. = 1972.
b. = 1976.
c. = 1973/4.
d. = 1976/7.
e. = 1974.
f. = 1975.
Sources: *Interim Evaluation Report: Two Projects for the Feeding of Primary School Children and Vulnerable Groups in Lesotho and Swaziland,* WFP/IGC: 24/10 Add 42, (WFP, Rome, August 1973), Annex 1, para. 8; *Lesotho Second Five Year Development Plan 1975/76–1979/80,* vol. 1 (Maseru), Table 12.1; *L'Economie de la Tunisie en Chiffres 1973* (Institut National de la Statistique, Tunis), p. 33; Information from CRS and CARE-MEDICO, Tunis; *Réforme de l'Education – Dossier Initial* (Ministère de l'Education Nationale et de la Culture, Direction de la Planification, Ouagadougou, 1976); Information from CRS, Ouagadougou; *Botswana Education Statistics 1975* (Central Statistics Office, Gaborone, 1975), Tables 1A and A19.

In Lesotho, the Save the Children Fund (SCF) delivers to virtually every primary school in the country: 1,048 at present.[5] Yet it appears from Table 5.1 that coverage is less good than in Botswana. One explanation advanced for this anomaly is that some parents are unable or unwilling to pay the charge of R0.70 p.a. which is levied on each of their first two children. As in Botswana this money is not for the food but for ancillary costs — transport in Lesotho's case. This explanation is somewhat dubious since the slightly smaller levy in Botswana does not seem to have had a similar effect. An alternative partial explanation is that the figure for total enrolment includes many who do not attend school regularly. Although the total for 1975 is 175,355, the *average* attendance at WFP assisted schools that year was only 134,800; the number of beneficiaries represents 82 per cent of this average figure.[6] The school ration is more varied than the Botswana lunch and consists of maize meal, blended food, vegetable oil, pulses, egg powder, and dried fruits. Details of its nutritional value are set out in Table 5.2, page 93, since it may be taken as roughly typical for WFP primary school rations elsewhere. As in Botswana, the meals have been food aided continuously since independence.

In Upper Volta the school lunch scheme has a longer history having begun in 1960; throughout the period since then the donor has been CRS. The current ration is 149 grammes of corn meal and 9.5 grammes of oil (630 calories) per day. In 1976/7 CRS supported 495 schools in seven of the country's ten départements. An estimated 90,000 children receive food periodically, but only about one-half of the schools are able to collect their supplies on a regular basis because of transport problems.[7] Thus the meal is received regularly by only 40 per cent of the school population, or 5 per cent of the school age group. From the selection of départements served, it would appear that the aid is concentrated on the middling-favoured areas, with both extremes doing rather badly. No aid at all is given to the département with the highest attendance rate (Hauts-Bassin), but other well provided départements receive significant support, while at the other extreme, the départements with lowest attendance rates (Sahel and Est) are also relatively neglected by CRS.

Some one-third of the supplies go to rural schools, of which in 1970/1 there were 750 providing an education to 30,005 pupils.[8] When these schools were conceived in 1961 they were designed to provide an education related to rural life and, with a minimum entry age of 15 years, to be reserved for the non-formal teaching of older children. However, in practice the education has been similar but of a lower standard to that provided in the primary schools; two of the three years' instruction is in French instead of the vernacular as planned, and the minimum entry age has been reduced. Nevertheless, the rural schools may still cater for less fortunate children than do the primary schools,

Table 5.2: Nutritional Value of WFP Daily Primary School Ration in Lesotho

Commodity	Amount (g)	Calories	Protein (g)	Fat (g)	Carbohydrates (g)	Calcium (mg)	Iron (mg)	Vitamin A (iu)	Thiamin (mg)	Riboflavin (mg)	Nicotin amide (mg)
Maize meal	80	292.2	11.6	0.96	62.72	4.8	2.32	352	0.35	0.21	2.8
Dried skim milk	40	142.8	14.4	0.4	20.4	504	0.4	16	0.18	0.61	0.44
Edible oil	10	90	–	10	–	–	–	–	–	–	–
Egg powder	10	65.8	5.4	4.76	0.2	22.9	1.16	417	0.05	0.15	0.04
Pulses	30	101.1	7.5	0.3	17.1	21	1.5	30	0.24	0.06	0.75
Dried fruits	15	46.2	0.3	–	11.25	7.5	0.3	–	0.01	0.01	0.06
Total		738.1	39.2	16.42	111.67	560.2	5.68	815	0.83	1.04	4.09

Note: this scale is based on the ration distributed in 1973. The current ration is slightly different — 40 grammes of blended food are supplied in place of DSM, and 15 g of vegetable oil instead of 10 g.
Source: M. van der Wiel–van Heughten, *Field Report 1 July–30 September 1973* (WFP Maseru), Table III.

even though the great majority of school age children remain outside the school system altogether.

In Botswana, Lesotho and Upper Volta the aim is to supply food aid to all children attending the participating schools. In Tunisia this is not the case: the free lunch is intended only for children who come from poor families or who live far from the school; other pupils may receive the meal but they have to pay for it currently at the rate of 40 millimes per day. Those who benefit from free meals are selected by a committee of local notables which includes the administrative head of the délégation and a representative of the ruling political party, the PSD. There are no hard data on the background of those selected, but the view of some non-government observers is that the selection is roughly equitable and that the number of recipients is higher in the more remote rural areas than close to the towns.

Although the food aid is channelled through CRS/CARE, which have divided the country between them,[9] the voluntary agencies act largely as an accounting office with the practical organisation being undertaken by the education ministry and CNSS: the former estimates annually the number of children to be fed and fixes a set of approved menus in conjunction with the Tunisian nutrition institute, while the latter is responsible for logistics. The menus are considerably more sophisticated than those found in the other three countries, with daily variations and a choice of hot meals if cooking facilities are available (as they are in about 60 per cent of schools) and cold meals if they are not.

Food aid has been supplied for use in school lunches since 1959, and is used to make bread and biscuits as well as macaroni for the hot meals. Before 1974, aid shipments included hard wheat that could be used directly to produce macaroni. In December 1974, after hard wheat had been dropped, an agreement was reached for the Tunisians to swap some Title II flour for local semolina to make into macaroni. The agreement was for one year only, but it has been extended each subsequent year. The exchange is made on an equal weight basis, and since semolina has a higher unit value than flour this results in a deficit that is financed by the Tunisian Government.

Over the past three years the number of pupils receiving a free lunch has been significantly reduced as a result of two influences. The first, but not in the event the critical influence, has been some American suggestions that resources might be directed away from school lunches to other vulnerable group feeding activities. The second and decisive influence has been a Tunisian desire to phase out food aid

coupled with budgetary stringency. In 1974 the government decided
to reduce the number of beneficiaries by over one-third and although
the value of the ration was increased this only took account of
inflation; the following year the number of beneficiaries was reduced
still further. Thus while over 522,000 children received a free lunch in
1975, by 1977 the number had dwindled to some 271,365. The effect
of these reductions has been to keep the Tunisian budgetary
contribution constant in money terms despite the decline in food aid
and the effects of inflation. The adverse consequences of this fall in
coverage may have been partly offset by what seems to have been an
increase in concentration on the poorer districts. There are no detailed
statistics on the relative wealth of different governorates, but it is
thought that the coastal ones are more affluent. In Nabeul, with a
school enrolment of 79 per cent of the 6-14 year age cohort, the
number of beneficiaries was cut by 69 per cent between 1974 and
1977. In Kasserine, by contrast, which has only 45 per cent school
enrolment, the cuts were only 1 per cent. Similarly, the cuts in Sousse
and Monastir were 76 per cent and 87 per cent respectively; in Gafsa
they were only 7 per cent while in Sidi Bouzid the number of
beneficiaries actually rose by 18 per cent.[10]

The Mother and Pre-school Child (MCH) Projects

A rough measure of the size of the mother and pre-school child (MCH)
feeding schemes in the four countries is given in Table 5.3, page 96.
The table must be used with caution because the figures for different
countries are often not directly comparable, and even within countries
there are unavoidable inconsistencies: the years for columns (3)-(5)
are not always the same; in Tunisia, column (4) refers to the 3-6 year
cohort but column (5) includes all under 6-year-olds; while in Upper
Volta the figure for beneficiaries covers only those who receive CRS
food, while column (6) includes all children up to the age of 6 even
though the centres do not cater for those over age 5. Despite these
shortcomings, the table indicates some salient facts about the scheme,
and shows that even allowing for a wide margin of error the extent to
which the target group is covered varies considerably between the four
countries. In many parts of the world there are two types of
supplementary feeding project: residential and take-home. The former
provide accommodation and intensive care, usually for severely
malnourished children, while the latter simply provide quantities of
food for a mother to take home and cook. Except for a small number
of centres in Tunisia, which do not now use food aid, all the

supplementary feeding with which food aid has been associated in the four countries is of the take-home variety.

Table 5.3: Size of Mother and Pre-school Child Feeding Schemes in Botswana, Lesotho, Upper Volta and Tunisia

(1) Country	(2) Donor	(3) No. of beneficiaries Mothers	(4) Children	(5) Size of total 0—5 age group	(6) (4) as % of (5)	
Tunisia	CRS/CARE	0	160,000[a]	1,093,000[b]	15	
Botswana	WFP	21,630[c]	82,839[c]	117,463[d]	71	
Upper Volta	CRS/EEC	n.a.	23,000[e]	1,261,597[f]	20	
Lesotho	CRS/WFP	13,708[g]	67,852[g]	n.a.	approx.	33.3

a. = 1977 data for 3—6 year age group.
b. = 1976 data.
c. = 1975 data.
d. = 1971 data.
e. = 1973 data for CRS beneficiaries only.
f. = 1973 data for 0—6 year age group.
g. = 1973 data.
Source: USAID, Tunis; Bechir Hamza, Noureddine Chamakh, Hedi M'Henni, *La Santé de la Mère et de l'Enfant* (Tunis, Maison Tunisienne de l'Edition, 1976), p. 14; *Feeding of Primary School Children and Vulnerable Groups: Interim Evaluation Report,* doc WFP/IGC: 28/11 Add A4 (World Food Programme, Rome, August 1975); *Report on The Population Census 1971* (Garborone, Central Statistics Office, August 1972), Table 9; *Field Bulletin No. 21* (Catholic Relief Services—USCC Office of the Pre-School Health Program, 15 August 1974, Nairobi), p. 17; Ministère de la Santé Publique et des Affaires Sociales, Ouagadougou; WFP, Maseru; *Lesotho Second Five Year Development Plan 1975/76—1979/80,* vol. 1, para. 13.12.

As with the primary school lunch scheme, the best coverage is achieved by Botswana. However, the percentages given in column (6) for each country undoubtedly overstate the proportion of the target group that is assisted on a sustained basis, because not all participants attend regularly. The same caveat applies to the school lunch scheme but it applies *a fortiori* to MCH projects. The precise level of regular attendance is not known, but in Botswana not more than 50 per cent of nominal beneficiaries receive their ration regularly.[11] The major part of MCH food handouts are disbursed through voluntary feeding centres staffed by untrained members of voluntary groups and through village development committees. Only some 14 per cent of the 312 distribution points are located in health facilities and are thus able regularly to combine food distribution with preventive health measures.

This proportion is smaller than that in the other three countries and not only explains why the rate of coverage in Botswana is so much better than elsewhere, but also suggests that the rate of regular attendance may be higher elsewhere since participation in a scheme run from a clinic which combines supplementary feeding, health care and education requires a greater commitment from a mother than does a voluntary feeding centre. The current monthly ration in Botswana is 2.4 kg of blended food (CSM/CSB) and 450 g of vegetable oil (equivalent to 415 calories per day).[12] Before 1973, the ration included dried skim milk (DSM) and when this was phased out it was noted that some mothers dropped out of the scheme possibly because they disliked the replacement food, or possibly because, when it is reconstituted, DSM can be used in a variety of ways which differ from those intended, e.g. milk in tea. Rations are normally distributed uncooked at weekly or monthly intervals.

The link between supplementary feeding and preventive health measures is much closer in Lesotho although this is achieved at the expense of coverage. This is well illustrated by contrasting the relationship between school and MCH distribution points in the two countries: in Botswana the ratio of MCH feeding centres to schools is 1:0.98, while in Lesotho it is 1:4.[13] Part of the reason for the closer link may be the involvement of CRS which provides technical assistance to 160 of the 265 participating clinics. Its main interest in food aid is as part of a package to improve child health. Other elements of the package include educational talks and demonstrations, and regular weighing of the child. The child's progress is recorded on a special CRS chart which plots his weight against his age. The chart is filled in each time the child visits the clinic so that his growth from birth to five years is shown as a graph. Superimposed on the chart is what CRS call 'the road to good health': two lines that indicate for each age a recommended maximum and minimum weight. If the child's weight is between the two lines, he is on 'the road to good health'. The lines are drawn in relation to the Harvard standard of weight for age and except for the ages 0-11 months and 48-59 months, the top line corresponds to 100 per cent and the bottom line to 80 per cent of the Harvard standard. The chart is intended to combine the functions of a record and an educational device.

Collaboration between the donors in Lesotho is good, and although their rations differ this does not appear to give rise to serious problems. Details of the rations are given in Table 5.4, page 98. Collaboration between donors in Upper Volta is much less good, a characteristic that food for nutrition shares there with all other forms of development food aid. A comparison of the two countries emphasises that the host government may have to play an active role in encouraging donor co-ordination. Another difference between the two countries is that whereas in Lesotho all government health clinics distribute food aid, in Upper Volta many do not. This is because there is significant resistance to the concept of supplementary feeding among some civil servants and doctors; the implications of this are considered in Chapter 7. No systematic information is available on the number of beneficiaries or rations at the clinics that do distribute food aid other than those assisted by CRS. In the CRS clinics, the monthly ration is 2.4 kg of cornmeal and 454 g of vegetable oil (410 calories per day). In both Upper Volta and Lesotho, mothers attending the CRS assisted clinics are charged a small fee to cover internal transport costs. The rate in Upper Volta is $0.12, and in Lesotho it is $0.20-$0.30 per child per month.

Table 5.4: CRS and WFP Monthly Rations for the MCH Project in Lesotho (kg)

	CRS	WFP
Dried skim milk	0.9	0.9
Blended food	—	1.8
Wheat	1.8	
Oil	0.9	

Note: WFP rations are expressed in daily amounts; monthly figure obtained by multiplying by 30.
Source: WFP, CRS, Maseru.

In Botswana, Lesotho and Upper Volta supplementary feeding to preschool children begins at six months and officially ends when they reach five years of age. In Tunisia, it continues up to their sixth birthday, but is split into two separate projects: an MCH scheme for the under three year olds and their mothers; and a preschool project for the three to six year age group. In recent years this has been an important distinction since food aid has been phased out of MCH but not out of the preschool programme. Currently, no food aid at all is channelled to the 92 MCH centres and 18 URNs (Unité de Récuperation Nutritionelle) run by the health ministry, although the centres do give food to mothers and children judged on medical grounds to be especially needy. The food is a locally produced commodity called

Saha made from chick peas, flour, lentils, wheat, and dried skim milk with added vitamins and calcium. The Saha project is a joint operation between the national nutrition institute, the cereals office, Swedish International Development Authority (SIDA) and UNICEF. Production began in 1976 with 400 tonnes, and is planned to rise to 1,200 tonnes p.a. by 1978. It will be supplied to hospitals and sold to the public in addition to its use for feeding vulnerable individuals. The MCH project has been non-food aided since June 1976. From 1974 to 1976 CRS and CARE distributed food aid, and before that the scheme utilised PL 480 aid directly and, until 1972, UNICEF food aid as well. The bilateral US food carried harder terms than the CRS and CARE aid: although in both cases the food was given as a grant, Tunisia paid 50 per cent of the transport cost and all the survey expenses for the bilateral aid. It is clear that the voluntary agencies' two-year experience was not a happy one. The MCH philosophy of both organisations is that food aid serves a threefold function: to boost the nutritional intake of recipients; to act as a family income supplement; and, most importantly, to be a form of learning by doing, demonstrating that the recommended dietary habits do produce healthier mothers and children. Their normal practice is to distribute food rations to all who take part in an MCH project. This does not accord with the government's view of the MCH scheme, at least as it has been put into practice in recent years. The current government practice is for MCH clinics to provide health education and preventive medical care, but not to distribute food to all who come; rather food is prescribed only on an individual basis as a medicine. The years of CRS/CARE involvement saw both approaches adopted at different times and in different places, which was clearly unsatisfactory for both sides. In the event, the government took the initiative and ended the use of food aid in the MCH project.

By contrast, the pre-school feeding scheme which began in 1957 still absorbs a full measure of food aid. Until 1977 the aid was supplied on a direct bilateral basis by the USA, but it is now being channelled through CRS/CARE following the decline in these voluntary organisations' responsibilities towards the MCH and primary school projects.

Non-nutritional Benefits

The nutritional goals of these projects are considered in Chapter 7, but there are in addition a number of other objectives. These mainly apply to the school lunch projects, although in Botswana MCH food distribution has stimulated the formation of women's groups which run the voluntary feeding centres. The two most important non-nutritional benefits of the school lunch scheme are an improvement in scholastic performance and an increase in school attendance. The argument on performance is that by the middle of the school day the children have become hungry, inattentive and unreceptive to teaching. By supplying them with a midday snack, their learning capacity during the second half of lessons is improved. Although this is a stated goal of the lunch projects in all the countries studied, its validity has not been tested empirically. Interestingly, the same idea has recently been put forward by a teachers' organisation in the UK, although again on the basis of belief rather than controlled experiment.[14] The situation in respect of both school hours and meal patterns will clearly vary between countries. However, there is a *prima facie* case for investigating the likely impact of a midday snack on the efficiency of learning, since school attendance in ldcs often requires a young child to leave home very early before breakfast, and not to return home until after lunch.[15] Teaching can and does occur without food aid, just as it does occur without class-rooms, desks, or books, but there is some reason to believe that its efficiency is improved by the provision of all four facilities.

There are three ways in which food aid may increase school attendance. The first is a corollary of the general nutritional impact: if school food improves a child's health he will spend less time away from class owing to sickness. Second, food aid may act as an incentive for parents to send their children to school. Whether or not this happens will depend on the popularity of education among various social groups, and this will clearly differ between countries. In Botswana for example, it seems unlikely that the meal increases the attractions of primary education which is already well regarded. The situation may be different elsewhere, and it has been suggested that in Lesotho the lunch scheme has attracted boys to school.[16] Third, even if it does not act as an incentive, food aid may be a useful income supplement to help poorer households meet the cost of fees and other education costs. In this case, food aid can be considered as a form of income-in-kind, and this concept recurs frequently in the chapters below.

Notes

1. See Bibliography: Botswana (1974a), Table 14.
2. This is not quite as strange as it may seem at first sight, because the district councils, which fall under the Ministry of Local Government and Lands'

purview, have important responsibilities for primary education. See Bibliography: Botswana (1976a).

3. See Bibliography: WFP (1975a), para. 26.

4. Fees were P54 p.a. in 1976, but between 1977 and 1979 they will be progressively increased to P370. Following the government decision to raise fees, one of the schools decided to go private.

5. See Bibliography: SCF (1976).

6. See Bibliography: WFP (1973b), Annex 1, para. 8.

7. See Bibliography: CRS (1977a), p. 9.

8. See Bibliography: Upper Volta (1972a), p. 257.

9. CRS deals with a central belt of the country, while the CARE assisted schools are located in the extreme north and south.

10. Information from CRS, Tunis.

11. See for example Bibliography: Botswana (1975a) which states that utilisation (taking account of both over-issuing and non-attendance) is 49.25 per cent for CSM and 33 per cent for vegetable oil and that these rates are consistent with those recorded for previous quarters.

12. The WFP ration is expressed in daily amounts; these monthly figures are obtained by multiplying by 30.

13. The actual figures are: Botswana – 305 schools, and 312 MCH feeding centres; Lesotho – 1,048 schools and 265 MCH feeding centres; See Bibliography: Botswana (1975c), Table A1; WFP (1975a); WFP (1973b), Annex I, paras. 14–15. Information from CRS, Maseru.

14. *Concentration in Schools: How it Can be Helped and Hindered,* AAM Discussion Document (Association of Assistant Mistresses, London, July 1977).

15. For the situation in Botswana see Bibliography: Stevens (1978a), p. 23.

16. WFP (1976a), Annex II, p. 10, para. c.

6 FOOD FOR WAGES

The term 'food for wages' describes projects in which food aid is given to workers as full or part payment for some kind of activity. In many projects, known collectively as 'food for work', the beneficiaries provide unskilled or semiskilled labour on a public works scheme. However, food for wages also covers settlement schemes and projects in which farmers are encouraged to innovate or extend their activities. There is no widely accepted generic term for this second group but 'food for farmers' will serve as a convenient shorthand description. The distinction between these two types of food for wages is an important one because it will be argued that, at least in respect of the four countries studied, while food for work provides employment for the poor (if not for the poorest), productivity tends to be very low, and by contrast that although productivity rates with food for farmers projects are much higher, they do not reach the poor.

Organising Food for Work

Food for work absorbs directly some 16 per cent of the food aid supplied each year.[1] In addition, some of the revenue derived from food for cash may be used to finance labour intensive public works. At least four practical reasons have been advanced for disbursing food aid in this way: it may encourage governments to undertake labour intensive projects that would not otherwise have occurred; it may stimulate local participation; it may be a convenient transition from emergency food handouts to development food aid; and, importantly, it may be an effective mechanism for providing income-in-kind to poorer people. However, in addition to these practical arguments, which are assessed below, there is an economic argument for food for work where countries face inflationary or balance of payments problems. In such circumstances, public works programmes may aggravate either or both difficulties, through adding to excess demand. Since part of such demand will be for food, food aid can help. A further argument is that payment in food dampens the multiplier effect. It should be noted, however, that this will hold only if recipients do not resell any of their rations and do not reduce food expenditure, neither of which are particularly plausible assumptions (see Chapter 7). There is, however, no evidence from Botswana, Tunisia, Lesotho, or

Upper Volta as to the macroeconomic impact of public works
programmes, and it is therefore not possible to assess the effect of food
aid in this area. Instead this type of food aid has to be justified or
criticised on the basis of its practical characteristics and their
suitability for the problems that the four countries have faced. The
countries studied have experienced a bewildering variety of food for
work projects, which have sometimes overlapped and which have
involved different kinds of public works. Table 6.1, below, provides
some basic data on these schemes to set the scene. The multifarious
projects provide examples of three types of food for work: sporadic
projects designed to assist and encourage local self-help; schemes that
are related to emergency feeding; and long-term employment creating
projects.

Table 6.1: Food for Work Projects in Botswana, Lesotho, Upper Volta
and Tunisia

Country	Donor	Year	Type of activity
Botswana	WFP	1966-7	Buildings, dams
	WFP	1969-71	
	WFP	1973-4	Brick making
Lesotho	WFP	1966—	Conservation, roads,
	CRS	1968—	afforestation, fish ponds, irrigation
Upper Volta	WFP	1969-73	Wells, dams, reclamation
	WFP	1974-5	Wells, dams, reclamation,
	WFP	1975-6	afforestation, roads,
	WFP	1976—	buildings
	CRS	1968—	Wells, dams, reclamation
Tunisia	USA	1956-73	Various[a]
	WFP	1968-9	Afforestation
	WFP	1968-73	Buildings, roads, afforestation
	WFP	1968—	Dams and erosion control

a. The Tunisian food for work project aided by the USA lasted for 17 years
and covered a wide variety of projects. Details of the broad categories of works
undertaken are given in the text.

Of these, the first is rare, with the only clearcut example coming from Upper Volta. Between 1969 and 1974, the first World Food Programme food for work scheme in the country supplied food aid to various construction projects for wells, reservoirs, and small dams for domestic and livestock use, and also to prepare the land served by these new facilities for agriculture. The typical way in which the work was organised for this project, and also for CRS aided food for work, seems to have been for a village to take the initiative and ask the appropriate government technical branch,[2] usually through a local official (who might be a Peace Corps volunteer) or the ORD (Organisme Régional de Développement), for advice on repairing and/or extending an existing structure, or to build a new one. Villagers would provide the labour, although not necessarily on an organised basis, and WFP or CRS would be asked for an allocation of food aid.[3] Work periods were therefore relatively short, around four months, and the allocation of projects fairly haphazard. No records are available on participants so it is conceivable that workers went from one project to another and obtained semipermanent employment. However, this is improbable. During its five years of operation, the WFP project supplied rations for 847,689 man-days of labour;[4] this would have provided permanent employment for only some 950 persons per year (assuming a 15-days working month), but in practice it appears that many more than this participated for short periods.

Upper Volta is unique among the four countries in that the first project was not related to a drought, although in 1974 it was superseded by a one-year and then by a two-year project both of which were drought related. The link between food for work and drought has profoundly influenced the nature of the tasks set and the manner in which they are performed, the attitude of government towards food aided public works, and the type of people prepared to participate. In Tunisia and Lesotho an initial drought-related project turned into a permanent, nationwide system of public works executed with the assistance of food aid. In Botswana, however, there has not been a permanent system of food for work; instead there have been three relatively short campaigns each related to an actual or an expected drought. The first two concentrated on using food for work gangs, usually under the direction of the Department of Community Development, to construct classrooms, houses for teachers and other officials, and dams. As with supplementary feeding, the food aid has been distributed by the Institutional Food Programme (IFP) and its predecessors. The aim was to construct the buildings in their entirety

Food for Wages   105

using bricks moulded as part of the campaign. The results were not
auspicious except in the Etsha area of north west Botswana where,
during the second campaign (1969-71) food aid was supplied to a group
of Angolan refugees to support them while they built villages to live
in and cleared fields to plough. The third campaign tried to learn from
the mistakes of the first two, and concentrated on site clearance and
brick making in the belief that government technical supervision
would be adequate for these tasks but not for the more complex
activities attempted during the previous projects. Arrangements were
made for 7,500 workers, and the ration set at 50 lbs of maize meal per
2 weeks of work. The decision to supply maize meal instead of a
blended food which would normally have been provided is an
illustration of WFP's flexibility: in order to launch the project quickly
it was able to permit the food to be purchased in the Southern
African region and hence cut transport time. In the event the campaign
was truncated. It was planned following bad rains in 1972/3 and in the
expectation that there would be a second year of drought. However, as
it turned out 1973/4 was wet and the project petered out after a few
months as good rains began to fall.

Lesotho's first food for work project arose from the same mid 1960s
drought that gave birth to Botswana's. However, in the case of Lesotho,
the project has been continuously extended and almost half the length
of roads and tracks in the country have been either built or improved
using food for work. At June 1975, some 13,475 people were engaged
on food aided public works in the following proportions:

(1)	Conservation	7,075	(52%)
(2)	Access tracks, roads and bridle paths	4,205	(31%)
(3)	Tree planting	1,310	(10%)
(4)	Fish ponds	360	(3%)
(5)	Irrigation	250	(2%)
(6)	Special projects	275	(2%)
	Total	13,475	

At present, food aid is supplied by WFP and also by CRS, which began
to assist food for work in 1968 although in 1974 it withdrew from
road construction as part of an arrangement whereby the two donors
improved the integration of their programmes. Although WFP and
CRS supply different rations (see Table 6.2, page 106) with a different
local value, this does not appear to have caused any major problems.

The World Food Programme has estimated the local replacement value of their ration (at August 1975 prices) as R6.59. Participants work for five hours per day, for 15 days a month (divided into three weeks of five days), so that the ration represents payment of 44 cents per day. The Catholic Relief Services have not calculated the value of their ration, but on the basis of WFP figures it is roughly equivalent to R6.11 per month or 41 cents per day. The rations from both donors are designed to be sufficient for the worker and four dependents. Participants are selected by the appropriate village development committee and, in theory, a rotation occurs to enable the largest number of people to benefit and to ensure that food for work does not become a permanent source of employment to the detriment, for example, of agriculture. However, since work records are not collated, it is not possible to check whether or not a rotation occurs in practice.

Table 6.2: WFP and CRS Monthly Food for Work Rations in Lesotho (in lbs per 15 Days' Work)

Commodity	WFP	CRS
Maize meal	100	90
Wheat flour	—	10
Edible oil	3.2	4
Pulses	5	—

Source: World Food Programme and Catholic Relief Services, Maseru.

Lesotho's food for work projects may be divided into two categories according to the way in which they are implemented. Some are undertaken directly by the Ministry of Rural Development (Minrudev) in liaison with local village development committees, while others occur as part of a larger development scheme. The most extensive type of work in the first category is the construction and upgrading of roads and access tracks. The road building and maintenance activities of the Lesotho Government fall into two almost perfectly discrete parts: those roads that are the responsibility of the Ministry of Works and receive capital intensive treatment, and those that are the responsibility of Minrudev where labour intensive methods are used. Although during 1968-70 the government's Chief Engineer: Roads and Transport used to make regular inspections of food for work road projects on behalf of the food aid office, there is currently no crosscutting assistance of this kind and overall technical responsibility for the roads lies with Minrudev

which, unlike the Institutional Food Programme in Botswana, is not
simply a food aid distributing agency but also includes a technical
section. The only link between the two organisations is that the
Ministry of Works has a programme for taking over responsibility for
food aid tracks that have been upgraded to certain minimum technical
standards. Despite this takeover programme, Minrudev still has
responsibility for maintaining an important part of Lesotho's road
network, as indicated in Table 6.3, below.

Table 6.3: Lesotho's Road Inventory, 1974

Type	Maintained by	Total (km)
Bitumen	Ministry of Works	201.3
Gravel 2 lanes	Ministry of Works	367.5
Gravel 1 lane	Ministry of Works	499.7
Tracks	Minrudev	1,126.0
	Traders and Missions	530.4
Total	—	2,724.9

Source: Based on *Lesotho Transportation Study* (Roughton and Partners, 1974).

In the remainder of the food for work scheme, Minrudev is not itself
the executing agency, but merely distributes food to labour intensive
works organised by other bodies. In some cases, the executing agency is
another government ministry, often the Ministry of Agriculture through
its Soil Conservation Division or Fisheries Officer, or it may be an
organisation set up to manage a larger project that uses food aid labour
for a part of its activities. The most important of these latter are three
area development projects for the Thaba Bosiu, Khomokhoana and
Senqu River areas, and a reafforestation scheme known as the Woodlots
project. The Thaba Bosiu project covers 300,000 acres near Maseru and
aims to increase agricultural productivity and farmer incomes by
arresting soil erosion and providing extension services, farm inputs,
credit, research and improved marketing services. Work on the USAID/
IDA project, which it is estimated will cost $9.8 million, began in
April 1973. Food aid is used in some road building and conservation
activities included in the project and normally employs 400 workers.
The Khomokhoana project has similar objectives and covers an area of

48,000 acres near Leribe. Total project costs are estimated at over $4 million and finance is from the Swedish International Development Authority (SIDA) and the Lesotho Government. It uses roughly 850 food workers, although up to 1,200 could be absorbed if the project had sufficient supervisors. The Senqu River project is designed to improve the difficult conditions of agriculture in the southern districts of Mohale's Hoek and Quthing, which have a combined area of 1.6 million acres, of which half is mountainous, and uses some 300 food aid workers. The project cost of $1.26 million is jointly financed by the UN Development Programme (UNDP) and the Lesotho Government. All three projects are run by management units and all use capital intensive as well as food for work methods in their infrastructure development. The Woodlots Project is financed by Anglo De Beers Forest Services and the government, and aims to develop a national forestry policy and a balanced administrative and technical forestry infrastructure, to establish woodlots for provision of fuel and building materials and to provide trees for the stabilisation of river catchment areas. The scheme, which began in 1973, is scheduled to last for 12 years and by the end of March 1976 some 1,038 acres had been planted. The labourers used in preparation of the land for planting are paid in food if they work for five hours per day, or in food and cash (R0.50) for a full day.

Of the four countries, Tunisia has experienced the longest and largest food for work programme, but unlike Lesotho's it is no longer a nationwide operation. The project, which was entitled La lutte contre le sous-développement (LCSD), was begun in 1956/7 to help cope with largescale unemployment following independence. The years 1955/7 saw a heavy exodus of capital and foreign nationals (mainly French) and a consequent fall in the level of economic activity. At the same time, there was a drought throughout the three years, and a political dispute between France and Tunisia as a result of which the former reduced the level of budgetary assistance and some of the trade preferences accorded to the latter. In 1956/7 the United States provided an emergency shipment of 45,000 tonnes of wheat under PL 480 Title II, most of which was distributed between the governorates for use in food for work. In 1959/60, this was followed by 90,000 tonnes of wheat, and by this time the concept of LCSD had been enunciated by the government. Between 1958 and 1969, the USA donated food aid for a largescale programme which employed up to 231,870 workers, and only in two years fell below 70,000 workers. Details are given in Table 6.4, page 109.

Table 6.4: Size of Tunisian LCSD Programme

(1) Year	(2) Number of man-days worked (million)		(3) Estimated number of men employed[a]	(4) Estimated cash expenditure on ancillary[b] services (million Dinars)	(5) Estimated food processing costs[c] (Dinars)	(6) Estimated value of food aid[d] (million Dinars)
1958/9	29.580		118,320	3.40	666,000	3.807
1960	31.043		124,170	7.70	323,000	1.777
1961	55.491		221,960	13.10	607,000	3.179
1962	57.968		231,870	13.70	752,000	3.935
1963	35.325		141,300	10.70	438,000	2.172
	Regional	National				
1964	11.000	17.000	120,000	8.75	115,000	0.602
1965	4.800	21.000	103,200	7.76	269,000	1.753
1966	5.394	11.056	65,800	6.70	182,000	1.156
1967	7.538	12.921	88,510	8.24	231,000	1.575
1968	6.764	9.800	55,960	6.37	205,000	1.722
1969[e]	10.944	7.606	74,200	6.57	350,000	2.160

a. Assuming 250 days worked per man per year.
b. Wages, equipment and supervision; does not include administration and materials such as cement, which are estimated at 10% of cash wages.
c. Cost of milling and distributing semolina made from food aid.
d. c.i.f.
e. Does not include WFP projects.

Source: A. Grissa, *Agricultural Policies and Employment: Case Study of Tunisia* (Organisation for Economic Co-operation and Development, Paris, 1973), p. 134.

During the first few years the food aid was regarded as a temporary emergency measure, and food for work was administered by the Ministry of Social Affairs. In 1959, portfolio responsibility was transferred to the Ministry of Finance and Economics as part of a move designed to stress the development objectives of the work. However a detailed study of the LCSD records that 'there was no corresponding change in the actual choice, organisation, and supervision of projects at the regional level'.[5] During 1959/62 there was another drought, and the scale of operations increased substantially. Until 1963 the governorates were responsible for all planning and execution, but thereafter the work was split between a national programme under the Ministry of Agriculture and regional programmes.

At first, the LCSD was not integrated into the country's national economic and investment plans but in 1962 this was changed and the Tunisian Government's financial contribution to the scheme was included in the budget. Possibly as a result of this move, which improved the government's scrutiny of its financial contribution, the scale of activities fell sharply, and increased only slightly in 1966/9 when the country experienced another drought. Food aid covers only a small part of the total cost of LCSD, as is clear from Table 6.4, and during 1960/3 the government's financial contribution was very high, representing almost 14 per cent of total government expenditure, and almost 32 per cent of its capital expenditure.[6] As the decade progressed, however, government expenditure rose, while outlays on LCSD fell so that by 1966/9 the Tunisian contribution represented only 4 per cent of the government's total expenditure and 9.5 per cent of its capital expenditure, which itself formed over 65 per cent of gross domestic investment.[7]

This major, nationwide programme of public works came to an end in 1973. At present, the only food for work project in operation is a WFP assisted scheme to improve soil and water conservation by constructing small dams and embankments in the Matmata hills of the two southern governorates, Gabès and Médenine. The project forms part of the Ministry of Agriculture's erosion control activities which are now undertaken by cash-paid labour in other parts of the country.

Productivity of Food for Work

The evidence that has been acquired on labour productivity in the four countries studied shows without exception that it is extremely low. The primary reasons appear to be that food for work attracts people with a low work capacity, and that supervision and ancillary equipment are inadequate. This much is clear; what is more open to question is whether the low productivity is necessarily a bad thing since it may be a corollary of reaching the poor.

Despite its brevity, the 1973-4 food for work project in Botswana provides an important illustration of the possibilities and limitations of such short-term drought-related campaigns. This is not only because it is better documented than some other projects, but also because the government made a serious attempt to make it a success. In a number of respects it was not a success, but the effort put into running the project was probably as high as can reasonably be expected in a country at Botswana's level of development, so that other countries in a similar position are unlikely to achieve better results. It is easy to forget that precisely because it is labour intensive, food for work has to face a full range of human problems. Thus, it may have an impact on the micropolitical scene where, for instance, it may appear to bolster the authority of the headteacher who has supervisory responsibility and thus incur the opposition of the local councillor and headman who are his rivals for influence. Such rivalries and the resulting bickering may affect the morale of the workforce which will also lose enthusiasm if work is delayed because machinery does not arrive on time, or if food deliveries are not made promptly.

There were undoubtedly many such social and micropolitical problems in Botswana, but in addition there were also a number of organisational difficulties. First, more people reported for work than had been anticipated. Each village was set a quota when the project was planned, but in almost all cases these were exceeded during the first half of the project period. This was partly owing to bad luck: estimating the number of people made destitute by drought is a hazardous affair, and the forecasts can be little more than 'guesstimates'. However, the excess turnout was also partly due to the government's own actions. When the project was planned, destitute families were categorised as:

Class A — households with no visible means of support but able to provide an ablebodied worker aged 14-60 years;

Class B — households with similar characteristics to Class A, but owning five or less small stock;

Class C — households qualifying for admission to Classes A and B but unable to supply an ablebodied worker aged 14-60 years.

The WFP assisted food for work project was designed to help Classes A and B who were assumed to be temporarily destitute as a result of the drought. It was not intended that Class C should be included for obvious reasons: destitute families with no ablebodied workers are unlikely to be able to participate in a programme of physical labour, and their destitution is unlikely to be a temporary consequence of the drought. It was therefore intended that Class C destitutes would receive from the government a cash allowance to enable them to purchase food. In the event, however, no such government programme materialised, and Class C destitutes tended to join the food for work projects.

The excess numbers had two corollaries. First, productivity suffered. In some cases overcrowding on the work site was such that the marginal productivity of the workers was negative, i.e. they tended to get in each other's way. The presence of large numbers of Class C destitutes who, by definition, could not work did not improve the situation. Second, consumption at higher levels than had been planned exacerbated shortages of food which had been ordered in batches. The first batch was for the WFP financed regional purchase of maize meal which began to arrive in September 1973 and was expected to last until Christmas, when further supplies obtained by the government would be available. In the event, however, the WFP food did not last this long, and some areas experienced a lengthy break in supplies. This potentially difficult situation was defused when heavy rains fell and some workers returned to their lands. There were also problems of poor supervision and ancillary support. A great deal was achieved by the personal initiative of those administering the scheme but the obstacles to be overcome were severe. In one district brick making machines that had been ordered before the project began had still not arrived by the time it had finished. In all there were 198 work sites, each of which had to be supplied at short notice with food, tools, sand, cement and supervision. Inevitably, this could not always be done.

The campaign had three stated objectives: to assist the destitute, to safeguard their self-respect, and to produce valuable public works that would offset the cost of the programme. Although differences in the scope of records kept by the districts make a national assessment of the project's cost effectiveness difficult, it is safe to conclude that it failed in its third objective. The value of the public works created did not offset the cost of the project; indeed, it would have been cheaper for the government to have handed out the food aid free of charge than it was to make people work for it. Excluding the value of the food, the project cost a good R35,000 more than it was worth in terms of the value of works produced.[8] Whether or not this expenditure can be justified in terms of the second objective of the project — to safeguard the destitute's self-respect — is a topic that is dealt with later in this chapter.

The Botswana campaign faced special problems because of the speed with which it had to be organised and the large number of work sites. It is possible that a permanent system of food for work would achieve higher levels of productivity. However, there is little doubt that food for work in Lesotho is also inefficient when measured against most conventional yardsticks. Two obvious reasons for this are a shortage of supervisors and of equipment. Conventional practice in the projects organised directly by Minrudev is for the work gang to elect a supervisor from among its own number. Such a person frequently lacks the authority or the resolve to enforce rigorous work practices. As for equipment, it is commonplace to see rocks for roadbuilding being carried one at a time in tin dishes from the quarry to the road site perhaps 200 yards away. Apart from these two specific problems there seems to be a more general one that food for work is seen less as work than as a vehicle for community development. It is considered to be 'women's work' and is normally the preserve of the elderly.

No detailed national comparison has been made of the efficiency of food for work and capital intensive or cash-paid labour intensive construction methods. However, one careful assessment of fish pond construction in three villages falling within the Leribe Pilot Agricultural Scheme (forerunner of the Khomokhoana Project) suggests that the average volume of excavation achieved per worker over 15 days is 2 cubic metres.[9] Given the estimated local value of WFP rations, this means the food cost of excavating 2 cubic metres is R6.59 at mid 1975 prices. This is not an altogether satisfactory example because the construction of a fish pond is a fairly complex operation. Better results were achieved in one dam building project in which 4.35 cubic metres of earth were moved per 15 man-days.[10] Nevertheless these are still extremely low figures. A fairly consecutive estimate for excavation by unskilled labour in normal soil is 2 cubic metres per man-day.[11] In other words, food workers have achieved in 15 days what ought to be a target for one day, although, of course, the food for work 'day' is relatively short. Such low productivity is partly offset by low rates of payment. Tender prices submitted by commercial contractors in 1973 gave a rate of R0.79 per cubic metre for cut-to-fill soil.[12] The rate for food for work, using mid 1975 prices and taking the highest rate of productivity achieved in the Leribe examples, is R1.52 per cubic metre. Contract prices rose considerably during the period 1973-5 and it is probable that by mid 1975 the commercial rate approached the food aid rate. Nevertheless, the cost of food for work has been calculated using the most productive example from a well supervised project. If instead a productivity norm of 2 cubic metres per work period is taken, the cost rises to R3.30 per cubic metre. In addition there are food distribution costs to be considered.

A comparison with commercial rates is thus not very flattering to food for work. The comparison is not completely satisfactory because commercial contractors use capital intensive methods and the market prices of labour and capital may diverge markedly from their opportunity costs. No direct comparison may be made with other forms of labour intensive construction in Lesotho because they do not exist. However, a 1975 interagency report on the feasibility of labour intensive techniques in Lesotho calculated that they would be competitive with capital intensive methods if the wage rates for unskilled labour did not exceed 80 cents per day. Since the report assumed labour productivity of 2 cubic metres of excavation per man-day, the competitive labour intensive rate may be given as 40 cents per cubic metre, which can be compared with the R1.52 or R3.30 per cubic metre paid under food for work.

What is particularly significant about these Lesotho figures is not so much that they are poor as that they may be considerably better than those in some other countries. Data on productivity in Upper Volta are very rudimentary. However, the indications are that it is lower than in Lesotho, and may be only one-third as great; productivity is probably so low that, as in Lesotho, it offsets the low value of the food aid ration and, in purely financial terms, makes food for work uncompetitive with commercial contractors. Even in Tunisia, where the government has considerably greater resources than exist in the other three countries, productivity in the LCSD was very low. Projects were chosen with inadequate care, supervision was poor, and the quality of labour was appropriate to an activity regarded as employment of the last resort. When it was begun, the LCSD was seen as essentially a welfare programme, and little attempt was made to attain high levels of productivity. At this stage the task of selecting and implementing projects lay with the governorates. The change of portfolio responsibility in 1959 to the Ministry of Finance and Economics saw the start of an attempt to link food for work with certain development objectives, and in 1964 a part of the programme was taken out of the hands of the governorates. However, by 1969 the regional programmes were still being allocated 59 per cent of the total number of work days, even though 'probably the lowest rate of labour productivity in the Tunisian food for work programmes is found in the regional ones.'[13] Communication and collaboration between the national government and the governorates was poor. A report by the Tunisian Office de la Formation Professionelle et de l'Emploi records:

> All attempts at controlling the local authorities by the central administration being deliberately ignored, it is difficult to admit that labour has been fully employed in the realisation of directly productive projects. Further, a preliminary orientation of governors towards a more vigorous choice of projects remains without response. The consequences are a very low labour productivity, and a very high cost of operations.[14]

The national programme was split between two departments of the Ministry of Agriculture: the Direction des Forêts, and the Direction de l'Hydraulique et du Développement Rural. The former used food for work in its afforestation programme, while the latter incorporated food aid labour in its erosion control work — conservation des eaux et des sols (CES). The work of the Direction des Forêts was generally more efficient than that of the CES programme, and an increasing share of the national allocation was channelled through it.[15] Nevertheless, neither department achieved any great success in maintaining a high level of productivity. Detailed rates are unavailable but there is some anecdotal information on various food aided projects such as:

Marth: (Governorate of Gabès) 20,000 man-days were authorised for building a 2 metre wall around a football ground representing a productivity rate of 25 man-days per linear metre;

Remada: A desert village in the governorate of Medenine, where even drinking water is scarce, was authorised to spend 19,000 man-days on a public garden;

Nabeul governorate: The repairing of non-paved country roads was authorised at a rate of 1.25 man-days per linear metre;

Le Kef governorate: 30,000 man-days were reported spent on repairing a 12 km road; a rate of 2.5 man-days per linear metre.[16]

The experience of these four countries is by no means untypical of labour intensive public works, whether or not they are food aided. Although a World Bank survey of 24 public works projects in 14 countries found that 'Tunisia appeared to have more than most [tasks] that could be classified as make-work . . .',[17] it also reported many other instances of low productivity on low priority projects. A survey of the literature has concluded that 'Productivity on most public works is abysmally low' and adds, further, that 'maintenance of completed assets is often so poor that very little benefit is derived'.[18]

What Are the Advantages of Food for Work?

It is difficult to disentangle the discussion of food for work from that on labour intensive public works generally; the preceding quotations are a case in point. There is a substantial literature discussing the merits of public works generally, and it is not possible to dwell here on all the issues raised. The essential economic argument in favour of labour intensive public works is that they benefit the poor, both in the short term by utilising a labour surplus and in the long term because the assets created yield income and employment over time. However, 75 per cent of the cases analysed by the World Bank study were executed in a policy environment that was generally unfavourable to employment,[19] and the long-run impact of public works is unlikely to be significant in such an environment. There is also some doubt over the impact of assets created by public works. In the first place, they may not yield a stream of financial benefits, as in the cases of Marth and Remada noted above. Second, assets with an economic use may not benefit the poor. A number of studies have argued that although public works may support poorer regions, they actually tend to worsen the distribution of asset ownership within the region, so that the main long-term benefits for the poor may come from working on newly created assets belonging to others.[20] It is important to distinguish between short- and long-term employment, and there is evidence that directly productive projects, such as irrigation, land reclamation and fisheries produce more employment during their operating phase, while economic infrastructure projects, such as roads, create more jobs during the construction phase.[21]

From the data available on Tunisia, Lesotho, Botswana and Upper Volta it appears that the bulk of the work undertaken with food aid would fall into the economic infrastructure category. For this reason,

and no less because there has been no serious attempt in the recipients
to list precisely the works created let alone to calculate their benefits,
this analysis will concentrate on employment created during the
construction phase of food aided public works. Whatever the merits
or otherwise of public works, the relevant question for this book is why
they should be linked to food aid. The question has two aspects: given
that there are public works, does it make sense to finance them with
food aid rather than cash; and, given that there is food aid, is it better
to channel it to food for work rather than to some other use. Many
arguments have been advanced on both aspects, but this discussion will
concentrate on the four listed at the beginning of the chapter.

Additionality

First there is the issue of additionality: food for work may encourage
governments to undertake labour intensive projects that would not
otherwise have occurred. Additionality is impossible to prove, but there
is every reason to suppose that it has occurred. This is partly owing to
the curious political position of food aid in recipient countries. Project
food aid has the potential to be simultaneously both more politicised
and less politicised than other forms of aid. Its high political value
derives from the fact that it can be used to reward individuals and is
therefore a more delicate political tool than is financial aid with which
a government can normally only reward communities by locating new
capital assets in their area. For this reason, food for work participants
(and indeed beneficiaries of supplementary feeding) may be selected on
partisan or ethnic grounds. However, at the same time both labour
intensive works and food aid tend to have a low priority in recipient
government circles. Thus, while there are many claims on the
government's resources of cash, there is little interest in food aid and
little opposition to its being used in the way suggested by the donor or
the local community development department. This may not be true of
bulk food aid, because it is effectively cash, or of very extensive
projects like LCSD, but it does reflect the situation with even relatively
large schemes such as in Lesotho.

Indeed, Lesotho provides a fascinating example of how food aid can
avoid budgetary problems that afflict cash derived from financial aid
or general revenue. Food aid has been used to build or improve half of
the country's roads, mainly those in the mountains where 40 per cent
of the population live. Had there been no food aid it is likely that the
roads would not exist. One criticism levelled at the scheme is that
villagers now refuse to maintain their roads without further food aid.[22]

It may be that this is less satisfactory than if the roads were taken over and maintained by the government or by voluntary self-help. Nevertheless, the point is that with the stimulus of food aid they *are* maintained, whereas the roads of the Ministry of Works are not. The Roads Department recurrent budget allocation for 1976/77 was some R800,000, which represents only half the estimated cost of keeping maintained all the roads for which it is responsible. In consequence, maintenance activities were generally restricted to the main tarred roads, with the gravel roads being left to deteriorate. The advantages of food aid in this case are that it has been available for recurrent expenditure whereas financial aid usually is not, and that the government has been more willing to use food aid for road maintenance than it has its general revenue, probably because of an excessive (although possibly temporary) financial cautiousness. This suggests, of course, that if it is desired to use food aid to finance the construction of physical assets it is better to channel it directly to food for work than indirectly by selling it on the open market and using the resulting revenue to pay cash wages to labourers. The apparent merit of open market sales linked to cash wages is that cash-paid labour is likely to have a higher rate of productivity than food-paid labour. However, the problem is that the cash may not, in practice, be used to finance labour-intensive public works, but will be spirited away to support development projects with a higher government priority.

The other side of the additionality coin is that lack of interest by key elements in the recipient government may mean that administration and supporting services are inadequate.[23] Much advice has been tendered that food for work productivity could be improved by better supervision and work organisation. Such advice is undoubtedly valid, and startling improvements have been achieved as, for example, in the Lesotho Woodlots Project in which the daily rate of digging pits increased from 4-10 to 30-70 after a system of targets was introduced.[24] In the Lesotho Thaba Bosiu Project there is one foreman for every 25 workers and he is selected by the project staff, not by his workmates, and paid in cash as well as food. As a result the project is believed to achieve a higher than average rate of productivity. However, to argue that better supervision would improve productivity is possibly to miss the point. Food for work schemes are not starved of supervisors and equipment because those administering them are unaware that more is required, but because they lack sufficient political weight to obtain more. A WFP team calculated in 1973 that the cost of providing the additional staff needed to bring the existing Lesotho food for work supervisory establishment up to a recommended level plus the cost of providing ancillary support such as vehicles was $36,000.[25] This represents an increase of only 19 per cent on actual expenditure on personal emoluments, travel and transport by the Food Aid Programme in 1972/3.[26] Nonetheless, even this modest proposal remained unimplemented even though domestic revenue rose by 65 per cent and recurrent expenditure by 15 per cent (in money terms) in 1973/4.[27]

Self-help

The second argument advanced in favour of food for work is that it encourages local self-help. This is a lively issue because food aid critics not only disagree, but have turned the proposition on its head and argued that it actually undermines self-help! Only the sporadic Upper Volta food for work projects before the drought had the potential to encourage self-help. In the other cases, food for work has been a vehicle for destitute relief or employment creation and the main issue is to defend it against charges that it has undermined the spirit of self-help. This is a nebulous area with question marks over the role of truly voluntary labour, as opposed to obligatory communal activity, in traditional life before food aid made its appearance, and the part played by a general extension of the money economy and its associated values in undermining such a role. Clearly the situation will vary widely between different countries, but it is wise not to romanticise the role of self-help both past and present, or to underestimate the power and pervasiveness of money economy values.

The three modes for financing public works — free self-help labour, food for work and cash-paid labour — are interrelated, and to a certain extent mutually exclusive. It is true that there are cases where all three exist side by side. In Lesotho there are the Ministry of Works and food for work roads, which exist next to a system for village water reticulation in which the government supplies the pipes free of charge and voluntary labour digs the trenches. For such peaceful coexistence, however, there needs to be an understanding that some activities are the preserve of self-help, others of food aid, and that in others cash wages are the norm. The division of tasks into these categories may be arbitrary and illogical, but so long as it is popularly accepted it may be possible to avoid problems. Confusion arises when the same activity is financed in different ways in different places or at different times. A village is unlikely to look kindly on self-help if its neighbour is receiving food aid for the same activity. Similarly, if in year 1 villagers make bricks for community projects using voluntary labour but in year 2 receive food aid for doing the same thing, they may become resentful if, in year 3 when the drought is over, they are expected to continue brick making but no longer receive the food. One possible reason for linking food for work to self-help has less to do with encouraging popular participation than with circumventing the recipient government's own labour laws. The cash value of the food for work ration is normally less than the government minimum wage. By stressing the role of food aid as a stimulus to local self-help, its role as a system of low wage employment can be obscured. The standing ILO/WFP practice is to distinguish between projects where the participants produce works that will benefit themselves directly e.g. community access roads and projects to undertake major public works. In the latter case, workers should receive food plus a cash payment of at least half the prevailing wage for comparable work. However, although the distinction between these two types of projects is fine in theory, in practice it is often hazy. The mutually exclusive nature of food for work and cash-paid labour is an important constraint on the scope for the former. Once cash wages have been paid for any specific activity it may be very difficult to introduce food wages for the same work. Significantly, the WFP assisted project in the Tunisian Matmata hills is experiencing difficulty in attracting labourers even though payment is in cash and food with a combined value slightly in excess of the cash-only rate paid for other CES work.[28]

From Emergency to Development

The third argument in favour of food for work is that it is a convenient transition from emergency food handouts to development food aid. It is common after a major emergency, as in the Sahel, for donors to introduce food for work to replace free handouts. There are two reasons for this. The first is that food for work can be used as a barometer of the emergency. It is very difficult to be sure when an emergency food shortage has disappeared, but if food aid is distributed through food for work, the length of the worker roll may provide a clue. When good rains fell unexpectedly in Botswana in 1974 it was observed that those who could do so quit the food for work gang and returned to their lands to plough. The second reason is that food for work safeguards the self-respect of those receiving food aid. This was a stated objective of the 1973/4 campaign in Botswana, and is an often unstated consideration elsewhere. It is difficult to assess the validity of such claims. At first sight it seems strange that projects in which productivity is so abysmally low could be personally satisfying for the participants. However, despite its cost, almost all districts in Botswana reported good morale among participants in the 1973/4 project, and asserted that it was a social success. The reason for this incongruity is that the participants see only one side of the cost/benefit ratio: they can see the benefit they have produced; they do not know the cost.

So there may be merit in linking food for work to emergencies. Against this, however, the prospects for achieving better rates of productivity are reduced by emphasising food for work as an occupation for emergency victims. Food for work becomes tarred in popular opinion with the stigma of destitute relief. People who are not destitute therefore do not like to become involved, even in schemes quite unrelated to an emergency. In Southern Africa it is viewed as 'women's work' and therefore not fit for men. In Tunisia, food workers are predominantly male, reflecting the different socioeconomic role of women, but nevertheless participation in food for work has low social status. Since age and infirmity are frequent causes of destitution, it follows that food for work tends to attract precisely those people who are ill equipped to work.

Income-in-Kind

This leads to the fourth proposition, that food for work is an effective mechanism for providing income-in-kind to poorer people. If this is accepted as a desirable goal, then paradoxically the low social status of food for work and the dismal rates of productivity that go with it may not be as undesirable as they appear on first sight. The low social status provides some assurance that only poor people will be prepared to accept the stigma, and in so far as the low productivity is the result of an infirm workforce (rather than poor supervision, etc.) and there exists a correlation between infirmity and poverty, it implies that the poor do indeed enrol. Of course, a neatly organised scheme which carefully selected the needy would be preferable to this haphazard arrangement, but it is rarely practical either on administrative grounds, or on political grounds if it is assumed that poverty is a result of political weakness. Arguably, food for work which has a social stigma is one of the few forms of aid that will not be monopolised or distorted by the affluent, although if the number of people prepared to accept the stigma exceeds the work places available (or sometimes even if it does not) there is scope for the participants to be selected according to their political or ethnic attributes. It is not possible to judge from the evidence of the four countries studied whether food for work reaches the poor better than other public works because only the former has been tried on any scale. However, it is interesting that the

Table 6.5: Male Unemployment and the Food for Work Project in Tunisia

Governorate	Male labour force	Unemployed males reported by census	% of labour force	Unemployed males in absence of food projects	% of labour force
Tunis	201,900	24,300	12.0	30,700	15.0
Pizerte	78,300	12,600	16.1	19,000	24.0
Beja	74,400	11,700	15.7	21,600	29.0
Jendouba	58,300	13,300	22.8	31,800	55.0
Le Kef	71,300	14,000	19.6	19,500	27.0
Nabeul	76,100	6,100	8.0	9,800	13.0
Sousse	103,300	15,600	15.1	21,200	21.0
Sfax	89,100	12,600	14.4	15,500	17.0
Kairouan	64,400	10,800	16.8	14,900	23.0
Kasserine	47,000	11,900	25.3	17,600	37.0
Gafsa	71,600	8,700	12.2	13,700	19.0
Gabes	41,400	6,400	15.5	11,100	27.0
Medinine	50,300	9,700	19.3	15,200	30.0
Total	1,027,700	157,700	15.3	241,600	23.0

Note: in this table we have retained the 20,000 working as semipermanent because we do not know their distribution by governorate.

Source: A. Grissa, *Agricultural Policies and Employment: Case Study of Tunisia*, Employment Series No. 9 (Paris, OECD Development Centre Studies, 1973), p. 119.

World Bank study of public works concluded that while they could benefit the landless, small farmers and unemployed they were 'generally unable to reach other poverty groups at even lower income levels, including the malnourished, the sick, the very young and very old, and frequently women or nomadic groups.'[29] This is in contrast to the results results of the current study which, although it uncovered no evidence of food for work helping the very young or nomads, has found instances of all the other groups listed benefiting from the food for work work programmes of Botswana, Lesotho, Upper Volta and Tunisia. Participants may use some of their income to increase food consumption, and food for work may therefore have a role to play in fighting malnutrition. This aspect is considered in the next chapter.

The relationship between food for work and unemployment deserves particular attention. If public works enrol those who would otherwise have been unemployed then the economic cost of the assets created will be less than the financial costs calculated in the section on productivity above. Furthermore, there are the political benefits of reducing high levels of unemployment. The most clearcut example of food aid being used to ameliorate the consequences of structural unemployment comes from Tunisia. Unemployment figures are not available for the years in which the LCSD was at its height, and may, in any case, be unreliable. However, a careful attempt has been made by Grissa to calculate unemployment levels for 1966 from the census data of that year, and to relate them to food for work (see Table 6.5, page 122). While the figures are not wholly reliable, they do seem to be sufficient to indicate the broad picture. Nationally, food for work reduced male unemployment by about one-third, and by more than this in some areas of high unemployment (Jendouba – 58 per cent, Béja – 46 per cent). When distributing the food, the government seems to have made a genuine attempt to give priority to areas with higher than average unemployment. Thus, the governorates of Jendouba, Kasserine, Médenine, Béja, Gabès, Le Kef, Kairouan and Gafsa, which have 47 per cent of the country's population, but which are generally considered to be relatively depressed, received between 67 per cent and 74 per cent of total LCSD allocations during 1965-9.[30]

Food for Farmers

Although food for work is the most extensive form of food for wages, it is not the only kind. Upper Volta has experienced a settlement scheme in which settlers have been given food aid until they became self-sufficient while in Botswana and Tunisia farmers have been

encouraged to adopt new practices or to extend their activities. The
Upper Volta settlement scheme began in 1970 and was designed to
resettle some 1,800 farm families on to 1,260 hectares of reclaimed
land in the Kou Valley, and subsequently also in the Comoe Valley.
Food aid rations were given to help the farmers survive until their first
adequate harvest, which was estimated to be one year (two harvests)
after settlement. The farmers were encouraged to grow rice, and assistance was received initially from Taiwan, but in September 1973 the
People's Republic of China (PRC) took over this aspect of the project
following a change in Upper Volta's policy on diplomatic recognition
of China. The World Bank, the EEC and France also provided financial
assistance for the water supply aspects of the work, while the Peace
Corps supplied some technical assistance. To put WFP's efforts into
perspective, the estimated value of the other external assistance
(excluding PRC and Peace Corps) was $7.3 million,[31] while on WFP's
own valuation its food aid stood at $2.5 million as at December
1975. In 1973 the WFP project was extended to take over the food
for work activities in the project area formerly provided under the
terminating predrought food aided scheme. There is little evidence on
its success. It appears that the departure of the Taiwanese caused
some problems, and that reporting has been poor. However, by mid
1976, 793 families had been settled in the Kou Valley, while in the
Comoe Valley 163 hectares had been prepared for agriculture and 450
farmers settled.[32] The main criterion for judging the success of
settlement projects is whether the farmers remain settled and achieve
selfsufficiency. It is probably too early to judge but so far it seems
that results and the speed at which farmers can subsist without food
aid has been variable: a survey in mid 1975, for example, found that in
the village of Mogtedo, none of the farmers settled in 1973 or 1974
were still receiving food aid and that in the village of Linoghin, only
two out of 28 families settled in 1973 were still receiving food aid; but
in Kaibo South 50 out of 100 farmers settled in 1973 were still receiving
WFP rations.[33]

The Botswana experiment was only short lived and occurred in
1973/4 alongside the drought-linked food for work campaign. Fears
had been expressed in the government following the 1969/71 food for
work project that food aid might be acting as a disincentive to
agricultural production. In an attempt to assess the validity of these
fears, the government with FAO assistance conducted a field survey
during 1971-2 into the background and motivation of food for work
participants.[34] The results were not available in time to assist the

planning of the 1973/4 campaign, but it was considered prudent to link a part of the drought relief programme to agricultural improvement schemes administered by the Ministry of Agriculture. These plans crystallised into a scheme to use food aid as an incentive to encourage farmers to plough their lands at the end of the previous season, which acquired the title of the 'food for fallow' project, and a scheme to encourage them to build small water catchment tanks, the 'food for tank dam' project. The term 'food for fallow' can be misleading as it implies that farmers were encouraged to take land out of production. This was not the case. Traditional practice is roughly for farmers to plough and sow during November to January and to harvest in June to August. Research at the Ministry of Agriculture has suggested that bringing forward ploughing and weeding to just after the harvest has two advantages. First, the amount of moisture retained in the earth during the dry winter can be increased, thereby improving the yield of crops sown during the following agricultural year. Second, early ploughing also means that sowing can begin as soon as the rains start to fall in the spring. Under the food for fallow scheme, therefore, farmers were offered a risk insurance of a 45 kg bag of food sorghum per acre if they altered their traditional farming practice, and adopted the new, improved regime.

In terms of speed of implementation, the food for fallow scheme was most impressive. It was formulated between the Ministry of Agriculture and the local WFP office in January 1973. A formal request was submitted to WFP in Rome in early February, approved within 10 days, and a formal agreement was signed at the end of February. The project commenced on 1 March 1973, and the participating farmers were approached and persuaded to plough within two months. The project also achieved some of its objectives. Of the farmers who ploughed early 97 per cent also weeded early, and 78 per cent of them had planted by the end of November. The distribution of food was thus associated with a genuine change in agricultural practices by the recipients. The new methods also resulted in better yields, although the improvement over the old methods was less spectacular than had been anticipated because, contrary to expectations, the 1973/4 rains generally proved to be very good. The good rains had two effects. First, of course, harvests generally were very good so that the demonstration effect of the improved practice was less than it might have been in a bad year. Second, the improvement was designed specifically to benefit farmers in periods of low rainfall, and involved a danger that in times of very heavy rain production could actually fall as a result of early ploughing. Nevertheless, despite these problems participating farmers did record startling yield increases averaging 37 per cent on fallowed land.[35]

Yet the project was only a partial success. Its failures arise from its origins. First, because it was an emergency project devised in response to a drought that had already occurred, it had to be put into operation rapidly. This inevitably meant that many farmers were missed. Only 1,714 farmers participated, and only 516 of these came from the northern areas. This shortfall would not have been a major setback if the project had been continued and extended in subsequent years. Unfortunately it was not. The food for fallow scheme was in no sense a 'make work' project drummed up to provide an excuse for distributing emergency food aid. It was a project that had received support in the Ministry of Agriculture before the question of supporting it with food aid had been raised, and it is now incorporated into the National Development Plan as a bona fide aspect of the agricultural development strategy. However, it is not at the forefront of government's priorities. There is still disagreement over whether agricultural improvements should be encouraged by 'rewards' or whether new techniques will never be successfully transplanted unless the farmer can recognise their advantages without needing to be persuaded by a reward. Added to this, there have been good rains in every summer since 1973/4, which has banished food aid to the back of people's minds and makes winter fallowing appear less urgent. In consequence, although the Ministry of Agriculture prepared a proposal for a followup project in February 1974, it was not possible to reach agreement within the government in time for it to become operative that autumn, and it has not been revived since.

Despite these negative aspects, food for fallow was an admirable example of an imaginative use of food aid, and although it has not been followed up it has shown that it is feasible to use food aid to encourage agricultural development. The food for tank-dam scheme was less successful. It did not become operational until the 1973/4 agricultural year, and then broke down because the rains, far from being scanty, were some of the heaviest on record. The rains hit the scheme in two ways. First, the project was designed to provide useful work for farmers with time on their hands; in the event the bumper rains produced a bumper harvest and so there was no shortage of work. Second, the heavy rains themselves hindered the construction of dams by saturating partially completed structures. Nonetheless, some success was achieved since 318 farmers completed tank dams.

The Tunisian food for farmers project is much larger and has been in operation longer although it, too, has been somewhat crippled by external factors. A series of UNDP Special Fund research projects[36] completed during the 1960s concluded that the climate and soils of the rainfed areas of the Centre and South do not permit any other agricultural strategy than a mix of tree crops, cereals and sheep. Instead of this ideal mix, the area was in fact carrying too much cereals and sheep, thus leading to erosion problems. Thus, a UNDP/FAO study[37] found that although only 21 per cent of the land in the high steppes is suitable for cereals, in practice 59 per cent is under cereals at any one time. A major government project was therefore launched in 1969 with FAO and WFP assistance to provide a package of inputs to farmers in the area via the co-operative movement and to encourage planting new olive, almond and pistaccio trees, maintenance of earlier plantations, regeneration of old olive trees, planting of forage reserves, and erosion control. The WFP contribution was to supply food rations to participating farmers and also 20,000 tonnes of wheat for market sale to raise finance for locally produced tools and equipment. In addition to food rations, farmers were to receive cash grants and loans on completion of specified tasks. The aim was thus to improve the mix of farming activities in the area, and to boost the co-operative movement.

The achievements of the project are given in Table 6.6, page 128, which shows that there has been considerable variation in the extent to which the targets for various activities have been reached. Targets for establishing new plantations and maintaining old ones have been met, but very little has been done on soil conservation. One negative implication of this discontinuity is that more trees may have been planted than can be maintained in the long term. Essentially, the activities that can be undertaken on an individual-farmer basis have prospered, while those best done in a co-operative context have not. The reason for this is that in September 1969, less than half a year after WFP approved the project, the co-operative movement collapsed. So traumatic was the co-operative experience and the subsequent policy reversal that government involvement in group activity since then has been extremely circumspect. Indeed, although farmers' groups are required for participation in the WFP project, they are known as *groupements* rather than *coopératives.*

This change in government policy has influenced considerably the ability of the project to achieve its original objectives. The WFP assistance was intended to boost the co-operative movement, but in

Table 6.6: Tunisia; WFP Project 482 Targets and Achievements, by Year (in hectares, unless stated otherwise)

	(1) 1968/9	(1) 1969/70	(2) 1970/1	(2) 1971/2	(3) 1972/3	(3) 1973/4	(4) 1974/5	(4) 1975/6
New plantations and their maintenance								
Target	12,000	16,000	14,000	12,000	12,000	16,000	11,500	7,500
Actual	–	3,453	2,442	7,640	22,592	21,667	22,886	17,472
Maintenance of earlier plantations								
Target	70,000	70,000	70,000	70,000	70,000	143,500	123,000	102,000
Actual	90,031	69,601	81,204	101,880	129,036	166,728	134,299	110,062
Regeneration of olive trees								
Target	4,000	6,000	6,000	6,000	6,000	–	200	200
Actual	500	–	–	–	–	–	–	200
Cactus plantations								
Target	4,000	6,000	6,000	4,000	2,000	19,000	25,000	25,000
Actual	4,537	1,845	6,247	8,654	13,787	17,192	25,392	12,890
Soil conservation								
Target	120,000	120,000	120,000	120,000	120,000	1,400,000[a]	1,800,000[a]	2,200,000[a]
Actual	29,945	7,008	8,352	2,192	450	1,653	–	–

Note: data sources vary in different years, but are revised on the basis of latest available information. Targets for 1973/4, 1974/5 and 1975/6 are *additional* to those of the Original Plan of Operations.

(1) Figures taken from the report of the 1971 Evaluation Mission, based on government reports.
(2) Figures taken from the report of the 1973 Evaluation Mission, based on government reports.
(3) Figures taken from the 1975 government request for Project 482 Expansion.
(4) Figures taken from the government report to the 1976 Evaluation Mission.
a. The area in hectares has been changed to volume units (cubic metres).

practice the co-operatives have continued to exist largely in order to distribute WFP food. The co-operatives themselves are now service co-operatives rather than the pre-1969 production co-operatives. Their income, out of which are paid staff salaries and food transport costs, is derived almost entirely from a fixed 10 per cent of the total credits and subventions provided to members under the project. As the scheme progresses, the plantation and maintenance activities of the co-operatives are phased out and their income falls correspondingly. Already some groups are having difficulty in paying their officials. At a national level, project staff are recruited on special contracts and they have been drifting away towards posts that are better integrated into the civil service career structure.

Clearly there is no way in which the food aid donor could have influenced the government shift away from co-operatives. The fact that even under these difficult circumstances the project has succeeded in encouraging tree plantation underlines the potential of this use of food aid, which appears to be more cost effective at producing given results than more conventional food for work. However, the Tunisian and Botswana examples suggest that unlike food for work it is not well designed to alleviate unemployment/underemployment or to reach the poor. An investigation in 1975 of the Tunisian project activities in the Gafsa governorate has suggested that the main beneficiaries are the larger more prosperous farmers, and the same was true of the Botswana food for fallow scheme. In Tunisia, it is the larger farmers who generally are able to gather together the minimum number of clients needed to start a service co-operative; they stand a better chance of being selected because their land titles are better established; and they have access to the labour required to complete the tasks on time. These factors are all specific to the Tunisian experience, but the method of payment, in credits and food, itself favours the large farmer who can afford to wait up to a year or more to be paid for the costs he has to incur at the beginning. Hence the statement made at the start of this chapter, that while food for work reaches poor people productivity is low, and while food for farmers achieves higher productivity it does not reach the poor.

Notes

1. See Bibliography: Singer (1978a), p. 26.
2. Service de l'Hydraulique et de l'Equipement (HER).
3. See E.S. Seligman, *Project Proposal: Earthen Dam Repairs and Construction in Upper Volta* (Ouagadougou, 1 October 1972), mimeo.), pp. 16–17.
4. See Bibliography: WFP (1974a).
5. Grissa, see Bibliography: (1973), p. 137.

6. Ibid., p. 139.

7. Ibid., p. 140.

8. All but three districts (Kgalagadi, North East, and Southern) produced figures on the non-food costs of the project and the number of bricks produced. These six districts spent R96,470 and made 1,574,707 bricks, worth R22,046 if they are valued at R14 per thousand. Part of this expenditure was on tools and equipment which have a residual value. Not all districts reported on the amount spent on tools, but from the figures supplied by five districts it seems that approximately one-third of total expenditure is accounted for in this way. If the cost of tools is discounted, the non-food costs of the project are reduced to R64,346. Some gangs undertook other development projects in addition to brick making and these have a value. Unfortunately, only one district attempted to estimate their value, and reckoned it to be 37 per cent of the value of bricks. If this figure is taken as a rough guide for other districts, the total value of work is increased to R30,203. It is improbable that the value of other works exceeded this proportion since brickmaking was the main activity. Thus, the project cost a good R35,000 more than it was worth in terms of the value of works produced. Since the figure for expenditure does not include either transport or the cost of government personnel, the true cost must be higher. In particular the opportunity cost of the time devoted to the project by key development staff must be considerable.

9. *Some Comparisons and Costs of Earthworks Built by Food Aid Labour* (Leribe Pilot Agricultural Scheme, April 1974), Table 5.

10. Ibid.

11. See, for example, *Lesotho: Transportation Study* (Roughton and Partners, March 1974) and data from the World Bank.

12. Ibid., figure 5.20.

13. Grissa (1973), p. 145.

14. Office de la Formation Professionelle et de l'Emploi, *L'expérience tunisienne de mobilisation de la main-d'oeuvre* (Tunis, 1969), p. 5, cited in Grissa (1973), p. 144.

15. WFP project 425, the successor to the LCSD, is also organised by the Direction des Forêts, but since it is concerned with CES work this presumably reflects a reorganisation of the Ministry of Agriculture.

16. Grissa (1973), pp. 165–7.

17. See Bibliography: Thomas *et al.* (1976); and also World Bank (1976a).

18. See Bibliography: Maxwell (1978a), p. 40; see also Singer (1978a), p. 30.

19. World Bank (1976a), p. 21.

20. See Bibliography: Singer (1978a), pp. 36–7.

21. World Bank (1976a), p. 29.

22. WFP (1976a), Annex II, para. 29 (i).

23. A point confirmed by the World Bank study, Thomas *et al.* (1976a), p. 458.

24. *Lesotho Woodlots Project – First Annual Report for the Period 1 April 1973–31 March 1974* (Maseru, mimeo.).

25. WFP (1973d), paras 8.3, 8.4.

26. See Bibliography: Lesotho (1973a).

27. Lesotho (1976a), Table 4.1, p. 27.

28. The 1977 daily rate for food for work is 500 millimes cash and a ration worth something under 300 millimes; cash-paid CES workers receive 700 millimes per day. Information from the Direction des Forêts.

29. Thomas *et al.* (1976a), p. 454.

30. Grissa (1973), p. 151.

31. WFP (1975e), paras 8, 10.

32. *Quarterly Progress Report Project 446 — 2nd Quarter 1976.*

33. WFP, Ouagadougou.

34. Botswana (1974b).

35. Evaluation was not undertaken very rigorously, and so the records may be fairly inaccurate. Nevertheless, it is clear that large yield increases were experienced.

36. Tunisia 3, Tunisia 8 and Tunisia 17.

37. TUN/72/004.

SECTION THREE: THE IMPACT OF FOOD AID

7 THE IMPACT OF FOOD AID ON NUTRITION

At first sight it might appear to be rather easy to judge the impact of food aid on nutrition. After all, this type of aid involves transferring food from rich to poor countries, and any which is not wasted is eaten by someone either directly or, if it is supplied as animal feed, indirectly. Furthermore, the task of fighting malnutrition is a constant theme of the largest food aid donors.[1] However, despite appearances the topic is a minefield of conflicting opinions and major gaps in information. There is controversy over whether investment in nutrition is either necessary or cost effective, and whether nutrition programmes, if they do occur, should include food handouts. Even among those who accept a need for rations, there is disagreement over whether these should be based on food aid or on locally purchased commodities. In addition to such general questions there are a host of practical issues concerning the extent to which specific food aided projects achieve their goals.

Probably all the projects associated with food aid have been accorded nutritional objectives by some observers at some time. However, this chapter will concentrate on the schemes that are most likely to have a major impact on nutrition. They include those schemes described as 'food for nutrition' in Chapter 5, and the food for work projects dealt with in Chapter 6. Food for nutrition schemes are obvious candidates because they concentrate on a section of society that is assumed to be especially vulnerable to malnutrition. The nutritional impact of food for work is less obvious, and to an extent linking the two causes confusion as well as illumination. Food for work participants may be malnourished, but unlike mother/pre-school child (MCH) beneficiaries they are not selected specifically because they are vulnerable. Nonetheless, it was noted in Chapter 6 that food for work tends to reach poor people who may face real problems of malnutrition because of their poverty. Furthermore, food for work projects are often accorded major nutritional goals by the donors, and such claims should be tested. The procedure in this chapter will be to consider first the claims of food for nutrition projects, to which most of the relevant data refer, and then to see whether such advantages or defects as have been identified can also be found in food for work.

Table 7.1: Energy Supply and Number of Undernourished Persons by Region

	Daily per caput calorie supply, 1972/4	No. of persons with food intake below 1.2 BMR, 1972/4	
		Millions	As % of population
Africa	2,110	83	28
Latin America	2,540	46	15
Near East	2,440	29	16
Far East	2,040	297	29
Developing market economies	2,180	455	25

Source: World Food Programme, *Interim Report on the Assessment of Food Aid Requirements, Including the Question of Food Aid Targets,* WFP/CFA: 5/5—B (Rome, March 1978), Table 2.

Approximately one-sixth of total food aid is used in projects which have over-riding nutritional objectives. In 1974, 11 per cent of food aid flows worth $150 million was absorbed in supplementary feeding programmes, while a further 7 per cent was used for emergency feeding; some 40 million people benefited directly from these schemes.[2] The number of beneficiaries, though large, is but a small proportion of those who may be vulnerable. The number of young mothers and pre-school children who would be eligible for MCH feeding was estimated at over 200 million in 1971, while the number of people with insufficient calories has been put at 900-1,200 million.[3] The regional distribution of malnutrition is shown in Table 7.1, above, which reveals Africa to be one of the most vulnerable continents. Apart from this obvious limitation that food for nutrition programmes, numerically important though they are, cover only a fraction of the potential target population, there are other, more fundamental, questions about the validity of such schemes.

The main justification for supplementary feeding is that malnutrition is a major and persisting problem with unacceptable moral and economic consequences which will not be solved effectively by economic growth alone since it is normally as much the result of poor distribution as of low production.[4] Feeding programmes attempt to identify pockets of special vulnerability and to relieve the problem directly by supplying food rations. They are thus seen best as a method of providing income-in-kind to selected groups with a view to improving

income distribution; this is an important definition of supplementary
feeding to which we return later in the chapter.

There appears to be a large measure of support for the idea that the
problem of malnutrition is essentially one of poverty and poor
distribution. Thus, the first hurdle for food aid is not on this basic
point, but on whether food for nutrition projects have accurately
identified pockets of particular vulnerability. The question, in short, is
whether the people who receive food aid are liable to suffer mental or
physical damage as a result of malnutrition and, above all, whether the
damage is permanent. There exists a link, which is particularly marked
among young children, between malnutrition and both mortality[5] and
mental development.[6] However, while good nutrition may be a
necessary condition for adequate mental development it is questionable
whether it is a sufficient condition since other environmental factors,
notably social stimulation, also have a part to play. Further, it has been
argued that the damage caused by malnutrition is only permanent in
severe cases which may afflict under 5 per cent of the preschool
population in ldcs, whereas reversible, mild malnutrition affects up to
40 per cent.[7] The issue cannot be taken much further here because
none of the sub-Saharan case studies has base-line nutrition data
adequate to show the extent of different degrees of malnutrition. In
Tunisia, there has been a nutrition survey which has concluded that:

> It is clear that significant growth retardation exists in Tunisian
> children. The problem is essentially nationwide. During the second
> year of life, Tunisian children undergo a particularly great food
> deficit and weight relative to height drops considerably below that
> of European and North American children. . . . Although the
> retardation is not as severe as observed in some developing
> countries, it nevertheless is sufficiently marked to warrant major
> attention in future planning.[8]

Although it identified a nutrition problem, the survey was generally
optimistic about the severity of malnutrition and the possibilities for
improvement. However, the same optimism may well not apply to the
other case studies where standards of living are generally much lower.
In all of the countries studied, and probably in the majority of
countries receiving food aid, the data on nutrition are too inadequate
to justify any firm conclusions on the degree, location and socioeconomic consequences of malnutrition. In three of the case studies,
however, there are reasonable indications that malnutrition exists to

some degree and in some places, and it will be assumed for the remainder of this chapter that it is sufficiently severe to justify government action and for such action to be able to hold its own on economic as well as social grounds with other claims on national resources. The question then becomes one of whether supplementary feeding is an appropriate vehicle for such action, and whether food aid can satisfactorily be incorporated into such programmes. In turn, these issues depend on whether the problem is caused by an absolute shortage of food (and if so, which foods) or by poor nutrition practices, as well as whether supplementary feeding programmes reach those families with members at risk and, if they do, whether the ration is consumed by those who need it.

Who Receives the Food?

The two main vehicles for supplementary feeding are the primary school lunch and MCH schemes. In Lesotho all primary school children, and in Botswana the great majority of them, have access to a food aid meal; those who do not are either relatively advantaged like children at the English-medium schools in Botswana, or probably underprivileged, such as those at unregistered schools. In Upper Volta, distribution is much more haphazard since transport has to be provided by the recipient school. In Tunisia, there is a deliberate policy of selecting poor children to receive the meal free of charge; others may also receive it but they have to pay. However, in none of these four countries is primary education universal: the highest rate of enrolment is achieved by Tunisia with 70-75 per cent of the primary school age population at school, while the lowest rate is recorded in Upper Volta with only 10 per cent.[9] Thus, even if all schools were covered, the lunch programme would still miss substantial sections of the population, and there is every reason to believe that those children who do not attend school are more vulnerable than those who do. This is particularly true since national statistics conceal regional variations which often mirror differences in relative affluence. Thus, the richer coastal governorates of Tunisia have an attendance rate of some 75 per cent, while in the poorer interior the figure falls to 57 per cent. Similarly, in Upper Volta the low national figure conceals an even lower 4 per cent for the Sahel département in the extreme north of the country.

This would not necessarily be a major criticism if at least the school population contained a substantial proportion of poorer people even if it excluded the poorest. The poorest groups are often inaccessible not only to school feeding but also to other government programmes. Before deciding that school lunches are an unsatisfactory method of combating malnutrition their problems of coverage need to be compared with those of alternative schemes. However, there is some evidence that the lunch programme does not simply miss the poorest groups, but positively discriminates against them because primary school children come from essentially non-vulnerable backgrounds. In the case of Botswana it has been possible to relate school attendance to economic background.[10] The conclusion is that students tend to come from households which have an income of over $560 p.a., and which obtain less than half their income in kind and are not heavily dependent on transfers and income-in-kind. This conclusion may households whose children do not attend school: they are particularly dependent on transfers and income in kind. This conclusion may differ in the other case studies for which information on food aid and income distribution is too rudimentary to make such comparisons. However, with 71 per cent of the 7-13 year age cohort at primary school,[11] Botswana comes a close second to Tunisia in terms of educational coverage. Only if income distribution is less skewed in Lesotho, Upper Volta or Tunisia than it is in Botswana will the primary school population be more representative. Botswana certainly does have a fairly unequal distribution of income, with a Gini coefficient of 52 per cent for the rural areas.[12] No directly comparable measures are available for Upper Volta or Lesotho, but in Tunisia the Gini coefficient has been estimated on 1970 data at 50 per cent[13] which is close to the Botswana figure. It seems improbable that income distribution in Upper Volta could be sufficiently egalitarian to compensate for the very limited primary school coverage. The only country in which the conclusions reached for Botswana might be tempered is Lesotho, in which some 60 per cent of the primary school age population are at school, and which has an unusually even distribution of income, at least for the rural population. No Gini coefficient has been calculated for Lesotho, but it has been estimated that the poorest 5 per cent of the rural population earn 4 per cent of total income and that the bottom 20 per cent earn 16 per cent of income; in Botswana the comparable figures are 0.7 per cent and 4.3 per cent.[14]

This problem of built-in bias does not apply to MCH projects. Furthermore, it has been argued that MCH beneficiaries, especially pre-school children, are a more satisfactory target group than are school children who may already have suffered irreversible damage by the time they reach school age. However, even with MCH programmes there is likely to be an element of bias against the poor because some of them are inaccessible, and possibly also because relatively affluent mothers are adept at taking a disproportionate share of food supplies. Supplementary food rations directed at mothers and pre-school children may be distributed either from health clinics or from other points that in some cases have been set up expressly to disburse food aid, like the voluntary feeding centres in Botswana. In either case organising the scheme requires a fairly heavy administrative input, even though the government may be able to share this burden with international and local voluntary groups. In cases where the ration is distributed from a clinic, the geographical coverage of the scheme will be limited by the number of health facilities that the country can operate. In other cases, the limiting factors will be transport, storage and administrative capacity. In either event, total coverage of the country is unlikely. Some mothers will be able to travel from their home to the nearest feeding centre in another village, but this will not always be possible, particularly in the less densely populated areas. Yet often those living in inaccessible parts may be particularly vulnerable. In Botswana, the national ratio of food distribution centres to settlements of over 200 people is 1:1.7, but in the Ngamiland district of the north west it is 1:3.4.[15] Furthermore, a recent rural income distribution survey has found the median income in the north and north west (Ngamiland and Chobe) to be 29 per cent less than the national average, and it also observed a similar difference between the median annual income of residents of large villages (R887) and those of small villages, lands areas and cattle posts (R610). Botswana is a very large country with a very small population and so has special difficulties. However, Lesotho and Upper Volta are also badly served by geography and infrastructure. Lesotho is compact, but 40 per cent of the population live in the mountain region where transport is difficult. The figures on the geographical distribution of beneficiaries in Table 7.2, page 141, give only a partial picture of the adequacy of coverage. They are donor estimates of the numbers served by each district depot, but most districts contain both lowland and mountain areas, and, in any case, a depot in one district may supply food to another area. Nevertheless, it is interesting to note from column (3), which gives MCH beneficiaries as a proportion of district population, that the highest percentages are recorded in Quthing and Berea, which include relatively small areas of mountains, while the lowest percentages refer to the only district that is almost completely mountainous,

Mokhotlong, and its neighbour Butha Buthe. In Lesotho this geographic bias may not adversely affect the project's capacity to reach the poor because, contrary to what might be expected, there is no significant difference between rural incomes in the mountains and in the lowlands. An estimate for 1970 put average annual household income at R198 for the mountains and R199 for lowlands; the relatively poor areas are the foothills (where the estimated income was R161),[16] which are not distinguishable from Table 7.2.

Table 7.2: Distribution of MCH Food Aid Beneficiaries in Lesotho by Depot

District depot	(1) No. of beneficiaries	(2) Estimated de facto population	(3) (1) as % of (2)
Berea	14,139	116,800	12
Butha Buthe	3,370	65,100	5
Leribe	15,476	164,900	9
Mafeteng	11,576	118,700	10
Maseru	16,376	219,600	8
Mohale's Hoek	8,320	118,900	7
Mokhotlong	3,763	66,000	6
Qacha's Nek	5,309	66,300	8
Quthing	14,516	79,600	18
Total	92,845	1,015,900	

Source: WFP, CRS, Maseru.

In Upper Volta there is no adequate information on the distribution of MCH food aid, largely because of the administrative system which requires each centre to collect its own supplies from a limited number of depots. However, there is reason to suppose both that the more remote départements are less well supplied under this system than they would be under a more centralised regime, and also that they are poorer than the average. Of the four countries, Tunisia is best placed to organise a good geographical coverage for its supplementary feeding. However, until it ceased altogether, MCH food aid was distributed only from health clinics. There were thus only 110 distribution points, which is less than the number in either Botswana (312) or Lesotho (265).

Thus, MCH programmes probably miss some of the poor because of inadequate geographic coverage. It has also been argued that relatively affluent mothers manage to shoulder aside their poor compatriots in the great food grab. By its nature, it is difficult to obtain hard facts about this sort of thing, but there have certainly been reports from field staff associated with MCH programmes (often health workers) that it has occurred, with Northern Ghana during the 1977 drought being a case in point. Clearly, this will be a problem only if demand for food at a particular distribution point exceeds supply. If it does not, then rich mothers may still get a disproportionate share but the potential of supplementary feeding to help vulnerable individuals will not be reduced, although the cost effectiveness of the exercise may be impaired. Unfortunately, in none of the four countries studied are records kept to indicate supply and demand, and in none is there any official policy of selection to favour economically disadvantaged people (although in Tunisia there was a practice of medical selection, contrary to the wishes of the donors). This is an area in which donors could improve on their control procedures. All that can be reported in the absence of any such data is that there were no reports in the four case studies of this sort of problem. Although this certainly does not prove that the problem does not exist, it does suggest that it is not a universal difficulty of major proportions. To an extent, the problem affects both food and financial aid, with the capacity of local elites to cream off the benefits of aid varying from one ldc to another. The decision whether to continue a programme despite corruption is clearly very delicate because some benefits may still reach the poor. However, although food and financial aid face similar problems, those of food aid may well be the more severe for reasons summed up in the aphorism that 'nothing falls off the back of a lorry more easily than a sack of food aid!'

An extensive evaluation by CARE in 1976 of its preschool take-home feeding programmes in Colombia, the Dominican Republic and Pakistan, as well as its on-site projects in Tamil Nadu, India and Costa Rica, provides some further evidence on the coverage of MCH. It concluded that 'the feeding programmes enrol many children who are not malnourished.'[17]

Food for work differs from supplementary feeding both on the count of geographic coverage and on that of diversion to the rich. Since a food for work project requires a greater administrative input than a voluntary feeding centre, it is unlikely to achieve as wide a geographic coverage as supplementary feeding. However, it may be possible to compensate for this narrow front, and also for the fact that participants as a group are not vulnerable in the same way as mothers and children, by concentrating on the poorest areas. The Tunisian LCSD (La lutte contre le sous-développement) put more resources into the poorer governorates than into the richer ones, and to the extent that food for work is linked to emergency relief it is likely to concentrate on the more vulnerable regions. On the other hand, the problem that the most vulnerable people may also be the most remote applies equally to both supplementary feeding and food for work. Where food for work really scores is that in cases where participation has acquired a social stigma, the affluent are less likely to crowd out the poor than they may with supplementary feeding.

Who Consumes the Food?

Leaving aside the problem of distribution, there remains the issue of who actually consumes the food after it has been handed over, and whether it is fully absorbed in additional consumption or whether it partly displaces food from other sources. Here the positions of MCH and the school lunch programmes are reversed, with the latter providing the more satisfactory answers. School children may not be among the poorest, but at least there is no doubt that they receive the food ration: they are offered a midday meal with the option only of whether to take it or leave it. With MCH there is no such certainty, except in the limited number of residential, remedial feeding centres. The mother is given a ration to last a week or a month and takes it home. The rations are designed to make a significant contribution to the nutritional requirements of the mother and her baby; Table 7.3, page 144, illustrates this by comparing the calories supplied by the World Food Programme and the Catholic Relief Services in Lesotho with the FAO/WHO recommended allowance. However, the ration will achieve this result only if it is consumed solely by the initial beneficiary. In practice, this is unlikely to happen: it is improbable that a mother would store her food aid ration completely separately from the family supplies, and equally unlikely that she would refuse to share it with other members of the household. The 1976 CARE survey found that half the children from the take-home programmes had not eaten the ration the previous day, and that the most frequent reason for this was that the mother had run out of food ahead of schedule because she had shared it with the rest of the family.[18] The conclusion that MCH rations are probably inadequate because of sharing is hardly earth shattering, but it is highly significant because donors have not taken it into account in their actions. The average de facto rural family size in Lesotho is 4.4

persons, with roughly one child in the preschool age group.[19] In a
four-member family with two MCH beneficiaries in which the food
ration was shared equally, the preschool child would get only 21 per
cent, and his mother only 12 per cent of their daily requirements, or
half the levels estimated in Table 7.3, below. In a situation where
social custom favours age and males, the sharing might not be equal
so that the intended beneficiaries would receive even less. One way
around this problem would be simply to increase the ration, but this
would also increase the cost of the programme and could have
implications for local commerce and agriculture (which are considered
in the next two chapters) since some of the ration might be sold or
displace local production. Interestingly, this is precisely the solution
adopted in food for work in which rations are typically calculated on
the needs of both the actual participant and four or five dependents.

Table 7.3: Comparison of Calories Supplied by WFP/CRS Ration in
Lesotho and Allowance of Calories Recommended by FAO/WHO

Recipient	(1) Supplied calories	(2) Recommended calories	(3) (1) as % of (2)
Pregnant woman	586	2,500	23
Preschool child	586	1,400	42
Primary school child	740	2,400	31

Source: M. van der Wiel—van Heughten, *Field Report 1 July — 30 September 1973*
(World Food Programme, Maseru), Table II.

The possibility that the ration is sold or displaces local production
has obvious implications for nutrition as well as consumer prices
and agriculture. The notion of supplementary feeding is based
on the assumption that rations will be completely absorbed by increased
consumption, if not by the direct beneficiary then at least by her kith
and kin. If this does not happen then of course the nutritional impact
will be smaller than expected, and increasing the size of the ration will
not necessarily improve the situation. There is no firm evidence from
the four case studies of what happens on this score, and a fairly
extensive socioeconomic survey would be needed to fill the gap, but the
finding of the CARE evaluation is that 'In all five countries mothers
stated that they were able to spend less on foods for their family since
being enrolled in the CARE feeding program . . .'[20] It should be

emphasised that this does not mean the food aid goes to waste: the actual impact will depend on what the recipients do with their savings/earnings, and this is a recurring theme in the remainder of this book. Nor does it necessarily mean that the recipients were not malnourished to begin with: even malnourished people may prefer to use their income-in-kind on purchases other than food. However, it does reduce the attractions of supplementary feeding as a method of combating malnutrition.

The possibility that the receipt of food rations may provoke a complex change in the recipient's economic relations (a sort of household fungibility) applies equally to the school lunch and food for work programmes. Although we can be sure that the school children actually eat the ration, it does not follow that their total food consumption increases by the same amount. They may be provided with less at home during term time or, indeed, being accustomed to a certain level of food intake, they may simply not want as much food at home. Anecdotal information, but no hard data, has been collected from all the case studies suggesting that this does occur to a certain extent.

Is Food Aid the Right Answer?

This question comes in two parts: first, apart from the problems of coverage discussed above, is supplementary feeding the most appropriate response to malnutrition; and second, should it be undertaken using food aid? If the recipients do not eat all the extra food they have been given, perhaps this is a sign that the problem is more one of ignorance and poor nutrition practices than a shortage of food, and that education not handouts is the appropriate response. Even if this issue is resolved in favour of supplementary feeding, it is possible that giving rations based on food aid instead of commodities obtained locally can undermine its effectiveness.

There is little disagreement among the supporters of supplementary feeding that its impact is improved if it goes hand in hand with nutrition education. Indeed it is argued that the one improves the other, either because the promise of free food acts as an incentive to encourage mothers to attend a clinic where they may be subjected to a battery of preventive health measures, or, more positively, because supplementary feeding represents a form of learning by doing. The argument in this second case is that before adopting a new and unknown dietary pattern an illiterate mother will want to be assured that it actually works, and to convince her a demonstration is needed — a talk or a booklet expounding the virtues of, for example, dried skim milk (DSM) will not work; only when she sees that her child grows faster and suffers from less ailments than the children of mothers who do not attend the clinic will she be prepared to maintain the new diet on her own initiative. However, this is not the only view on the subject. Some observers and practitioners have argued exactly the opposite: that supplementary feeding undermines preventive health measures because education will be effective only if mothers are well motivated and attend clinics because they understand the need for improved health care. The provision of food rations reduces the likelihood that participants will be attending in order to learn better health practices, and increases the probability that they will be motivated by a desire for a free handout. Worse, they may refuse to participate in other programmes that do not give rations. Only in Tunisia and Upper Volta has this issue been hotly debated by practitioners. In Botswana and Lesotho there is a considerable measure of agreement that the distribution of food aid rations should form an integral part of MCH activity; for technical reasons this goal is not always achieved, but it remains the generally accepted ideal. In the two francophone countries there is no such agreement, and differences of opinion exist both between the food aid donors and the host government and, within the government, between different departments. This clear split between the anglophone and francophone countries may owe much to their different colonial traditions, sources of expatriate technical assistance and the fact that it is the Americans who are the most prominent in propounding the virtues of supplementary feeding. Since the argument has been conducted on a fairly high level of generality unsupported by hard data, it is neither possible nor desirable for this book to adjudicate between the two camps. However, it is relevant to observe both that the existence of important pockets of opposition to supplementary feeding is likely to reduce the effectiveness and hence the nutritional impact of the scheme, and also that opposition is much more marked towards MCH than towards the school lunch programme, which even in Tunisia and Upper Volta has a wide measure of support, and more marked towards both of them than it is towards food for work.

Even if the desirability of supplementary feeding is accepted, there remains a potential conflict between the goals of relating feeding schemes closely to education and of improving coverage. If the main aim is to make feeding schemes available to as many people as possible in order to reduce the likelihood of missing those in need, the voluntary feeding centres used in Botswana have much to recommend them. However, such centres are less effective at dispensing health education than are clinics. It is possible to devise a dual system to provide education plus food from clinics wherever possible, and food only from voluntary feeding centres elsewhere. However, care is needed to ensure that there is no competition between the two types of distribution point. Such care has not always been taken, and in both Botswana and Upper Volta there have been complaints that supplementary feeding schemes with a high education input have at times been partly undermined by rival schemes with less education.

Assuming that supplementary feeding is good, there remains the question of whether it can satisfactorily incorporate food aid. There is little doubt that domestic purchase of foods grown locally is the ideal. Even commercial imports may be superior to food aid because the range of foods available is wider, and because they are more likely to be available on a continuing basis. To take just one example of this, the educational rub-off of supplementary feeding is likely to be smaller if the food distributed is a concoction like corn soya milk (CSM) which cannot be obtained elsewhere than if it is a more common food that can be purchased from the local shop. However, the case for food aid is not that it is ideal but that it is available at little cost to the recipient country. The case against food aid has, therefore, to show that this cheapness is offset by major disadvantages, the most frequently cited being that it may damage health, and that it may encourage an undesirable change in consumer tastes. As far as health is concerned, the problem commodity is dried skim milk. A human's capacity to absorb DSM is reduced if he has a deficiency of lactase, an enzyme capable of hydrolysing lactose into glucose and galactose. A deficiency can occur through either heredity or malnutrition. In cases of severe malnutrition the administration of DSM unfortified with Vitamin A in large quantities can lead to blindness and death. Less dramatically, if DSM is given to children who have a lactase deficiency it will cause diarrhoea which, at the very least, may lead the alarmed mother to stop feeding it to the child, thus undermining the object of the exercise. A further problem is that DSM forms an excellent breeding ground for bacteria if reconstituted with polluted water. While these are all potential hazards they can be avoided by a carefully run programme and virtually all DSM is now fortified with Vitamin A. No evidence was found in any of the four country studies of major health problems resulting from food aid. Indeed, the willingness of the Catholic Relief Services in Upper Volta to accept the administrative problems of multiple donors to ensure a continued supply of DSM suggests that it has some attractions. However, DSM is clearly a potential health hazard and should therefore be used only in well controlled feeding programmes. This is an important point because now that the USA has switched to blended food, the EEC is the main donor of DSM, but its capacity to supervise supplementary feeding programmes directly is limited.

Another serious charge levelled at food aid is that it discourages breast feeding. There is certainly some evidence linking the two[21] but it seems that the causes of a decline in breast feeding are fairly complex and that even if food aid is a contributory factor it is a very small one. Social and cultural influences may be particularly important. One analyst has noted that 'in most developing countries, the greater the sophistication, the worse the lactation: the bottle has become a status symbol.'[22] Of course, food aid should not contribute to this trend even in a small way, but it would seem fairly easy to overcome any such tendency in a well organised supplementary feeding/education programme. The CARE evaluation found no evidence to support the fear that food aid programmes reduce breast feeding.[23] Again, the way to avoid the problem seems to be to link food aid, especially DSM, only to well organised schemes which combine both supplementary feeding and education.

The charge that food aid provokes undesirable changes in consumer tastes is not limited to its use in supplementary feeding, and was referred to specifically in Chapter 4. However, since the beneficiaries of supplementary feeding are mainly young children whose tastes are still being formed, the criticism has particular force in this context. It has been argued that food aid encourages a consumer shift away from locally available foods towards imported varieties, either accidentally as an unintended consequence of feeding schemes or intentionally with donors thinking of food aid as a kind of loss leader.[24] As with breast feeding, it appears that there are undesirable shifts in consumer tastes but that these can be ascribed to a host of social and economic factors which may or may not include food aid. In none of the four countries studied were taste changes observed that could be directly related to supplementary feeding. In Botswana, for example, there is a worrying shift away from sorghum, which is well adapted to the climate, towards maize, which is not. Maize has certainly been used for supplementary feeding, although it has now been replaced by blended foods, but the general opinion is that the problem has little to do with food aid but is owing to the greater convenience of maize which, unlike sorghum, can be purchased in a processed form as flour or 'mealie meal'. There is a growing reluctance among young people to spend time and energy stamping their own grain,[25] so they switch to maize products. The most fruitful way to reverse the trend is to develop a local sorghum milling capacity, which the government is attempting to do.

To an extent, there is a conflict between the goal of education through food aid and the fear of taste changes. If supplementary feeding is based on exotic blended foods, the educational rub-off may be low, but so will the dangers of taste changes since the product cannot be obtained once the MCH rations have ended. However, the use of blended foods may not provide a complete safeguard against taste changes; the danger is not that mothers and children will become hooked on Wheat soya blend (WSB), an unlikely event as anyone who has tasted the stuff will testify, but that they will believe that a modern, healthy diet must contain a 'miracle white powder' and will increase their milk consumption accordingly. This leads into yet another area of fierce medical controversy which concerns the role of proteins and calories. Dried skim milk, and many of the blended commodities supplied as food aid, are high protein foods. Cynical observers assume that their use is not unrelated to current and past milk mountains, although others argue that they are necessary because the beneficiaries need a high protein food supplement. It is likely that both views are partially correct: DSM is currently in surplus supply in Europe and was available from the USA until the early 1970s; however, the fabrication of completely new, protein rich foods in the USA cannot be explained as surplus disposal. The view that the beneficiaries of supplementary feeding need protein rich foods is by no means shared universally. The opposing view is that they need extra calories, not extra proteins, and that DSM and the blended foods are an expensive way of providing the calories. The main significance for the economist of this medical argument is that (a) calories tend to be cheaper than proteins; and (b) in countries like the four studied here which are relatively rich in cereals, there is a good local supply of calories. Since all the donors supply protein foods to supplementary feeding as a grant, the extra cost is not a major concern for the recipient, but it is a factor that has to be taken into account (as was done in Chapter 3) when calculating the value of the aid both to the recipient government and to the ultimate beneficiary. However, if the arguments of the 'pro-calorie school' are accepted, it does mean that DSM and blended foods cannot be justified on the grounds that they are an essential ingredient in nutrition feeding, but must stand or fall simply on the basis that they are available. The only evidence on this controversy collected during the case studies favours the 'pro-calorie' school. It comes from Tunisia where a nutrition survey reported that:

'The absence of evidence of major protein deficits suggests total calories and micro nutrient deficits as principal causative factors [of growth retardation].' and that the 'survey reveals a reasonably satisfactory state of nutrition relative to protein. Calorie deficit problems seem most obvious in the 1 to 2 year old children.'[26]

The CARE evaluation also investigated the issue and concluded that:

Calorie deficiency is the major problem among program participants. There are far fewer children with protein deficiency, making the high protein content of the present rations excessive except in the case of the approximately one-out-of five children who are severely protein deficient.[27]

There is one further twist to the debate over which foods to supply. Cereals combine cheapness, abundance and social acceptability in all four countries and, therefore, might be assumed to be the ideal source of calories. However, they are also bulky, and it is argued that a young child simply cannot consume a sufficient quantity to satisfy his calorie needs. Oil is a much less bulky medium for supplying calories, and so there is a genuine demand in feeding programmes for the soya-bean oil of the USA and the butteroil of the EEC.

Does Supplementary Feeding Work?

All the foregoing palaver would be unnecessary, of course, if it could be shown convincingly that in practice food aided supplementary feeding either does or does not work. Unfortunately, neither of these possibilities can be convincingly demonstrated. There have been very few surveys designed to measure the nutritional impact of food aided projects, and those that have been undertaken supply only partial answers. It is well to remember that because of household fungibility a very extensive survey is needed to evaluate the success of supplementary feeding. Nevertheless, it is somewhat alarming, given the emphasis on nutrition by food aid donors, that so little work has been done to measure its effects. A recent review of eleven nutrition evaluations has classified their findings according to whether or not they report a significant short-term and, in some cases, long-term impact. The results, which are reproduced in Table 7.4, page 152, are not conclusive either way and, in any case, some of the surveys need to be treated with considerable caution.[28] The CARE evaluation compared the nutritional status of participants and non-participants, but because of the absence of adequate base-line data it was not possible to analyse the growth of participating children over time.[29] In an attempt to discover the effect of participation in an MCH scheme it compared the nutritional status of long-term and recent attenders, but found no significant reduction in rates of malnutrition by weight for height criteria attributable to length of participation except in the Dominican Republic.[30] Since different results were observed in the six country projects, correlations were established between the success of each programme and a number of possible influences. The strongest correlation was found to be with the incidence of malnutrition among new entrants: the schemes appeared to produce little nutritional impact because many of those who enrolled were not malnourished.[31]

There have been two useful surveys of the impact of MCH in the four countries studied in this book but none on school feeding or food for work. Both have been undertaken by CRS, one in Upper Volta and the other in Lesotho. Neither has produced conclusive evidence, but their results are suggestive. The Upper Volta survey was undertaken in 1973 and covered a sample of 1,000 children attending CRS assisted clinics.[32] The sample, which represented 6 per cent of the children attending the selected clinics, was drawn from 12 per cent of the total number of centres supported by CRS with the following geographic spread (number of centres sampled in parentheses):

Ouagadougou	(6)
Bobo-Dioulasso	(1)
Yako	(5)
Fada N'Gourma	(5)
Koudougou	(5)
Kaya	(2)

The survey consisted of an examination of the CRS weight charts that had been sent by each clinic to the national office either because the children had reached five years of age or because they had stopped attending the clinic for some other reason. The charts were analysed to discover whether children who attend the programme have on average a better nutritional status than those who do not; and whether the probability of a child maintaining an adequate rate of growth increases with length of attendance. The sample was stratified according to the age of the child when it first attended the clinic, and according to the length of attendance. The relationship between weight and length of attendance is given in Table 7.5, page 153. For most of the subsamples there is clear evidence that the proportion of children with an acceptable body weight increases with length of attendance. The exceptions to this trend are children who were under a year old at first attendance: with this group there was a fall in the proportion with an acceptable body weight during the first year of attendance, although after this first year the general trend asserted itself and the proportion increased. No explanation of this anomaly is given in the survey report except that it may be related to its coincidence with the weaning age – one of the most critical periods in a child's life; possibly children are so vulnerable at this stage that the MCH programme succeeds only in reducing and not in eliminating the fall in weight.

Table 7.4: Nutritional Impact of Supplementary Feeding

Part I: Type of programme considered

Recipients		Food distribution method		Nutrition rehabilitation centres
	Take-home		On-site	
Mothers			A Colombia (WFP 095 and 549)	
			B Guatemala (INCAP)	
Pre-school children	C India (Project Poshak)		E India (Project Poshak)	H Haiti (a)
	D Bangladesh (WFP 2226)		F Mexico (WFP 307)	I Haiti (b)
			G Colombia (WFP 095 and 549)	J Guatemala
Primary school children			K Andhra Pradesh, India	
			L Orissa, India	
			M Coimbatore, India (a)	
			N Coimbatore, India (b)	

Part II: Impact of programme

	Significant	Not significant	Not assessed
Short-term	H, I, N, J, A, G, C, E, F, B	D, K, L, M	
Long-term	H, I, N	J	A, G, C, E, F, B, D, K, L, M

Source: S.S. Maxwell, 'Food Aid for Supplementary Feeding: An Analysis', *Food Policy*, vol. 3, no. 4 (November 1978), Tables 1 and 2, pp. 292–3.

Table 7.5: Proportion of CRS Upper Volta Survey Population with an Acceptable Body Weight (by Length of Clinic Attendance)

Age on first visit	1st visit	Length of attendance % with acceptable body weight after:					Total length of attendance (months)	Number in sample
		6–11 months	12–23 months	24–35 months	36–47 months	48–50 months		
0–11 months	64	46					6–12	28
	63	63	75				13–24	59
	75	67	81	86			25–36	57
	67	67	87	87	93		37–48	15
	37	31	44	69	75		49–60	16
12–23 months	66	71					6–12	35
	49	67	67				13–24	45
	67	80	93	94			25–36	89
	34	71	85	95	95	94	37–48	41
24–35 months	50	60					6–12	10
	60	90	90				13–24	40
	54	77	90	93			25–36	190
36–47 months	100	100					6–12	8
	74	87	93				13–24	255

Source: Catholic Relief Services USCC, Nairobi, Office of the Pre-School Health Program, *Field Bulletin No. 21*, 15 August (1974) p. 24.

Table 7.6: Comparison between Proportion of Children Attending CRS Upper Volta MCH Centres with an Acceptable Weight and Proportion of Non-attenders with an Acceptable Weight

| Age of children in group (months) | Children just registered at centre (control group) | | Children who have attended centre for | | | |
| | | | 12 months | | 24 months | |
	No.	%	No.	%	No.	%
0–11	114	65	–	–	–	–
12–23	119	57	90	61	–	–
24–35	132	55	130	74	66	75
36–47	196	75	182	79	118	91

Source: *Field Bulletin No. 21,* p. 27.

A majority of the sample had an acceptable weight on their first visit. This suggests that the role of the programme in keeping children on the 'road to good health' may be critical only for a minority – the remainder would have been all right even in the absence of the programme. In an attempt to test this hypothesis, the survey compared the weights of children who had been attending the clinic for 12 or more months with others of the same age who had just registered for the first time; the latter group were taken as a control typical of non-attending children. The results of the comparison are reproduced in Table 7.6, above. A significantly higher proportion of attenders in the over two years old age groups had an acceptable weight. However, no comparison was possible, obviously, for children under one year of age, while for the one to two year olds the difference between attenders and the control group was not very significant. There are clearly a number of weaknesses with this comparison. The background of the children was not examined. It is assumed that the acceptable nutrition of the attenders derived from their attendance; contrarily, it could be that the clinics attract precisely those people with the motivation and income to provide their children with an adequate diet. Another area for possible contradictory conclusions is the growing disparity between the nutritional status of attenders and the control with increasing age. The report interprets this as evidence that the longer the children attend, the greater is the improvement in their nutrition over non-attenders. However, an alternative explanation would be that parents of, for example, three year olds who have not attended in the past only begin to do so if their offspring are obviously malnourished;

Table 7.7: Comparison of Average Weights of Children just Registered at CRS Centres in Upper Volta with Average Weights of Children of Same Age Who Have Attended Centres for One or More Years

Average age (months)	Average weight at first attendance (lbs)	No. of children	Average weight after 12 months' attendance (lbs)	No. of children	Average weight after 24 months' attendance (lbs)	No. of children
1	3.6	67				
4	5.6	36				
7	7.1	43				
10	7.6	30				
13	8.0	64	7.9	53		
16	8.7	40	8.5	31		
19	8.4	38	9.5	37		
22	9.1	47	9.9	26		
25	9.9	56	10.3	58	11.8	34
28	10.4	53	10.9	37	10.9	15
31	10.6	64	11.1	35	11.8	23
34	11.3	63	11.5	40	12.2	17
37	12.2	111	12.2	49	12.0	39
40	12.6	72	12.6	48	12.9	33
43	12.9	44	12.7	61	13.6	31
46	13.1	36	13.2	66	13.4	32

Source: *Field Bulletin No. 21*, p. 29.

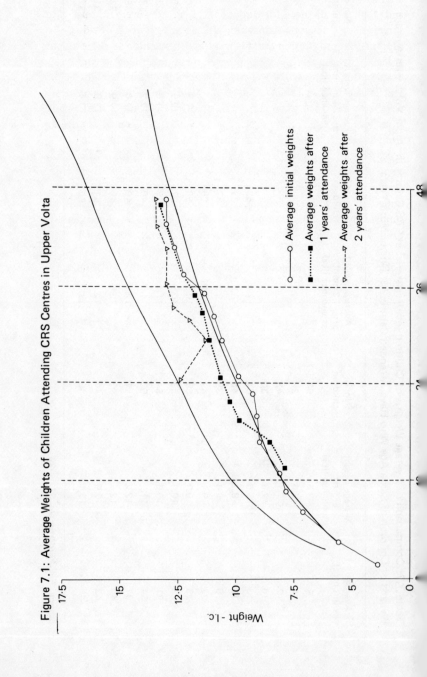

Figure 7.1: Average Weights of Children Attending CRS Centres in Upper Volta

Weight - l.c.

○ Average initial weights

■ Average weights after
    1 years' attendance

▽ Average weights after
    2 years' attendance

those with healthy children do not bother to change their ways. Such alternative hypotheses could only be tested by a much broader survey, and emphasise the need for work of this kind. However, although the survey leaves questions unanswered the evidence it does provide supports the proposition that MCH improves nutrition to some extent at least. The importance of the programme is underlined by an examination of the actual weights of the children considered in Table 7.6. This is done in Table 7.7, page 155, and the relationship of these weights to the 'road to good health' is plotted in Figure 7.1. The picture from Table 7.7 and Figure 7.1 appears much less sanguine than it did from Table 7.6: although a high proportion of children have an *acceptable* weight, they are very close to the lower limits of the 'road to good health' i.e. their weight is only just acceptable and there are no grounds for complacency. Of course, the survey only considers the impact of the MCH programme as a whole; it does not show whether supplementary feeding as opposed to preventive health education has produced the results which have been measured.

Table 7.8: Lesotho Evaluation, January 1973-April 1974 — Clinics Selected

	District	Average monthly attendance (1973)
Lowlands		
Loretto	Maseru (central)	1,040
Mafeteng	Mafeteng (southern)	1,530
St Charles	Butha Buthe (northern)	790
Teyateyaneng	Berea (northern)	1,380
Quthing	Quthing (southern)	1,528
Mountains		
Christ the King	Qachas Nek (southern)	7,505
St James	Mokhotlong (northern)	972

The Lesotho evaluation was conducted between January 1973 and April 1974, and is the most recent of several similar CRS studies in the country.[33] As in Upper Volta, weight records were analysed for past and also for present attenders, and new entrants were used as a control to represent non-attenders. Since the survey used the same methodology as was employed in Upper Volta, the same reservations about the findings apply. Over 16,000 cards were analysed, taken from seven clinics selected as shown in Table 7.8, above. The sample rejected

Table 7.9: Lesotho Survey; Average Yearly Starting Weights Compared with Average Yearly Finishing Weights (as % of Harvard Standard)

	Starting (control) group			Finishing group		
	No. in group	Average starting age (months)	% of Harvard standard	No. in group	Finishing age (months)	% of Harvard standard
Past attenders	802	6	92.6	–	–	–
	940	17	83.1	45	18	89.1
	1,135	27	87.3	20	30	87.9
	1,250	40	87.4	45	42	90.6
	565	50	85.9	3,209	54	89.6
	–	–	–	3,100	59	89.3
Present attenders (Lowlands)	1,532	6	98.8	–	–	–
	780	15	87.1	236	18	88.3
	320	27	89.1	196	30	86.2
	152	40	85.0	192	42	90.6
	6	51	81.8	178	54	88.3
Present attenders (Mountains)	888	5	87.5	–	–	–
	247	16	81.1	146	18	84.5
	124	27	84.5	125	30	86.2
	12	38	82.6	93	42	86.5
	6	49	80.0	120	54	87.5

Source: Field Bulletin No. 20 – An Evaluation of the CRS-Sponsored Pre-School Health Program in Lesotho (CRS Regional Office, Nairobi, 15 June 1974).

Table 7.10: Lesotho Survey; Comparison of Percentages of Children Who Have Attained Acceptable Body Weight in Groups of Children Who Have Attended Centres for One, Two, Three, or Four Years with Groups of Children of Same Age Just Registered at Centre

Age of children in group (months)	Control group (%)	12 months (%)	Groups who have attended centre for: 24 months (%)	36 months (%)	48 months (%)
17–18	77	89	–		–
28–30	73	79	81		–
40–42	85	87	88	86	–
50–54	86	93	94	93	93
14–18	82	85	–	–	–
27–30	78	76	79	–	–
39–42	82	90	83	83	–
50–54	80	80	94	93	87
14–18	64	79	–	–	–
24–30	68	68	67	–	–

Source: CRS, *Field Bulletin No. 21.*

the records of children who had attended for less than three months, had been absent for six or more consecutive months, or whose attendance rate was less than 50 per cent. One finding which is significant for the earlier debate on coverage is that less than 10 per cent of cards had to be rejected for these reasons. A comparison of established attenders and the control group is given in Table 7.9, page 158. With one exception, all age groups show an improvement in terms of the Harvard standard between the starting and finishing groups. In the majority of cases, the difference is more than 3 per cent, which was calculated to be statistically significant. However, although participants may have improved, the table suggests that they were not very vulnerable in the first place — the lowest average for the starting group is 80 per cent of the Harvard standard (i.e. the bottom line of the 'road to good health'), while the highest is 98.8 per cent. Since these average figures may conceal some genuine malnutrition, Table 7.10, page 159, shows the percentage of selected age groups who have attained an acceptable body weight. Except among present attenders in the mountains, the number of new entrants with an unacceptable body weight never exceeds 27 per cent of those attending. In other words, the findings of the CARE evaluation are confirmed: many beneficiaries of supplementary feeding are not malnourished at all. This, of course, does not reduce the value of the scheme for those who are malnourished, but it does affect the cost effectiveness of the exercise. It would be possible to calculate the unit cost per malnourished child assisted but only if it is assumed that those who had an acceptable body weight on entering the programme would have maintained satisfactory progress even without supplementary feeding, i.e. that there is no 'immunisation effect'.[34] Since this assumption is of doubtful validity, no such exercise has been undertaken. However, it is clear that a scheme which provides food to three adequately nourished children for every one who is malnourished will be considerably less cost effective than one which concentrates more efficiently on pockets of vulnerability.

Indirect Effects of Food Aid

It is easy to dismiss supplementary feeding as irrelevant or of very limited use without comparing its effectiveness with that of alternative means of improving nutrition. Certainly, it is little help to suggest that education is the real answer. Education both of administrators and mothers is undoubtedly desirable, but as one sage has noted 'Whenever any country says of any problem that it is all a matter of education, one knows at once that nobody has any idea of how to solve it.'[35] Food aided supplementary feeding is one way of combating malnutrition which, despite its defects, is relatively cheap for ldc governments and has actually been put into practice in many countries.[36]

One of the most notable achievements of food aid in the field of nutrition is its indirect effect in popularising supplementary feeding among ldc governments. In none of the four countries studied did the government begin distributing food rations through MCH programmes and primary schools before the arrival of food aid. Unless it can be shown that supplementary feeding is harmful, this is an achievement of which the donors can feel justly proud.

However, there are two corollaries of this innovative donor role that may be less desirable. The first is that just as supplementary feeding did not exist before food aid arrived, so it may not continue after the aid ceases. The official dogma of the donors is that food aid is 'seed capital' which can be phased out once the programmes it has stimulated are fully operational and the recipient country's economy is sufficiently strong to finance them domestically. Only in Tunisia has food aid been phased out of food for nutrition projects, and in this case the results have not been auspicious: supplementary feeding has been removed from the MCH programme altogether, and domestic finance has not been increased to cover the loss of food aid to the school lunch programme. Tunisia's experience may paint too bleak a picture because supplementary feeding was never very popular, and there may be more success in an anglophone country. However, it certainly raises a question mark.

The second corollary is that if supplementary feeding schemes are run because donors have pressured ldc governments into accepting them and because food aid supplies the bulk of finance, the recipient government may not exhibit sufficient interest in ensuring effective operation. This may have serious implications since, as noted above, the potential hazards of food aid are best avoided by close supervision. None of the food aid donors apart from CRS and CARE is able to provide this degree of supervision. The World Food Programme has good control procedures, but it does not extend to oversight of individual distribution centres. Thus some degree of initiative on the part of the donors in gaining acceptance for supplementary feeding may be desirable, but there is a limit beyond which pressure may cause ldc governments to accept programmes which they lack the capacity or resolve to operate safely.

Conclusion

This chapter has argued that, despite initial appearances, the relationship between food aid and nutrition is not at all straightforward. Putting aside the problem of whether specific measures to combat malnutrition can be justified on economic as well as on social and moral grounds, there are a host of difficulties which limit the validity of donor claims that food aid is a powerful force for improving nutrition standards. Supplementary feeding programmes may miss the most vulnerable households, but even if they do not miss them, there is no guarantee either that the food rations are eaten by the intended beneficiaries or that they are additional consumption and do not merely displace food from other sources. There is an unresolved controversy over whether supplementary feeding should form part of preventive health measures and, if it does, whether it can accommodate food aid. The issues are unresolved partly because no adequate surveys have been undertaken to measure the precise impact of food aid; despite the difficulty of carrying out the extensive enquiry that would be required, this must be regarded as an unfortunate omission on the part of the donors. Two partial surveys from Upper Volta and Lesotho suggest that MCH programmes which include food aided supplementary feeding have some impact on nutritional levels, but they also confirm the evidence of other surveys that the overall impact of the schemes on combating malnutrition is weakened because many participants are not malnourished to begin with.

Despite all these caveats, supplementary feeding has some merits, given that it is cheap for the recipient country to operate, it has some impact on nutrition and it is actually in operation in many countries (which is a not insubstantial achievement). It could only be shown to be not worthwhile by evidence that other schemes can do the work just as well and are mutually exclusive, or that supplementary feeding has major disadvantages. On this second point, most of the potential hazards of food aid can be avoided by reasonably well organised programmes that, in the case of MCH, provide education as well as food. Food aid donors have achieved a notable success in popularising supplementary feeding, although influence to this end should not be taken too far.

Although it tends to proceed on a narrower front, food for work may avoid some of the problems associated with supplementary feeding, notably the diversion of aid to the affluent and to other members of the initial recipient's family. Thus, even though it is not specifically directed to areas of nutritional vulnerability, food for work may have a greater nutritional impact than supplementary feeding, particularly if it reaches the poor. However, while nutrition surveys relating to supplementary feeding are poor, none exist at all on food for work, so the analysis cannot proceed beyond such generalisations.

The analysis of this chapter does not suggest that food aid has no impact on nutrition. But what it does suggest is that the flamboyant claims of donors and others that food-aided supplementary feeding is a major weapon for combating malnutrition cannot be justified by the available evidence. Indeed, it is probably best to avoid justifying food aid primarily by its nutritional impact. It may be better to note that food aid can have a number of desirable effects, and that in some circumstances these may include an improvement of nutritional levels. This issue will be taken further in Chapter 10, but two points are worth noting here.

Table 7.11: Value of Food Aid Rations in Botswana as Proportion of Total Household Income

(1) Percentile of population[a]	(2) Annual household income	(3) R48 as % of (2)[b]	(4) R38 as % of (2)[c]
1	121	—	31
10	233	—	16
20	325	—	12
30	402	12	—
50	630	7	—

a. 1st percentile = poorest, 99th = richest.
b. Based on 3 rations for: mother, preschool child, primary school child.
c. Based on 2 rations for: mother, preschool child.
Source: *The Rural Income Distribution Survey in Botswana 1974/75* (Central Statistics Office, Gaborone, 1976); Christopher Stevens 'Food Aid and Nutrition: the Case of Botswana', *Food Policy,* Vol. 13, No. 1, February (1978), pp. 18—28.

The first is that the nutritional impact of supplementary feeding has not been demonstrated sufficiently to justify a shift in the balance between MCH and primary school feeding. There is some pressure, notably in the USA, to switch away from primary school feeding towards MCH on the grounds that preschool children are more vulnerable and may suffer irreversible damage before entering school.[37] The argument is probably valid, and if food for nutrition programmes operated perfectly it might well justify a change in emphasis. However, the programmes do not work perfectly. In countries where there are pockets of strong hostility to supplementary feeding, the opposition may be more severe towards MCH than towards school feeding. Further, although the preschool child may be more vulnerable than his primary school brother, there is a danger that he does not receive the intended ration. Finally, the primary school lunch scheme has potentially important objectives other than the fight against malnutrition which were noted in Chapter 5; of these, the most significant may be to improve educational performance.

The second corollary is that food aid rations are a form of income-in-kind. If they are viewed in this light, as a way of giving transfer income to selected groups, a number of the objections rehearsed above fall away. It is no longer of critical importance whether the initial beneficiary consumes the food, or even whether the ration is absorbed in additional consumption. What is important is whether it is sensible to provide income transfers to the recipient households, and whether the rations supply a significant addition to their income. The concept of food aid as transfer income-in-kind applies equally to food for wages projects, and for this reason it is sensible to pursue these two questions in the concluding chapter. However, it may be noted here that supplementary feeding can be a most significant addition to family income. In the case of Botswana it has been possible to relate the local value of supplementary feeding rations to total household income, and the results are shown in Table 7.11, page 163.[38] Column (3) represents the value of three rations (one for a mother, one for a pre-school child and one for a primary school child) but does not apply to the poorest 29 per cent of the population on the assumption that their children do not attend primary school; the value of the rations received by the poorest 29 per cent are shown in column (4) (one ration for a mother, and one for a pre-school child). Even on the assumption that the poorest families do not benefit from a school lunch, supplementary feeding could supply an important 31 per cent of the total income of the poorest percentile, and a not insignificant contribution for all families receiving less than the median income.

Notes

1. See, for example, Bibliography: WFP (1973a), p. 3; USDA (1977), p. 55; EEC (1974a), p. 4.

2. See Bibliography: Maxwell (1977a), pp. 1, 3.

3. See Bibliography: WFP (1971a); Reutlinger and Selowski (1976a).

4. See, for example, Bibliography: Joy (1973a); Dandekar and Rath (1970a); Levinson (1974a).

5. See, for example, Bibliography: Sommer and Loewenstein (1975), p. 289.

6. See Bibliography: Belli (1971a), p. 15; Jelliffe in Berg, Scrimshaw and Call (1973), p. 379; Scrimshaw and Gordon (1968), p. 310.

7. See Bibliography: WHO (1974), pp. 95 and 101. According to the report, depending on the country studied only 0.5–5 per cent of the population under six years old suffers from severe forms of malnutrition, whereas 4–40 per cent suffer from moderate forms.

8. See Bibliography: Tunisia (1976a), p. 5. The survey examined 11,000 people over two years.

9. See Bibliography: Upper Volta (1976a); Condette (1970a); Benoit (1974a).

10. For full details see Bibliography: Stevens (1978a), pp. 21–3.

11. Stevens (1978a), p. 21.

12. See Bibliography: Botswana (1976a), p. 86. The Gini coefficient of concentration is a measure of skewness; in the case of income distribution, the higher the coefficient the more unequal is the distribution.

13. See Bibliography: Jain (1975), p. 112.

14. See Bibliography: World Bank (1975a), p. 22; Botswana (1976a), p. 84.

15. Stevens (1978a), p. 24.

16. See Bibliography: World Bank (1975a), Table 5.3.

17. See Bibliography: Anderson (1977a), p. 63.

18. See Bibliography: Anderson (1977a), p. 37.

19. See Bibliography: Marres and van der Wiel (1975), Table VI, and p. 62.

20. Anderson (1977a), p. 87.

21. See Bibliography: Berg (1973a), p. 100 cites Chile as an example.

22. Berg (1973a), p. 99.

23. Anderson (1977a), p. 23. It also cites a study by Checchi and Co. of Colombia, Kenya and the Philippines which made similar findings.

24. See, for example, Bibliography: George (1976), Chapter 8, for the loss leader argument.

25. See Bibliography: Hamilton (1975), p. 35.

26. See Bibliography: Tunisia (1976a), pp. 5, 7.

27. Anderson (1977a), p. 34.

28. Maxwell (1977a), pp.24–32.

29. Anderson (1977a), p. 7.

30. Ibid, p. 58.

31. Ibid, p. 63.

32. See Bibliography: CRS (1974a).

33. CRS (1974b).

34. The exercise could, of course, also be undertaken on the basis of some other equally arbitrary assumption about the proportion of each ration which has an immunisation affect.

35. Leonard Barnes, *Africa in Eclipse* (Victor Gollancz, London, 1971), p.277.

36. How it compares with other uses of food aid is considered in the concluding chapter.

37. See Maxwell (1977a), p. 4.

38. For full details see Stevens (1978a), pp. 26–7.

8 CONSUMER PRICES

Just as nutrition is the watchword of food aid supporters, so prices have been a focus for the critics. This is less because of the intrinsic interest of price levels *per se* than because of the possible adverse impact price changes may have on local agricultural production. Ironically, an early study noted favourably the potential price effect of food aid. An FAO report on India[1] argued that there may be a food constraint on growth: development expenditure will create additional demand leading either to inflation or to a balance of payments deficit; food aid can provide extra real resources to stabilise prices or to support the balance of payments. However, there has been a tendency to regard with disfavour the possible impact of food aid on prices since 1960 when Schultz produced a seminal article[2] arguing that if food aid were sold on the open market without any countervailing government action, the supply of food would increase relative to demand, the equilibrium price would fall and farmers would respond by reducing production. If food aid displaces commercial imports or is matched by an equivalent increase in consumption, supply will not rise relative to demand and prices will be unaffected. But if it represents a net addition to supply relative to demand, it will tend to depress *consumer* prices; whether or not this is matched by a fall in *producer* prices will depend on whether the government takes any steps to insulate one from the other. Even if there is a fall in producer prices, this need not necessarily affect the income of farmers who would be cushioned if, for example, food aid displaced commercial imports of a related commodity or increased consumption of it or if the aid is accompanied by an increase in exports of the same or a related good. The variety of possible permutations underlines the need to establish empirically exactly what does happen in a country which receives food aid. Since the Schultz article there have been numerous attempts to do this, often by reference to India's experience.[3] The issues that have been considered include whether supply is price elastic, the income and growth effects of food aid, market imperfections arising from government action and the strength of the wholesale sector vis à vis farmers, as well as the effect of farmers switching to other crops/activities. A recent literature survey[4] has considered 20 empirical studies, 12 of which refer to India. It concludes that 'It does seem probable that a price disincentive effect on production can be and has mostly been avoided by an appropriate mix of policy tools.'[5]

The impact of food aid on agricultural production is considered specifically in Chapter 9. Suffice it to note here that although, in a perfect market, there exists the possibility that food aid will depress food prices, the empirical studies that have been undertaken do not indicate unambiguously whether or not this has happened in practice, but they certainly do indicate that it is possible to take effective countervailing action to avoid undesirable price changes.

Another aspect of the relationship between food aid and consumer prices concerns the indirect effect on government policy. Food aid may free government resources either because it is free foreign exchange or because of what is known in the jargon as 'shunting', where aid finances a project which the government would have undertaken anyway. A recipient government may use these resources in any number of ways, including food subsidies. Of course, such action is not the prerogative of food aid alone: any form of aid or other resource flow that frees government resources will permit similar policies. To an extent, therefore, critics of food aid who argue that it results in undesirable food subsidies are applying double standards if they do not adopt a similar stance towards schemes which, for example, improve ldc export earnings in a way which benefits the exporting government rather than producers, or towards project aid that results in shunting. Nevertheless, there is a plausible case that food aid is especially prone to be used in price control schemes, if only for psychological and institutional reasons that link together free food and subsidies in the minds of decision makers. Of itself a consumer subsidy need not affect producer prices, and food aid may have a positive role to play if it supplies the resources required for the subsidy. The main dangers are twofold. First, food aid may be sufficient to encourage a government to fix consumer prices at artificially low levels but may be insufficient to finance the subsidy, so that the government must either divert its resources away from other tasks or bring down producer prices. Second, even if food aid finances the subsidy in the short run, in the longer term as market price levels rise it may prove inadequate. The next two sections consider two price control schemes with which food aid has been associated: in Tunisia the government has successfully operated a dual price system for producers and consumers; in Upper Volta consumer price control has led to producer prices being depressed as well.

The Macro Effect: Differential Pricing in Tunisia

A large part of the food aid received by Tunisia has been in the form of food for cash, and has mainly been added to the general supplies of the Cereals Office and the Oil Office (see Chapter 4). The oil and grain markets in Tunisia are highly regulated and are subject to explicit government price policies. For the past 15 years, the government's cereals policy has been based on four criteria:

(1)   the producer price must be sufficiently high to be an incentive to production;
(2)   retail prices must be low enough for the poor;
(3)   production and productivity of cereals must be increased to selfsufficiency;
(4)   the state will intervene to control the commercial sector.

There is an inherent danger of conflict between objectives (1) and (2) since prices that are sufficiently high to encourage production may be too expensive for poor people, and vice versa. This conflict can be resolved only by the victory of one objective over the other or by a system of differential prices with the state paying the difference between high producer and low consumer rates. It is this second approach that has been adopted in Tunisia. Since the proceeds from bulk food aid sales have added to the general revenue of government, it is not possible to link them directly with any specific item of expenditure. Nevertheless, producer prices have been higher than consumer prices and it does not seem unreasonable to suggest that the revenue derived from food aid may have assisted the government in financing this dual system.

During the 1960s the Tunisian producer price for cereals was significantly higher in money terms than rates in the main producing countries. In 1966/7, for example, the Tunisian hard wheat producers received $84 per tonne, while their counterparts in USA, Canada and Argentina were paid only $46-50 per tonne.[6] The big increase in world cereal prices of the early 1970s was not matched by changes in domestic Tunisian prices, which therefore fell below world levels. However, the recent slump in the world price has brought the two back into line.[7] The important point for this analysis is that during the period in which the largest quantities of bulk food aid were being supplied, there is little doubt that there existed price incentives to encourage production.[8] The difference between what is considered an adequate producer price and an acceptable consumer price is made up by the government. In July 1974, the producer prices per tonne for hard and soft wheat paid at a buying station were D61 and D55 respectively, giving the farmer an after-tax return of D56.620 or D51.020. The cost covering sale price of the Cereals Office, taking into account the base price, marketing and transport, would have been D67.900 for hard wheat and D61.300 for soft wheat. However, the price at which the Cereals Office sold to the mills which make flour, semolina and livestock feed was subsidised by the government to the extent of D15.190 per tonne for hard wheat and D14.040 per tonne for soft wheat.[9] The subsidy is paid via the Caisse Générale de Compensation which paid out D20 million in 1975 and D14.148 million in 1976 to lower wheat, flour and animal feed prices. Cereals are not the only commodities that are subsidised by the Caisse: in 1975 its total budget was D83 million, of which D31 million was for sugar, and D10 million for fertilisers. The intention is that the subsidy should be passed on to the ultimate consumer of cereal products, and to this end retail prices are fixed.

The success of this differential price policy depends on whether farmers actually do sell through official channels and whether consumer price controls are enforceable. It was noted in Chapter 4 that possibly only 25 per cent of the harvest is sold to the Cereals Office or the two marketing co-operatives, and that up to 25 per cent is sold on the unofficial parallel market. The reasons for sale on the parallel market could either be because farmers have difficulty in selling through official channels, or because private traders offer better prices. While the former might undermine the government's policy of high producer prices, the latter would reinforce it. The exact reasons are unknown, but two points are worth noting. First, the offical network of collecting centres is adequate,[10] so that there should be no access problem. Second, the transport costing system of the Cereals Office does not necessarily reflect the lowest cost of moving grain from surplus to deficit areas, and this together with the tax levied on official grain sales creates opportunities for private traders to offer premium prices.[11] Undoubtedly, the consumer price control system is less effective in the rural areas than it is in the towns, and to this extent the policy benefits urban more than rural consumers. The urban consumers are also favoured because the subsidy on processed wheat is greater than that applied to sales by the Cereals Office of unprocessed wheat to farmers for seed or for home consumption. On the other hand, the very high level of subsistence consumption, which is particularly marked for small farmers, suggests that rural consumers are not heavily dependent on commercial grain purchases.

An intriguing, but unanswerable, question is what would have happened in the absence of food aid? The most likely answer is that the policy would have been maintained, but financed from domestic sources. At the present time, food aid contributes only a part of the cost of subsidies. In 1976, for example, Tunisia received some 20,000 tonnes of soft wheat under PL 480 Title I, valued by the donor at $2.9m (D1,166,670). This represents only 8 per cent of the wheat, flour and animal feed subsidy that year, although in earlier years, when the flows of food for cash were larger, the proportion was probably higher. If the government had been forced to abandon differential pricing, it is not at all clear which element would have been sacrificed: whether producer prices would have been reduced to 'acceptable' consumer levels, or whether consumers would have been forced to pay more. The main beneficiaries of the system are the large farmers, who use the official marketing network, and the urban consumers; both of these are powerful political forces. The main aim of this speculation is not to identify what might have been, but to suggest that it is quite simplistic to suppose that food aid has *caused* urban food prices to be subsidised.

Table 8.1: Quantity of Cereals Consumed per Head per Year (1975) in Tunisia (kg)

Cereal	Big towns	Urban	Rural	Average
Hard wheat	39.8	77.4	152.2	107.82
Soft wheat	101.5	80.6	34.3	61.27
Barley	1.8	2.4	15.5	9.13
Other cereal products	1.1	0.4	0.3	0.51
Products based on cereals	5.6	2.7	1.2	2.60
Total	149.8	163.5	203.6	181.33

Source: Institut National de la Statistique, *Projection de la consommation des ménages à l'horizon 1981 et 1986* (1976).

Food aid has in fact contributed in a small but important way to a system which has certainly provided price incentives to production. Such gains must be set against any adverse effect on consumer tastes, particularly as regards preferences between hard and soft wheat. Wheat consumption per head in Tunisia is high, and indeed, per capita consumption of hard wheat is reportedly one of the highest in the world. A 1965-8 survey found a mean annual per capita consumption of 147 kg of cereals,[12] while a 1975 survey recorded an average of 20 per cent of food expenditure going to cereals.[13] Consumption of different cereals according to place of residence is given in Table 8.1, page 170. It shows that per capita consumption has increased since the mid 1960s, and that there is a marked difference in hard and soft wheat consumption between the urban and rural areas. The diet of people in the rural areas is predominantly hard wheat which is used for couscous, while in the urban areas generally, and in the big towns especially, it is soft wheat used for bread. There has been a significant change in the proportion of cereal consumption accounted for by hard and soft wheat since the earlier consumption survey of the mid 1960s. This is illustrated in Table 8.2, page 172, which compares for big towns, urban and rural areas the share of the two varieties in total wheat consumption for 1965-8 and 1975. Soft wheat has become more important in the towns and less important in the rural areas; not only have percentages fallen but the actual quantity of hard wheat consumed per head has fallen in the towns, with the same occurring for soft wheat in the rural areas. The increasing use of soft wheat in the towns can be explained as a consequence of two factors: a growing taste for bread (a 'modern' food) and lower prices for soft wheat products. The average 1975 official price of bread was 91 millimes per kg, compared with 96 millimes/kg for semolina (*semoule fine*) 108 millimes/kg for pasta and 114 millimes/kg for couscous (*couscous rapide*).[14] Since food aid has been predominantly of the soft variety it can be argued that it has facilitated the government pricing policies that have encouraged this trend, although some increase in bread consumption would have been expected in any event because of taste changes.[15] It is not obvious whether this is a good or a bad thing. It certainly means that urban consumers have benefited more from bulk food aid than their rural brethren but this would be expected in any case because price controls are harder to enforce in the countryside. Had food aid lured country folk away from their traditional staple of couscous towards bread there might have been ground for some disquiet. However, this has not happened: in fact the trend has been quite the reverse, possibly because of the high proportion of rural autoconsumption and the increasing production of hard wheat. Further, although the government's prices discount soft wheat, it has been argued that the differential between the two varieties is too small, rather than too large, and does not reflect the true value of hard wheat.[16]

Table 8.2: Changes in Relative Share of Hard and Soft Wheat in Total Tunisian Wheat Consumption by Area, between 1965/8 and 1976

| | Consumption as a % of total wheat consumption | | | | | | | |
| | Big towns | | Urban | | Rural | | Average | |
	1965/8	1975	1965/8	1975	1965/8	1975	1965/8	1975
Hard wheat	38	28	56	49	62	82	56	64
Soft wheat	62	72	44	51	38	18	44	36

Source: Institut National de la Statistique.

A similar situation obtains with respect to vegetable oil which is also an important item in the Tunisian diet: in 1975, 7.5 per cent of average per capita food expenditure was on oils, making it the fifth most important item of food expenditure after cereals, meat, fresh vegetables and drinks, in that order.[17] The bulk of oil consumed is 'mixed oil' consisting of olive and soyabean oil; the proportion of olive oil has gradually been reduced from 50 per cent to 10 per cent. The reason for its popularity is its price: the average 1975 fixed price for mixed oil was 192 millimes/litre, while that for olive oil was 531 millimes/litre.[18] The difference in price partly reflects the lower cost of soyabean oil, but is also due to the fact that mixed oil is subsidised. Using much the same reasoning as applied to cereals, there are grounds for arguing that food aid has facilitated the government's policy of combining high producer and low consumer prices. Producers have received prices that reflect the high world value of olive oil, while domestic consumers have been able to satisfy their needs with mixed oil. This exchange policy could have been continued without food aid because the price margin between the two types of oil is sufficiently wide. Nevertheless, as with cereals, it seems reasonable to link food for cash directly with the differential price system even though the 'cash' it supplies goes into general revenue.

The Macro Effect: Price Stabilisation in Upper Volta

Domestic grain supply in Upper Volta comes from many small farmers who harvest after the rainy season, usually around October. A high proportion (perhaps 80 per cent) of production is stored on the farm for family consumption with any surplus to domestic requirements being marketed soon after the harvest. The flow is therefore very peaked, with most of the annual supply coming on to the market over a short period of time. Demand, by contrast, is steady throughout the

year although there are peaks at the time of religious festivals,
particularly those that fall during the period just before the next harvest
(the 'Soudure' season), when the effects of any miscalculation in the
level of household stocks are beginning to be felt. In addition, there
are fluctuations in domestic supply from one year to the next.
Traditionally, the task of levelling out the bunched supply to meet
steady demand has been the responsibility of private traders who buy,
store, transport if necessary and resell. There is some feeling that the
traders have used their dominant position in the market to reap
monopoly profits. The lack of data makes it impossible to judge the
validity of such views, but it is clear that they are sufficiently widespread to have become translated into a political demand, and it is also
clear that the serious droughts of recent years have required the
government to become actively involved in the grain trade.

The Upper Volta Government, with foreign assistance, has therefore
made a number of attempts to stabilise grain prices both within a given
year and between years. Insufficient attention seems to have been given
to the difference between producer and consumer prices. On the
occasions when the distinction has been explicitly recognised, it has
usually been assumed that the interests of producers and consumers
are sufficiently complementary for the scheme to benefit both parties.
The objectives of a regional grain stabilisation and marketing project
assisted by USAID between 1971 and 1975 were thus to provide a
'more stable market' characterised by 'reasonable prices to consumers'
and a 'fair return to producers'. However, there has been an observable
tendency for the government to give particular attention to the needs
of consumers. Food aid has been used as one input into these
stabilisation schemes, which have established central agencies to buy
and sell domestic grain for the purpose of intrayear stabilisation, and to
import and store grain for interyear stabilisation. Food aid has been
used for intrayear stabilisation as a substitute for commercial imports,
with the intention that the central agency should accumulate savings
to use in subsequent years to purchase either further imports or local
produce, depending on whether the harvest is good or bad. During
recent years the attempts to stabilise grain prices have been strongly
affected by the drought: the need to moderate price fluctuations around
a long-term secular trend has sometimes had to take second place to
more immediate problems of getting food to deficit areas.

A series of organisations have been formed by the government to
intervene in the local grain market. The first to receive food aid was
the Office de Commercialisation des Produits de la Haute Volta which

received WFP aid in 1966 to provide it with working capital.[19] The first consignment of yellow maize and sorghum arrived in August 1966 and realised some CFA 13 million. The 1966 harvest was poor and so only a small part of the cereals handled by the Office was purchased locally. In April 1967 the Office was disbanded, leaving heavy liabilities,[20] and its role was taken over by SOVOLCOM (Société Voltaique de Commercialisation) a newly created semi-public firm. The 1967 instalment of WFP grain (2,250 tonnes of yellow maize) was channelled through SOVOLCOM which also received 15,000 tonnes of cereals from USAID, requested after the 1966 drought. The combined deliveries realised some CFA 180 million,[21] of which CFA 26 million was made available as working capital while part of the remainder was placed into an account for expenditure on development projects. Unfortunately, SOVOLCOM made a loss on its other activities and at the end of the year faced a deficit of CFA 200 million. To prevent the firm absorbing the food aid fund into its deficit, a restraint was placed on the utilisation of revenue from WFP/USAID grain sales. During 1968 SOVOLCOM purchased 1,000 tonnes of sorghum at CFA 16 million but as the 1967 harvest had been a good one it did not sell the grain until 1969 when there were shortages following a poor harvest in 1968. It sold about half its stock of sorghum in shortage areas for CFA 21-23.50/kg (compared with an average purchase price of CFA 16/kg the previous year) but the quantities involved were not sufficiently large to produce a lasting effect on the price level which rose to CFA 36/kg.

No further food aid for price stabilisation was supplied until 1971 when the government created a National Cereals Office — OFNACER — to operate as a price stabilising agency, and since then it has received food aid grain from USAID, France and the EEC (see Chapter 4). During the 1971/2 crop year, OFNACER set its buying prices at levels recommended by an FAO expert. These prices ranged from CFA 15 to CFA 20 per kg for sorghum and millet, and a little more for maize. During 1973/4, however, it recommended, and the government accepted, a single producer price of CFA 18 and consumer price of CFA 30. It appears that the producer price was based on the 1971 FAO estimates, even though these were not designed for use in subsequent years without substantial updating. Probably as a result, OFNACER was able to purchase little grain locally and failed to prevent consumer prices rising to over CFA 40/kg. This failure may have undermined government confidence in OFNACER's judgement, since the cereals office was not consulted when the producer price for 1974-5 was set at CFA 22, and its requested consumer price of CFA 37 while initially accepted was later reduced to CFA 32, which reduced the margin to below the Office's cost covering limit.

Such difficulties were compounded by the drought, which had two corollaries. First, there was little local grain for OFNACER to buy. Its supply problems were made worse between 1974 and 1975 when the Regional Development Organisations[22] (ORDs) were given a monopoly of purchasing from the farmers and OFNACER had to obtain its stocks (not always successfully) from them. At the same time as the ORDs were given monopoly purchasing powers, OFNACER was given a monopoly to sell. Since neither organisation had the financial or administrative resources to handle these monopolies they made extensive use of local traders as agents, thus increasing their operating costs (by requiring up to five transactions instead of two) and therefore either their mark-up or their deficits. Even if OFNACER's coverage and administrative capacity had been perfect, it would have been hindered in buying grain at less than market prices because of the ease with which food may be smuggled across the border: it has been estimated that up to one-third of imports (and an unknown proportion of exports) are smuggled.[23]

The second corollary was that food aid destined for price stabilisation became confused with food aid for emergency relief. Until 1973 the confusion was especially likely because OFNACER was charged with distribution of both emergency and development food aid. It is clearly unsatisfactory to sell food aid that is intended for free distribution, but the reverse situation is also, although perhaps less obviously, undesirable in principle. The aim of food for price stabilisation is to help the agency involved become fully operational, and it is important for the success of the stabilisation project that the agency performs efficiently. If the grain, and therefore the working capital, the agency needs is diverted for free distribution or any other purpose, the likelihood of the organisation becoming self-supporting is reduced. In principle food aid required for emergency drought relief should be supplied independently of grain intended for sale. However, it is easy to understand how such principles may not work out in practice. Supplies intended for different uses may be muddled through administrative oversight. More importantly, during a drought the short-term need to get food to people in distress may outweigh the long-term task of putting price stabilisation on a good footing. Small wonder, therefore, that stabilisation and drought relief have been intertwined. In 1973 the EEC planned to supply 10,000 tonnes of grain to OFNACER, half to be sold for price stabilisation purposes and half to be distributed free for drought relief. An initial delivery of 5,000 tonnes was made with the intention that it should be split half and half. However, it became apparent that OFNACER was selling the whole consignment, whereupon the EEC redirected the supplies to the newly established Sous-comité Permanent de Lutte contre les Effets de la Sécheresse (hereinafter the Sous-comité) which had the function of distributing food aid for emergency relief. Since then, OFNACER has received no further food aid from the EEC. The opposite problem has faced USAID: the Sous-comité appropriated for free distribution some 10,000 tonnes of grain sent to OFNACER for price stabilisation.[24]

The diversion of PL 480 aid illustrates another problem. Food for price stabilisation involves evening-out short-term fluctuations while allowing a long-term secular trend to assert itself. Stabilisation is thus different from an attempt to hold down consumer prices to levels lower than those justified by long-term economic considerations. However, there is an obvious temptation to use food aid intended for one purpose for the other by fixing the sale price below the level required by the stabilisation agency to cover costs and build up working capital. In such a case, the surplus accruing from the provision of free food is transferred from the cereals office to the consumer. The temptation is likely to be more marked if, as in the Upper Volta case, there is a history of price controls linked to wage restraint, the government and not the cereals office is responsible for price fixing, and there is an artificial market situation following drought and massive inflows of relief food aid. During the 1960s, the Government of Upper Volta followed a policy of, on the one hand, restraining modern sector wage levels and, on the other hand as a *quid pro quo,* controlling the price of urban staples. This policy has also been pursued by other Sahelian countries. During the early 1970s when the area was hit simultaneously by drought and spiralling world food prices, all the governments attempted to some degree to insulate their urban populations from these increases. The episode has been described in graphic terms thus:

> This is a story of high drama. Men of power threw as many of the State's resources as they could muster into a struggle aimed at isolating the domestic economy from the price changes occurring outside. In the end they were forced to surrender, after pouring vast amounts of money and energy into the battle.[25]

The Upper Volta Government spent less than most of its neighbours in this attempt: bread prices were allowed to rise substantially during 1972-4 from CFA 89 to CFA 125 per kg, although sugar prices were held down, at a cost of CFA 400-500m in 1974.[26] The changes in the minimum industrial wage (SMIG), and consumer price index over the period 1970-5 are given in Table 8.3, below. The history of civil service pay has been rather complicated. In January 1967 wages were cut by 10 per cent and child allowances halved as part of an austerity drive. The salary cut was restored in January 1969, and in the following December there was a 2.6 per cent across-the-board increase. In December 1972 a graduated wage increase gave 10 per cent to the lowest and 3 per cent to the highest paid civil servants, and in April 1974 there was a flat rate rise of CFA 25,000 p.a. and a fixed 2 per cent increase for all civil servants.[27]

Table 8.3: Upper Volta Minimum Industrial Wages (SMIG) and Consumer Price Index (Traditional Family, Ouagadougou)

Year	SMIG[a]	General price index[b]	Food index[b]
1970	107	160	135
1971	107	172	164
1972	117	153	133
1973	117	177	192
1974	162	178	190
1975	162	206	245

a. 1963 = 100.
b. 1958 = 100, figure for December.
Sources: Banque Centrale des Etats de l'Afrique (BCEAO), *Indicateurs Economiques HV,* No. 238, April (1976); *Annual Report* (1971, 1975).

However, while the Voltaique policy was mild by Sahelian standards, the government did attempt to subsidise food prices, and it involved food aid in the attempt. In mid 1974 the government decided to reduce by one-third the price agreed with USAID for the sale of PL 480 commodities that year. The Americans were not informed of this decision in advance of its implementation, and do not appear to have been very happy with it because following the price cut the two parties agreed to transfer all the remaining stocks to the Sous-comité for free distribution, and since then OFNACER has not received any further PL 480 assistance.

Both of these examples of food for price stabilisation being used for other purposes illustrate potential pitfalls in future schemes of a similar nature. Their economic implications are similar: the economic effect of a diversion of food to free distribution can be seen simply as an extreme example of the use of food aid to hold prices below market levels. The problems of misuse were undoubtedly exacerbated by the drought and, indeed, it may be that the main problem of OFNACER is that price stabilisation was attempted at what, with hindsight, can be seen as a singularly unpropitious time. However, the difficulties experienced by the food for price stabilisation programme may reoccur in more normal times. The pressure to use such food aid for emergency relief is likely to be reduced in good years, but there remains the possibility that price depression may replace price stabilisation. A policy of keeping prices below market levels need not necessarily be unsatisfactory: in the 1960s it was clearly linked to wage controls. However, a more usual situation may be where a state introduces price control not as part of an overall package but as an isolated measure in response to political demands from the urban population, who are usually the group to benefit. The main danger from the government's point of view is that as the market level of prices rises, so the value of subsidy required increases until a situation is reached where any reform to bring controlled and market prices back into line would involve a quite unacceptably large jump in price. If food aid continues, the recipient becomes dependent upon the donor, and if it is terminated the government may have to divert a significant portion of its revenue to maintaining the subsidy. From the donor's point of view, the use of food aid for price depression will be desirable only if the consumers who benefit have some special economic significance or if there are other attractive features of a non-economic variety. After all, as was noted in Chapter 7, supplementary feeding is a form of consumer subsidy, or rather a way of increasing the effective demand of a certain group of consumers. However, the difference between the two schemes is that with MCH the target group of the project has a particular economic significance. There is no obvious reason why the general urban consumer should have any such significance. Clearly there can be a range of non-economic reasons for which a donor might approve of price subsidies. The most obvious is a belief that such a policy is conducive to political stability.

None of these problems is impossible to overcome; they are merely dangers that must be kept in mind, and they would seem to be no more difficult to remedy than problems caused by inefficiency in the stabilisation agency which will also tend to draw food aid funds away from their original purpose. A more significant limitation of price stabilisation as a long-term vehicle for food aid is the fact that demand is high only in the initial stages of the project; when the scheme is fully operational it will need to import food only during bad years.

The Micro Effect: Regional Commerce in Botswana

In none of the four countries studied is it possible to undertake the sort of sophisticated econometric analysis that has been attempted in India and Latin America to simulate the impact of food aid on national price levels. Only in Tunisia do the hardness and coverage of the data approach what would be required, but in Tunisia the system of price controls makes such analysis redundant. Upper Volta is the only other country to have received bulk food aid, but the records are too chaotic to allow anything but the simplest calculations. Botswana and Lesotho have received only project food aid. Price levels in the two countries are heavily influenced by those prevailing in South Africa, so that it is doubtful whether food aid could have affected national levels. However, because it is linked to projects it may have been concentrated in particular areas and thus had a greater than average impact, and it may have altered the level or pattern of purchases even if it has not affected prices. An indication of the potential of food aid to disrupt local trade can be obtained by comparing the value of aid entering a particular area with figures for local commerce. This has been possible in Botswana for only two villages, Moshupa and Molepolole. Both are about 50 km south west and west, respectively, of Gaborone, and although they are in the east of the country they are generally considered to be rather depressed. Thus the ratio of food aid to commercial activity is unlikely to be exceptionally low.

Moshupa, which is a small village, receives food aid only under the MCH and primary school lunch projects. Molepolole also receives food for cash to the brigades and secondary schools. Both received food for wages during the 1973-4 food for work campaign, although the number of beneficiaries in Moshupa is unknown. The food aid ration can be valued either on the basis of local replacement cost or, as noted in Chapter 3, by reference to the locally available commodities that would have been furnished in the absence of food aid and its exotic concoctions. The former will normally be higher, and so it is used here since the object is to estimate the greatest possible disruption that food aid could cause. The local Botswana value of WFP commodities has not been calculated, but this exercise has been undertaken for Lesotho which has very similar price levels. The Lesotho values are for August 1975, but the figures for retail activity refer to 1971; to make them roughly comparable, the retail figures are inflated in line with the South African wholesale price index. The results are that the primary school ration is given a value of R10 per year, while the MCH ration is worth R19 per year.[28] In 1971 there were 1,145 Moshupa children at primary school. The number of MCH beneficiaries is unknown, but a rough approximation is that they received one-half the value of food obtained by primary school children.[29] The total value of food aid entering the village is thus R17,175. The turnover for all goods of local shops in 1971 was estimated at approximately R240,000 p.a.,[30] or R362,530 in 1975. Food aid thus represents only 5 per cent of this turnover. A similar exercise can be undertaken for Molepolole, a major village. At the peak, during the 1973-4 food for work campaign, food was supplied simultaneously under four projects and totalled something in the order of R35,600.[31] This is 5 per cent of the annual estimated turnover of Molepolole shops (1973/4 prices) of R672,633.[32]

In both cases, the percentage is for the maximum disruption, assuming that none of the food aid results in additional consumption and that it is either sold locally or displaces local purchases. It is highly probable that the actual impact will have been much smaller. Some of the aid will have been absorbed by additional consumption and some of the money saved will be spent on other local purchases.

Of course, this does not prove that food aid has not affected price levels significantly, and it begs the question of what is meant by 'significant': perhaps food aid was the straw that broke the camel's back. The fact that project food aid was of relatively minor importance in Botswana does not necessarily indicate that the same applies elsewhere. However, a general point is that the insignificant results for Botswana may be typical for other countries with the same sort of food aided projects because the target groups involved are inherently limited in size. After all, Botswana has one of the highest school attendance rates of the four countries, and because of its use of voluntary feeding centres it has achieved a relatively good MCH coverage. It has a more limited experience of food for work than Lesotho or Tunisia, but as noted in Chapter 6, the social stigma attached to participation limits the scope of these projects. Thus, although the situation will vary from country to country, there is some basis for arguing that supplementary feeding and food for work projects are by their nature unlikely to cause a major disruption to local trade. Whether or not 'major' is equivalent to 'significant' will again vary between countries, but in this respect food aid is no different from many other development activities which have positive and negative aspects; the real issue is not just to list these but to prepare a balance sheet: are the potential gains sufficiently desirable and probable to justify the risk? This question is addressed in the final chapter, which considers not just the possible direct and indirect impact of food aid on consumer prices but also its effect on agricultural production, to which we now turn.

Notes

1. See Bibliography: FAO (1955).
2. See Bibliography: Schultz (1960).
3. See, for example, Bibliography: Fisher (1963); Goering (1962); Ginor (1963); Dudley and Sandilands (1975); Purvis (1963); Mann (1967); Srivastava (1968); Srivastava *et al.* (1975); Seevers (1968); Barnum (1971); Khatkhate (1962); Rath and Patvardhan (1967).
4. See Bibliography: Singer and Maxwell (1978).
5. Ibid., p. 32.
6. World Bank. The government has also subsidised the price of some farm inputs such as fertiliser.
7. The US producer price has fallen from $130/tonne in 1975 to $105/tonne in 1976 to a reported $79/tonne in September 1977: See Bibliography, FAO (1977a), p. 61; *The Times,* 5 September (1977).
8. Although cereal production is only a little more profitable than some other agricultural pursuits, such as livestock.
9. See Bibliography: Kansas State University (1974), p. 47.
10. Ibid., p. 58.
11. Ibid., p. 55.
12. Institut Nationale de la Statistique (INS), cited in M. Autret, *Rapport sur la situation alimentaire en Tunisie* (UNICEF, 1974).
13. See Bibliography: INS (1976a).
14. INS (1976b).
15. The INS has estimated the coefficient of elasticity of expenditure on cereals to be 0.18 for the big towns, 0.20 for urban areas and 0.27 for rural areas, all for 1975. These figures suggest that demand is inelastic, in which case the principal effect of subsidised and differential hard and soft wheat prices will be to switch consumption between cereal products rather than to cereals from other foods: INS (1976a).
16. Kansas State University (1974), pp. 52–4.
17. INS (1976a), Table 2.
18. INS (1976b), Table 8. The olive oil price was reduced to 380 millimes in December 1975.
19. See Bibliography: WFP (1969a), para. 3.
20. Ibid., para. 7.
21. Extrapolated from ibid., para. 8.
22. Organismes Régionaux de Développement.
23. See Bibliography: Berg, E. (1975), p. 9.

24. See Bibliography: USA (1975a), p. D–25.

25. E. Berg (1975), p. 101.

26. Ibid., p. 107.

27. Ibid., p. 123.

28. For further details, see Stevens (1978a), p. 26.

29. The total annual value of MCH food has been estimated at R582,714; divided among 104,469 beneficiaries; this represents R5.57 per head: Bibliography, Stevens (1978a), p. 27. The total number of beneficiaries of the two projects is very similar.

30. See Bibliography: Botswana (1972b).

31. R42,000 at August 1975 prices based on 3,011 primary school children at R10 each; 105 Brigadiers at R29.68; 684 secondary school students at R5.98; 19,870 man-days of food for work at R0.23 per man-day.

32. R525,000 in 1971: Botswana (1972b), para. 4.3.15.

9   FOOD AID AND AGRICULTURAL PRODUCTION

More attention has been given to its possible adverse effects on agricultural production than to any other aspect of food aid.[1] Indeed, it may be that the subject has received too much attention relative to the other corollaries of food aid.[2] Much of the literature continues the discussion of the price effect of food aid considered in the previous chapter, and attempts to quantify the fall in production that will follow from adverse price movements. There has been some suggestion that the supply of food has a negative price elasticity such that farmers reduce supplies when prices rise because they have fixed cash needs which they are able to satisfy with smaller deliveries when price levels are high.[3] However, the consensus is that, in India at least, farmers are responsive to price changes and elasticities are positive but low (around 0.2 for the relevant commodities).[4] Although there is widespread agreement that a fall in prices will lead to some fall in production, there is no such agreement over the likely scale of the production drop, or on whether the adverse effects of food aid can be mitigated by measures which reduce the price fall, such as differentiated markets, or which encourage farmers to switch to other crops. One literature survey concludes that 'The concept of disincentives to domestic agricultural production has validity. However, it can be accentuated or circumvented by the price and production policies of the recipient countries.'[5] The important issue is therefore, how often do recipient governments adopt such desirable policies?

    Much attention has been given to the impact of bulk food aid on local agriculture. Both Tunisia and Upper Volta have received significant quantities of bulk food for cash, and their experience is considered below. Of equal importance, however, is the impact of project food aid on agricultural production: on the one hand the projects may have improved production, for example, by creating needed infrastructure, but on the other hand the food may have formed a counterattraction to the agricultural efforts both of poor farmers and of their governments.

Bulk Food Aid and Local Agriculture

The Tunisian grain and oil monopolies have shielded farmers from any direct price effects of bulk food aid, most of which has been in the form of soft and hard wheat and soyabean oil (see Chapter 4). Any impact bulk food aid may have had on local production is therefore indirect: the availability of cheap imported food may have encouraged or enabled the government to give less attention to farmers' needs than it otherwise would. Over the past decade, Tunisia has switched from being a net exporter of food to a net importer because internal demand has grown faster than production. The turnaround date is 1966: before then agricultural exports exceeded imports, but in most years since there has been a food trade deficit. As two of the three main agricultural imports (cereals, fats and oil, livestock and livestock products) have been extensively supplied as food for cash, the role of food aid has to be clarified.

There is no question of an absolute decline in food production: the problem is that it has not been increasing sufficiently fast. As noted in Chapter 8, the government's grain policy has combined high producer and low consumer prices, arguably with the help of food aid, and there seems little point in speculating whether or not production would have increased even faster with different policies and without food aid. A more productive area for investigation is the relative importance of hard and soft wheat. Tunisia cultivates both varieties but is a net exporter of hard wheat and an importer of soft wheat, and it was argued in Chapter 4 that this is a deliberate policy, facilitated by food aid, designed to benefit the balance of payments. However, while this exchange policy may benefit the balance of payments in the short term it could have other less desirable effects, for instance by making the country more dependent on the vagaries of the international grain trade for its food. Table 9.1, page 185, gives the area, production and yield of hard and soft wheat. Inevitably, these figures are subject to some inaccuracy but they are probably adequate for the purposes of this study.[6] The area under hard wheat has increased by 25 per cent over the 13 years 1964-76, while the soft wheat area has fallen, also by 25 per cent. However, this change has not been matched by a fall in the share of soft wheat in total production because yields for soft wheat are significantly higher than for hard wheat. Between 1964 and 1975 production increased by 86 per cent in the case of hard wheat, and 100 per cent in the case of soft. The area given to the two varieties is a function of the higher producer price paid to hard wheat and the better yields of soft wheat. In the late 1960s high yielding varieties of soft wheat were introduced and the area under cultivation grew. However, in the early 1970s results were disappointing for those farmers using the new varieties because of bad seed quality, and interest tapered off.

In recent years, high yielding varieties of hard wheat have been
introduced and between 1973 and 1975 demand for the new seed
almost doubled while demand for the improved soft wheat seed grew
only slowly.[7] Thus the main reasons for the dominant position of
hard wheat are the higher producer price, which reflects its higher
international value, and the recent introduction of new seed varieties.
Although the producer price for hard wheat is higher than the rate for
soft wheat, there is some evidence that the differential is too narrow
rather than too wide (see Chapter 8).

Table 9.1: Production, Area and Yield of Hard and Soft Wheat in
Tunisia, 1964-76

Harvest Year	Hard wheat Production[a]	Area[b]	Yield[c]	Soft wheat Production[a]	Area[b]	Yield[c]
1964	431	950	0.453	81	160	0.506
1965	577	938	0.615	100	169	0.592
1966	432	700	0.617	49	145	0.338
1967	403	652	0.618	50	166	0.301
1968	425	700	0.607	73	133	0.549
1969	301	600	0.502	80	145	0.552
1970	369	750	0.492	150	280	0.536
1971	400	700	0.571	200	250	0.800
1972	707	920	0.768	258	260	0.992
1973	631	975	0.647	235	224	1.049
1974	655	990	0.662	202	195	1.036
1975	803	917	0.876	162	149	1.087
1976	—	1,186	—	—	119	—

a. thousand tonnes.
b. thousand hectares.
c. tonne/ha.
Sources: See Bibliography: Kansas State University Study of the *Tunisian Grain
Marketing System,* Table II–1; FAO, *Enquête Agricole de Base 1976* (Ministère
de l'Agriculture. October 1976).

The government's cereals policy has succeeded in coping with the
perennial problem that prices high enough for producers are too high
for consumers and vice versa. Its policy with respect to hard and soft
wheat is certainly commercially sensible at present, but it could
produce problems if, for example, the Southern European markets for
Tunisian hard wheat were blocked and world soft wheat prices soared.

Whether such a scenario is likely is another question. However, even if it did occur, and Tunisia had to import commercially large quantities of soft wheat to satisfy urban consumers, it is clear from Table 9.1 that the ratio of hard to soft wheat area can be changed fairly quickly, so that the balance of trade problem should not last very long. Since food aid has contributed to both policies, it would appear to have had a beneficial effect on cereal production rather than the reverse.

Table 9.2: Upper Volta Imports and Production of Cereals (tonnes)

Year	Imports	Production	Total
1961	5,500	726,000	731,500
1962	10,200	895,000	905,200
1963	12,800	918,000	930,800
1964	13,800	1,209,000	1,222,800
1965	15,200	1,034,000	1,049,200
1966	21,700	1,058,000	1,079,700
1967	25,100	1,081,000	1,106,100
1968	19,600	1,084,000	1,103,600
1969	21,600	1,032,000	1,053,600
1970	29,900	1,032,000	1,061,900
1971	19,100	1,308,000	1,327,100
1972	40,100	781,000	911,100
1973	39,200	829,000	868,200
1974	74,000	699,000	773,000

Source: FAO, *Trade Yearbook, Production Yearbook.*

The situation of vegetable oil is very similar: domestic and foreign trade are a state monopoly; domestic prices are fixed; production has increased rapidly in the past decade; and high priced olive oil is exported while lower priced soyabean oil is imported. Production and exports of olive oil as well as imports of soyabean oil between 1965/6 and 1975/6 were given in Table 4.4. Although production has increased by 243 per cent over the 11 years, the net domestic supply has risen much more slowly, with the difference accounted for by increased exports. This is confirmed by figures on consumption which show only a small increase in per capita oil intake between 1965/8 and 1975. The figure for all oils in the mid 1960s is 15 kg per person per year.[8] By 1975 the rate of consumption had risen to only 17 kg.[9] There is no evidence that the government's zeal in expanding olive production has been dampened by food aid or any other factor. Indeed, the point made in Chapter 6 was that olive cultivation may have expanded too fast rather than too slowly.

The situation in Upper Volta is less satisfactory. Again, food for cash probably did not adversely affect agricultural production, but in this case the conclusion is more of a reflection on the recent history of the country than on the merits of food aid. As in the other Sahelian countries, food imports were an important element in total food supplies even before the great drought of the 1970s. Between 1965 and 1970 food averaged 21 per cent of total imports,[10] although Upper Volta fared better than its neighbours in that food imports did not grow as fast as total imports. It is clear that the government's agricultural policies have not provided as much encouragement to domestic production as they might. Even so, it can be seen from Table 9.2, opposite, that during much of the 1960s cereal production grew rapidly (for example, at 6 per cent p.a. between 1961 and 1971), although imports grew slightly faster (7 per cent from 1962 to 1971). The Table also shows that even with food aid, the total supply of cereals was only a little higher in 1974 than it was in 1961.

While the drought may have been exacerbated by inadequate agricultural policies in the past, bulk food for cash did not begin to arrive regularly in large quantities until the end of the 1960s (see Chapter 4). Although food aid and production are related, the causal link is that low production has given rise to high food aid rather than the reverse. Much of the food has been emergency aid which has swamped any possible effects of food for cash which were small by comparison. In 1974 some 8,000 tonnes of US sorghum were transferred to the Sous-comité after the government had unilaterally reduced the retail price, but in the first three months of the year the Sous-comité received over 14,000 tonnes of emergency food aid grain for free distribution from various donors, and in the year as a whole commitments were received for some 16,000 tonnes. The same year, estimated local production of sorghum and millet was some 620,000 tonnes:[11] assuming 80 per cent went to subsistence consumption, some 124,000 tonnes would have come on to the market. Unfortunately, these production figures are very suspect but they do suggest that food aid for price stabilisation forms only a small part of total supplies. It is not very sensible to worry about possible adverse effects of development food aid when a country is perforce receiving much larger quantities of aid for emergency relief. This may seem to be a specious distinction designed to put food aid into a good light by splitting it into different types and showing that each type separately has been anodyne although the sum effect of all taken together may have been harmful. However, this is not the case. It was noted in Chapter 1 that the object of this book is to examine whether it is sensible to give and receive food aid on a continuing basis as a means of development assistance. The specific object of this section is to enquire whether bulk food for cash has depressed local agricultural production. In Upper Volta it probably has not, although the much larger quantities of emergency food aid may have had more severe adverse effects. Even a fervent supporter of emergency food aid would hesitate to deny that it may have serious corollaries, although he might argue that their seriousness was second only to the consequences of not providing relief.

The Direct Impact of Project Food Aid

Project food aid is premised on the assumption that the food consumption of the beneficiaries rises in line with the rations they receive so that there is no 'surplus' supply. However, it is clear from Chapters 5-7 that this assumption may be overoptimistic. If project rations are not matched by an equivalent increase in consumption, they might act as a disincentive to local agriculture in two ways. First, they could in theory be disposed of on the local market or displace local food purchases, thus depressing local prices. However, it was noted in Chapter 8 that this is unlikely to be a major problem. Second, they could lead to a reduction in the attention a farmer gives to his land either because participation in a food-aided project is time consuming or because the farmer has a fixed demand for food, for subsistence consumption or sale, so that the provision of food aid rations permits him to reduce his own farming activities.

The sporadic food for work campaigns in Botswana and Upper Volta are less likely to present a significant obstacle to agriculture than are the more permanent schemes of Lesotho and Tunisia. Facts on the Upper Volta food for work labour force are far too scanty to permit firm conclusions. However, during its five years of operation (1969-74) the WFP aided Project 243 employed 847,689 man-days of labour[12] which, assuming a 15-day working month, would only have provided permanent employment to some 950 persons per year. It is likely that in practice many more people were involved but for short periods only.

In Lesotho, where food for work is a permanent feature of the government's public works programme, each project is in theory kept to a short duration of 3-6 months and there is supposed to be a rotation of personnel in order to keep any distraction from agriculture to a minimum. However, records on participants are not collated and therefore do not permit checks on whether a rotation of personnel occurs in practice, and although each project is of limited duration there is nothing to prevent a particular locality receiving a succession of projects and so, effectively, receiving food aid on a long-term basis.[13]

There is some evidence that the Lesotho projects are organised in such a way that a conscientious farmer could participate and tend his land, although more rigorous record keeping is needed to be sure of this. However, this does not rule out the possibility that a less conscientious farmer could use food aid as an alternative to the fruits of farming. The argument that farmers have fixed wants is akin to the notion of the backward sloping supply curve noted and rejected above. It assumes that the people involved are content to remain at a fairly low consumption level; if they can reach their target with food aid rations they need not engage in the often laborious, high risk and low return activity of farming. Improbable as this may be as a general proposition, there are circumstances in which it could be valid. In Lesotho, for instance, farming typically forms quite a low proportion of total household income (see Table 9.3, page 190) and so the loss of income resulting from reduced agricultural activity may be small. Some 63 per cent of farm households with less than two acres of land, and a full 77 per cent of landless farming households have sideline jobs.[14] The dangers are likely to arise with the traditional labour intensive food for work activities described in Chapter 6, and also with supplementary feeding which, surprisingly, is not often listed as a potential threat to agriculture.[15] We may assume that there are few disincentive effects of projects like the Botswana 'food for fallow' scheme and Tunisia's olive, almond and pistaccio planting scheme because rations are disbursed only after completion of specified farming activities.

It is not possible to prove whether or not food aid is a counter-attraction to farming, but it is possible to give some idea of the probability by comparing the value of the rations given under various projects with the income that can be derived from farming. Of the four countries, only Lesotho currently has a permanent and extensive food for work system. It seems reasonable to assume that food for work is more likely to present a viable alternative to agriculture of it provides rewards that are comparable or better than those that may be obtained from farming. It also seems reasonable to look first to the poorer farming households as those most likely to be attracted by food aid, and to assume that there is some correlation between poverty and size of holding. The mean holding per farming household in Lesotho is 5

Table 9.3: Estimated Income of Lesotho Rural Households, 1970

	Lowlands	Foothills	Mountains	Orange River Valley	Total Lesotho
Number of households	72,080	57,740	39,590	18,020	187,430
Number of persons	388,670	291,030	211,480	96,770	987,950
Estimated annual income per household (Rand) of which:					
from crop cultivation	53.35	41.35	40.75	31.80	45.75
from livestock[a]	30.70	26.45	81.45	37.15	40.75
total farm income	84.05	67.80	122.20	68.95	86.50
from labour in South Africa	93.80	78.00	57.80	92.50	81.20
from labour in Lesotho	21.50	15.45	17.55	24.25	19.05
Total income	199.35	161.25	197.55	188.70	186.75

a. Includes cattle, sheep, goats, pigs, and poultry.

Source: *Lesotho: A Development Challenge* (World Bank, October 1975), Table 5.3, p. 40.

acres, and in 1973/4 the net return to the average farm household from agriculture was approximately R130.[16] For the purposes of comparing the rewards of farming and food for work it may be acceptable to adopt the rough and ready assumption that farm income will vary proportionately to the size of holding. A 2 acre farm would thus yield a net return of R52 p.a. The average holding size of the under 2 acre group is 1.2 acres which, by the same token, would yield R32 p.a. at 1973/4 values.

Table 9.4: Lesotho Holdings Reporting Fallow in 1960 and 1970, by Size of Holding

Size of holding (acres)	1960			1970		
	No.	No. with fallow land	%	No.	No. with fallow land	%
Under 2.00	26,849	2,244	8	36,848	5,593	15
2.00–3.99	41,727	6,461	16	55,733	10,638	19
4.00–5.99	34,230	8,130	24	40,651	10,567	26
6.00–7.99	21,691	7,394	34	22,380	6,071	27
8.00–9.99	11,452	4,565	40	13,277	4,822	36
10.00–14.99	13,487	6,570	49	11,285	3,383	30
15.00 and over	5,851	3,753	64	4,902	1,579	32

Note: 'fallow' defined as land uncultivated throughout the year.
Sources: *1970 Census of Agriculture Report* (Maseru, 1972), Table 2.0131; *1960 Agricultural Census Basutoland* (Maseru, 1963), Part 4, Table 13.

Clearly, a single period of food for work — 15 days for a ration worth R6.59[17] — would be a doubtful substitute for farm income. On the other hand a worker with a 1.2 acre holding would need to participate for only five months a year to equal his possible farm income. Further, if more than one person per household is involved the time taken to reach a farm income level is greatly reduced.

These figures can only be suggestive but they do illustrate the *potential* of food for work to be a counterattraction to agriculture. Another suggestive fact is that the area of fallow land in Lesotho increased from 75,176 acres in 1960 to 94,840 acres in 1970, a rise of 26 per cent.[18] The rise has not been proportionate for all sizes of holding: as may be seen from Table 9.4, above, the proportion of holdings of less than 2 acres that reported fallow land increased very significantly during the decade. This increase is, of course, not necessarily the result of food for work. The attractions of migratory employment in South Africa, for example, would seem to be more potent. The food ration of R0.44 per day compares unfavourably with the 1975 minimum daily wage of R2.20 (plus board and lodging) in the mines.

Rather more is known about the background of participants in Botswana's periodic food for work projects, following a sample survey of 1,021 households in 1971/2.[19] It was found that participants in food for work were mainly female (by a ratio of 6:1), that 41 per cent were under 40 years of age but that the younger people tended to participate for shorter periods of time. Only 25 per cent of participants worked for more than a year, and 51 per cent for less than six months. It was observed that participants planted smaller acreages of arable land than non-participants. Households that had participated for six months or more produced an average of 4.4 bags of grain from their holdings, compared with 9.5 bags produced by households that never undertook food for work. However, it was not clear whether they undertook food for work because their farms were small, or whether they planted less because food for work was available. There was no evidence that food aid encouraged people to give up ploughing altogether, but there was some suggestion that participants might reduce the area cultivated during periods when it was available to a greater degree than they would have done in its absence. However, since food for work tends to attract lower productivity farmers, the effect of any reduction in participants' ploughing on total arable output is not great. The survey concluded that in all probability

> the total effect on overall production of cereal grains in the country is small indeed, involving not more than two per cent of the households whose average production was less than half that of the non-participating households and involving fewer acres . . .[20]

It also suggested that food for work is not highly regarded as a means of livelihood. Households prefer working with their own livestock or land because they find it more profitable than working for food, and consider it offers better possibilities for self-improvement. This conclusion has been supported by observations during the 1973/4 campaign, launched following the 1972/3 drought and in the expectation that 1973/4 would be dry as well. In the event, there was no second year of drought and by Christmas 1973 it had become apparent that the rains were good. From then onwards, the number of food for work participants fell off rapidly. It was noted in some areas that a number of households left one of their members in the food for work gang to obtain food to support the others who returned to the lands. In such cases, farming was considered more attractive than food for work for those with the choice, but the two activities were closely related, with one providing support for the other.

Since the country has experienced only short-term food for work, it is possibly academic to compare the remunerative potential of food aid and agriculture. However, it is tempting to make use of Botswana's good data on rural income distribution to make a comparison which can serve as a general guide for other countries. The average annual farming income of the poorest 10 per cent of Botswana's rural population is estimated to be R19 and that of the 15-50 percentile group to be R67.[21] A household with one food for work participant would need only 16 weeks of food rations to equal the average farm income of the poorest 10 per cent, but even a full year's rations would not equal the farm income of the 15-50 percentile group.[22]

These calculations suggest that food for work in Lesotho and Botswana could form a counterattraction to agriculture but only for the smallest farmers who have very low agricultural incomes. However, food for work is not the only source of food aid. Some households also receive rations under the school lunch and MCH projects. It was argued in Chapter 7 that the school lunch is received mainly by relatively wealthy families, and so it is questionable whether its value should be considered here.[23] The MCH ration is, in theory at least, given to the poorest mothers and children. It is not usually as large as the food for work ration, but it is available for longer: it may be true that in some parts of Lesotho food for work projects have followed each other to provide semipermanent employment, but these are the exceptions; with MCH it is the rule that food is available for 365 days a year over almost six years.[24]

The WFP monthly MCH ration in Lesotho has been valued at R1.74 using August 1975 prices.[25] The Catholic Relief Services have not made a local valuation of their ration, but using WFP figures it would be approximately R2.46.[26] A 1974 study of poverty in Maseru calculated that the average monthly food expenditure of households earning less than R200 p.a. was R9.65, and that the average for all income groups was R19.54.[27] A rough comparison between these levels and the value of MCH rations is possible if the 1975 food aid value is deflated to 1974 levels in line with the South African wholesale price index; they then become R1.46 for WFP, and R2.10 for CRS. The average de facto rural family size is estimated to be 4.4 persons, with roughly one child in the preschool age group.[28] If the bold assumption is made that the figures for Maseru expenditure are adequate as a rough guide for the rural population, the preschool ration is worth 15-22 per cent of average food consumption by the under R200 income group, and 7-11 per cent of the average for all income groups. During the time that a young mother receives a ration for herself in addition to her child, these proportions will be increased.[29]

The maximum inflow of food aid would go to a household receiving rations under all three projects. The average 4.4 person household has one child in the primary school range as well as one preschool child. Over a year, assuming two periods of food for work, the household's income would be some R43 at 1973/4 prices, compared with an estimated agricultural income from a 2 acre farm of R52 in 1973/4. If the school lunch is subtracted, on the assumption that children of the poorest families do not go to school, the food aid value is reduced to R28.[30] In such a case, food aid might easily prove to be a counter-attraction to agriculture (always assuming fixed wants). However, while there may be cases in which food aid is concentrated on one household it is unlikely to be widespread. The total value of food aid received by Lesotho in 1973/4 was worth R2.37 million at local prices.[31] If it had been distributed on the basis of R43 worth for every group of three recipients, it could have reached only 165,000 beneficiaries, yet WFP and CRS claim to reach an average of 406,000 people between them.[32] The difference between these two figures may partly reflect donor overestimation, but it probably also stems from the irregular attendance of many participants. The donors are sometimes criticised for inflating their impact by citing figures of total beneficiaries without indicating how often each participates. However, the argument cuts both ways: if the total benefit of the programme is diminished because many participate infrequently, the potential adverse effects will also be diminished for the same reason.

It would seem that food aid *could* form an alternative to agriculture for marginal farmers, although whether it does do so is unknown; this is clearly an area where the donors could keep better records. Whether the risk of depressing agricultural production, however marginally, is worth taking depends on the potential benefits that may arise from food aid. There is, after all, nothing inherently unsatisfactory in a situation in which marginal farmers transfer to other occupations where they are more productively employed. All forms of labour intensive works would tend to have this effect, yet labour intensive development projects are generally held to be highly desirable for ldcs. The possible benefits of the MCH and school lunch projects were dealt with in Chapter 7, where it was concluded that their most important achievement was in providing income-in-kind to poorer people. Clearly, food aid cannot satisfy both those who want it to form a significant income transfer to poor people and those who assume that the poor have finite wants and will give up farming at the first opportunity (i.e. that they are lazy).

Food for work rations are also a form of income. However, in addition to this benefit, food for work activity does create physical infrastructure which has a value. The projects may be woefully inefficient, but they may result in infrastructure that is additional. Regrettably, neither donors nor recipients in the four countries have undertaken an economic evaluation of works constructed with food for work. Chapter 6 suggested that the 1973/4 project in Botswana made a negative contribution to the country's stock of physical assets, but this was a drought-related scheme much less likely to operate efficiently than a permanent system of food for work. In both Botswana and, on a vastly greater scale, Tunisia, the paramount object was to absorb unemployment and underemployment. Again, neither donors nor recipients have made a serious attempt to calculate the value of this objective, which has political and social as well as economic implications.

It is these unemployment and income transfer effects that form the core of fears that project food aid has an indirect adverse effect on agricultural production. Precisely because project food aid goes to marginal farmers, the unemployed and the underemployed, it is feared that it enables their government to neglect them. By supplying a palliative it may defuse a potential force for reform which would otherwise have exerted pressure on the government to alter the inadequate policies that led to such marginality. These are issues that are taken up in the last chapter.

Notes

1. Bibliography: see, for example the bibliographies of Schneider (1975a) and Witt (1975).
2. See Bibliography: Isenman and Singer (1977), p. 1.
3. See Bibliography: Khakhate (1962).
4. See Bibliography: Singer and Maxwell (1978), p. 28.
5. See Bibliography: Witt (1975), p. 17.

6. There are two Tunisian sources of cereal statistics – the Cereals Office and the Ministry of Agriculture. There is some evidence that Cereals Office figures have tended to underestimate production; Table 9.1 is derived mainly from Ministry of Agriculture figures.

7. See Bibliography: Tunisia (1976b), Vol. 1, p. 4.

8. INS survey cited in M. Autret, *Rapport sur la situation alimentaire en Tunisie* (UNICEF, 1974).

9. 6.04 litres of olive oil and 12.46 litres of mixed oil: see Bibliography, INS (1976a), Table 5.

10. See Bibliography: Berg, E. (1975), Table 23.

11. FAO, *Production Yearbook,* Vol. 28–1 (1974); and see Bibliography: Upper Volta (1975a).

12. See Bibliography: WFP (1974a).

13. WFP (1976a), para. 29.

14. See Bibliography: Lesotho (1970a), Table 1.0131.

15. See, for example, WFP (1976a), Annex II, para. 25.

16. Lesotho (1976a), para. 8.4.

17. See Chapter 6 for the derivation of this figure.

18. See Bibliography: Basutoland (1960), Part 4, Table 14; Lesotho (1970a), Table 2.0131.

19. Botswana (1974b).

20. Ibid., p. 40.

21. Botswana (1976a), pp. 97, 98. 'Farming income' includes income from crops and livestock; it excludes hunting and gathering.

22. The 1973/4 ration was 10 lbs of maize meal per 2 weeks (10 days), valued on Lesotho prices at R2.30.

23. Of course, since wealthy families may be less likely to absorb food aid rations in increased consumption than poor families, it is important to consider the effect of the primary school lunch on price levels. This was done, within the limitations of the data, in Chapter 8.

24. Preschool children receive the ration for 365 days a year while they are in the appropriate age group, while young mothers receive a ration for 120 days. The point has been made that food for work rations are more destabilising than MCH rations because they are very large, when they do arrive; this may have some validity, but does not rule out the possibility that MCH rations also displace home grown food.

25. WFP, Maseru.

26. The CRS assisted clinics levy a 15–20 cent monthly charge to cover overheads which should be deducted from this figure. However, this is not done here because the charge is waived if the beneficiary cannot pay.

27. See Bibliography: Marres and Van der Wiel (1975), para. 10.3.1 and n. 59.

28. Ibid., Table V1, p. 62.

29. For the sake of completeness, the primary school lunch represents 15 per cent and 8 per cent of average food expenditure, respectively, by the under R200 income group and by all income groups. The 1975 value of the meal is 8.7 cents per day or R1.74 per month (20 days); at 1974 prices it is R1.48 monthly.

30. Assuming a 39-week school year.

31. WFP (1976a), Annex II, Table 3.

32. *Information on the World Food Programme* (Lesotho National Nutrition Planning Conference, 7–13 December 1975, Maseru); CRS, *Annual Summary of Operations, July 1 1973–June 30 1974.*

10 FOOD AID: A CURATE'S EGG

The title of this chapter is not meant to be an exercise in fence-sitting; it is a positive statement that food aid is good in parts. Food aid is not a major solution to the problems of development; in many cases it is inferior to cash aid, and it is certainly not an adequate substitute for agricultural development in the ldcs. At the same time, there is no evidence from the four case studies that it is an inherently unsatisfactory form of development assistance. One recent and widely acclaimed book on world food problems asserts: 'the fact is that dumping large quantities of low-priced American grain on underdeveloped countries makes it economically *impossible* for the small domestic producer to compete . . .'[1] The evidence of this book suggests that as a general statement this is simply untrue.[2] The proposition that food aid is good in parts tells us little by itself. What is important is to discover how it is good and why it is bad and to develop some ground rules for assessing whether the particular circumstances of a given donor or recipient are likely to result in food aid having a positive or a negative impact.

The preceding chapters have attempted to categorise the multifarious activities supported by food aid in order to focus on their salient objectives, and have considered the available evidence on the impact of food aid on nutrition, consumer prices and agricultural production. There are three basic types of food aid — dubbed here food for cash, food for nutrition, and food for wages — which can be distinguished from each other on the basis of their major goals. Food for cash includes all schemes, be they open market sales, university feeding, dairy industry development or even, in some cases, market stabilisation, in which the primary goal is to turn the food into its money equivalent. In such cases, the food aid is best seen purely as a resource transfer. In the first instance the transfer is between donor and recipient governments, but in the medium term the situation may be different. Who the ultimate beneficiary will be depends on how the recipient government spends the money. Similarly, those affected on the supply side will depend on whether the food aid displaces commercial imports (in which case, it will be food exporters, but not necessarily the donor itself), or domestic production (in which case the ultimate 'donor' may be the farmers in the recipient country). Because the ultimate beneficiary may well be different from the immediate beneficiary, it is simplistic either to praise food for cash which is channelled initially to, say, a desirable training institution, or to criticise open market sales that occur in urban rather than rural areas. Deciding on who the ultimate donors and beneficiaries are is often as much a matter of art as of science. Even if food aid appears to substitute for commercial imports in the short term, there is the possibility that it will undermine domestic production in the medium term because it saps the government's resolve to promote agriculture, or induces it to subsidise consumer prices, or encourages new tastes, etc. Similarly, since it is argued in Chapter 4 that the use of counterpart funds does not, in practice, enable the donors to check on how their food aid has been used, it is often a moot point to decide who has benefited.

With food for nutrition, the main objective is to use project-tied aid to provide food to target groups who are considered to be vulnerable to malnutrition. Since it is project tied it would appear at first sight to be more easy to identify the ultimate beneficiaries of food for nutrition than those of food for cash. But in theory, because of the possibility of shunting, the real impact may not be in supplementary feeding but in some other activity that the government is able to finance with funds released by food aid. However, although such shunting is certainly possible, it seems probable that the real effect of food for nutrition has genuinely been to assist the projects to which it has been directed. This is because, at least in the four countries studied, supplementary feeding is truly additional. Had food aid not been available, it is doubtful whether these projects would have been started; indeed, in the case of two of the countries there is considerable doubt over whether they would be continued if food for nutrition were to cease.

Food for wages is similarly project tied, and seeks to finance part of the labour costs of some kind of work, usually involving the creation of physical assets. Some of the projects assisted are additional, notably many of the food for work schemes, but sometimes food aid simply replaces cash from other sources which is thus available for spending in other ways.

Thus the real impact of food aid can be quite different from its apparent effects. This applies even to food for nutrition, even though it results in genuinely additional supplementary feeding projects. This is because supplementary feeding may not actually result in improved nutrition. Chapter 7 examined the claims that food aid is a potent force for eliminating malnutrition, and considered the impact of both food for nutrition and those food for work projects that benefit poor people. In both cases it concluded that the claims were grossly exaggerated. Some of the reasons for and consequences of this overemphasis are considered below. Suffice it to note here that one of the main conclusions of this book is that food aid which is distributed to individuals through food for nutrition or food for wages projects is best thought of as income-in-kind. Like any other form of income, it may improve the nutrition of its recipients provided that they were inadequately nourished in the first place, and that their nutritional problems stem from poverty and not, for example, from ignorance. Since food aid is income in the form of food, it may have a better chance of improving nutrition than other forms of income, but this advantage should not be exaggerated. Considered as a form of income, it is clear that food aid could have an important impact on the family economy, at least if it goes to poor people. It was shown in Chapter 7, for example, that supplementary feeding in Botswana could increase the income of the poorest percentile of the population by almost one-third, and of the bottom 30 percentiles by almost one-eighth. Similarly, the data in Chapter 9 suggest that food for nutrition and wages projects in Lesotho could provide families with almost as much income as a 2 acre farm.

A Balance Sheet

Despite the problems of identifying precisely who wins and who loses from food aid, it has been possible to reach some reasonably sound conclusions as to what it has, and what it has not achieved. It is clear that food aid has potential dangers and problems. Whether these risks are worth incurring depends partly on their probability, and partly on the value of the potential gains. Even if risks are high, food aid may be worth having if the potential gains are also great; conversely, even small risks may not be worth taking if food aid is unlikely to achieve anything anyway. What is needed is a balance sheet which not only sets out the main costs and rewards, but also shows how they vary between recipients, donors, and uses to which food aid is put.

Some of the more general criticisms levelled at food aid were considered in Chapter 1, notably the view that it is a tool of foreign policy. A further general criticism is that it is a commercial tool: that food aid is the first step in a market development strategy whereby, for instance, the donors turn rice eaters into bread eaters and then proceed to sell them wheat. There is certainly evidence that countries which did not widely consume donor products before food aid have done so after food aid. There is no doubt that farmers and agribusiness in the major donor countries have benefited from food aid: no one has ever denied this. What is important when assessing the impact of food aid is whether this is to the detriment of ldcs. A recipient will suffer only if food aid results in a change in tastes either away from home grown foods to imported varieties, or from cheap imported foods to more expensive ones. The evidence from the case studies does not show any major taste changes resulting from food aid. This is not conclusive, of course, and one limitation of concentrating on Africa is that the possibilities for considering taste changes away from rice towards cereals have been limited. However, it does suggest that the problem should not be exaggerated; taste changes are rarely caused by a single factor and although food aid may be one element, it is wise to recall that prestige is also very important and that food aid commodities may acquire a social stigma rather than prestige. Possibly more worrying than taste changes in the recipient is a diversion of trade away from ldc food exporters: food aid from rich countries may displace commercial imports from poor countries. Although there is evidence in all of the four countries studied that food aid displaced commercial imports, it does not appear that ldc suppliers were involved. Nonetheless, this is clearly a potential problem.

A more specific criticism, which has been considered in some detail in Chapters 8 and 9, is that food aid has undermined its recipients' agricultural production in one of a number of ways: by depressing producer prices; by reducing government interest in agricultural development; or by forming a counterattraction to agriculture for marginal farmers. There is no evidence from the four case studies of food aid having caused a significant depression of producer prices. Indeed, in Tunisia it has arguably been used to maintain a dual system with higher prices for producers than are considered to be politically acceptable for consumers. In Upper Volta development food aid was part of a system that led to producer prices being depressed, but it was not an important cause of the policy.

There are two aspects to the second problem: that the existence of free or cheap food may permit an ldc government to neglect domestic agriculture. First, this could happen deliberately, perhaps because necessary reforms are politically unpalatable; this can be termed 'neglect by commission'. Additionally, governments may neglect agriculture through ignorance, because food aid suppresses the warning signs that would otherwise have prompted action; this might be called 'neglect by omission'. There is no significant evidence from the four countries studied of neglect by commission. Governments have not deliberately abandoned attempts to improve domestic production in the belief that development food aid would save the day.[3] It is much harder to be certain about neglect by omission: none of the governments concerned has followed the very best agricultural policies that could have been devised, and one result has been that marginal farmers have suffered. Since food aid has helped to alleviate that suffering it has conceivably reduced pressure on the governments to reform. However, the argument in Chapters 5 to 7 was that food aid reaches the poor because, like the poor themselves, it has a low social and political status. It follows that food aid has supplied a palliative to people who lack political clout, and it has not defused a potential force for reform.

The very success of food aid in providing income-in-kind to poor people makes it vulnerable to the criticism that it provides a counter-attraction to agriculture for marginal farmers. Again, there are two elements to this argument. The first is that participation in, say, food for work is time consuming so that workers are prevented from attending to their lands. This is a potential problem of programming, which can be avoided. There is little evidence of whether or not it is avoided, however, because donors and recipient governments fail to keep the necessary records; they should be encouraged to do so. The second element is that the poor have finite wants such that if they can satisfy them from food aid they will neglect their farms. The empirical evidence neither confirms nor contradicts this view. What is clear is that if this assumption is correct, then food aid cannot supply a significant income to the poor without some reduction in domestic agricultural output; the two goals are mutually exclusive, and the reader must make his own choice of which he considers the more desirable.

The potential dangers of food aid will vary according to the characteristics of the recipient. Of particular importance is whether the recipient has a food deficit or surplus. A country which has a chronic food deficit that is unlikely to be remedied in the medium term is less likely to be adversely affected by food aid than is a state in which the opposite is the case. This does not mean that food aid will always have adverse effects in a self-sufficient state. Although none of the four countries studied is self-sufficient, Tunisia has the potential to become so, yet its policy of using food aid to release commodities for export would continue to be attractive even if it became self-sufficient. Nonetheless, it is reasonable to demand much more rigorous justification for supplying food aid to a country which is, or could soon be self-sufficient than is necessary elsewhere, since the dangers of displacing

202 Food Aid: A Curate's Egg

local agriculture and of reducing government concern for food production are greater. Although this precept may influence the distribution
of food aid, it is unlikely to affect the total volume. One prediction of
world food supply and demand in 1990 forecasts a shortfall of 120-145
million tonnes in food deficit countries.[4] On the basis of these figures
and past donor performance it would appear that demand for food aid
will greatly outstrip supply.

The other side of the balance sheet concerns benefits: even if the
risks are low, is food aid sufficiently effective to be worth having?
Except in certain limited ways discussed below, food aid is generally
less effective than other forms of finance. Some brave attempts have
been made to put it on an equal footing with financial aid. Thus the
former executive director of WFP has argued that:

> Food aid is not second-class aid. When people need food, only food
> will serve their needs and direct distribution of the food to reach
> those in greatest need is often the most efficient way of meeting
> these needs.[5]

However, this claim seems to fit emergency relief better than it does
development food aid, particularly in the light of the evidence in
Chapter 7 which showed a very weak link between food aid and
nutritional improvement. The justification for supplying food on a
regular basis as a mode of development assistance must normally be
that it is additional: that it is not being supplied instead of financial
aid but in addition to any such aid. Whether or not, in the long term
from the donor perspective, food aid is additional is a moot point.
Except for food deficit countries like Britain, for whom bilateral food
aid almost certainly is not additional, the question is virtually
unanswerable with any certainty. Does the existence of food aid make
it easier for the EEC to avoid the embarrassment of food mountains,
and hence make it easier to avoid reform of the Common Agricultural
Policy? Or is the CAP the product of forces quite outside the realm of
food aid and uninfluenced by it?[6]

Although these questions are of the chicken and egg variety, there
are two aspects of additionality that merit further attention. The first
concerns the relationship between additionality and continuity. If
food aid is to be truly additional then it should be supplied only from
surpluses. But this means that it may vary in availability from year to
year. It has been argued that this has advantages.[7] Yet the shortage of
food aid in 1972/3 when it was badly needed was widely held to be a

bad thing. Furthermore, many of the projects which can absorb food aid demand continuity of supplies. Linking food aid handouts to a supplementary feeding project may or may not be a good idea, but it is quite certain that few of the benefits sought by its supporters will be achieved if rations are available one year and not the next. There is thus a tension between the requirements of pure additionality and those of effective utilisation. A rule of thumb for striking a balance between these two conflicting goals is that some uses of food aid need more continuity than others. Supplementary feeding or area development schemes probably need a five-year minimum guarantee of supplies. Bulk food aid can tolerate less security and, indeed, insecurity may be desirable if the aim is to prevent food aid acting as a 'fiscal drug', which tempts recipient governments to neglect opportunities for mobilising internal resources.[8] On the other hand, the administrative costs of the recipient in making frequent and sometimes unsuccessful requests for food aid have to be set against any such gains, and it must be remembered that similar arguments apply to virtually all project untied aid.

The second issue concerns the provision of ancillary equipment for food aid projects. It is common for donors to finance the construction of stores and the purchase of vehicles used by food aid. To this extent, food aid is doubly additional for the recipient because it attracts other types of aid for assets which may have a use outside the realm of food aid. However, to improve the effectiveness of food aided projects, it may be necessary for donors to do more. The extreme inefficiency of food for work was noted in Chapter 6 and linked to a dearth of tools and supervision which, in turn, resulted from recipient indifference. If the projects supported by food aid are to be efficient, the donor may be required to supply financial aid as well as food. Again, if this results in an increase in financial aid to the recipient, it will be doubly additional. On the other hand if, perhaps more realistically, there is no net increase, food aid will be drawing resources away from other uses. Whether or not this diversion is beneficial depends entirely on the projects in question, but there can be no presupposition that it will be.

The evidence of this book suggests that there are two ways in which food aid may in practice be superior to financial aid. However, these two virtues are rarely proclaimed by the donors. Their reticence on this score may be one of the reasons for the bad press that food aid has tended to receive. Although some of the criticisms of food aid considered above are valid some of the time, they are neither sufficiently great, nor so inexorable as to justify food aid's reputation *bête noire* of the aid system. One explanation of this puzzle is food aid's supporters both overstate and understate its achievements, while critics exaggerate its defects. The reasons for this confusing behaviour can be split into two groups under the headings 'the politics of food aid' and 'the psychology of food aid'.

The Politics of Food Aid

The subtitle 'the politics of food aid' is not the prelude to a discourse on the political aspects of the international grain trade, fascinating though these are. Rather, it refers to the fact that for political reasons it is difficult to focus openly on two of the most attractive features of food aid: first, that it often represents free foreign exchange, and second that it is a subtle means of providing income-in-kind to poorer people.

Viewed entirely from the viewpoint of the recipient, bulk food aid which substitutes for commercial imports is the best variety. It is easy to handle, allows the recipient government the greatest flexibility and should be fairly simple to monitor to ensure that there are no adverse effects. This is one area in which food aid may be superior to financial aid: while financial aid in the form of free foreign exchange may be the ideal, it is rare; food aid in this form, however, is common. Some two-thirds of the food aid that is supplied is sold by recipient countries on their domestic markets.[9] Not all of this need substitute for commercial imports, but the evidence of the four case studies suggests both that a significant part of it may do so, and also that some project food aid has the same effect.

Appealing though it may be, it is clearly not something the donors feel able to brag about. The rules governing food aid are designed to prevent it substituting for commercial imports. If despite the rules it does have this effect, then this is something to be hushed up rather than proclaimed in a loud voice. This attitude does not result simply from concern for the views of food exporters. To an extent food aid supporters have found themselves hoisted with the petard of their own public relations. For many, food aid is about feeding the starving millions even though the millions might benefit more from an agricultural development project financed from food aid revenue. A US Congressional aide is reported to have criticised the current practice of open-market sales on the grounds that 'This is simply a soft-loan window. It provides resources for assisting other governments. It's not food aid.'[10]

There are similar problems in publicising the effect of project food aid in supplying income-in-kind to poorer people. The argument in Chapters 6 and 7 was that supplementary feeding and food for work projects are better seen as a method of providing income transfers than as a way of improving nutrition or of creating physical assets. Undoubtedly they provide rations to some people who are not poor at all, but from the limited information available it seems likely that they also reach poorer people. Financial aid projects generally have not been notably successful at reaching the poorest.[11] Indeed, it may be the case that supplementary feeding and food for work reach poorer people more successfully than most other aid efforts. This may be partly because project food aid has low priority in the recipient government, and is therefore available for groups who are relatively neglected. It may also partly reflect donor preference for using its financial aid in large, visible projects. Supplementary feeding and food for work are, of course, roundabout ways of supplying income-in-kind to poorer people. It might be more sensible to make the whole affair overt and to select the needy with more care. Unfortunately, this is often not politically feasible in recipient countries where there is opposition to 'welfare'. The merit of food for work and supplementary feeding is that, rationally or irrationally, they are considered to be legitimate when overt social welfare distribution might not. This is the second way in which food aid may actually be superior to financial aid. Here again, however, it is a merit that cannot be proclaimed by the donors without fear of negating it. A related virtue of project food aid, which it shares with financial aid, is that most of it is disbursed in the rural areas. By providing income-in-kind to rural people it may reduce migration both to the urban areas and to neighbouring countries.

One problem which arises when the real impact of a project differs from its nominal effects is that reforms designed to improve efficiency may turn out to be misguided. Food for work provides a good example. The argument in Chapter 6 was that food for work attracts the disabled, who are also poor. As a result it reaches poor people, but productivity is very low. The donors are sincerely concerned at these low productivity rates and would like to improve them. One way of achieving this would be to use only ablebodied workers, but such a change would also reduce the extent to which food for work reaches the poor! It is, perhaps, too perverse to argue that low productivity should be encouraged, but it is clear that any attempt to improve productivity should be evaluated with these considerations in mind.

The Psychology of Food Aid

Food aid is low class. This is true at the recipient end, where it can be associated with destitute relief, and at the donor end where food aid is the poor relation. At the same time, it has been grossly oversold with harrowing pictures of starving children and encouragement for the popular but naive notion that poor people need food rather than money. The result seems to have been to provoke an overkill approach by the critics and in turn an overassertiveness by the donors.

There is an observable tendency in many critiques of food aid to take the line that parts of it may be all right but that scrupulous care is essential to check on any conceivable adverse effects. In itself this can hardly be a bad thing. One writer adjures her readers to give 'hawk-like scrutiny' to the EEC's food aid policies as its capacity to produce extra food grows.[12] Another warns that:

> Underdeveloped countries had better *assume* that the United States will use its food surpluses to help expand its commercial markets, to assist the penetration of agribusiness firms and to support the very regimes that work in direct opposition to the policies that would enable hungry people to feed themselves. Let anything else be a pleasant surprise.[13]

Who can take issue with either of these wise pieces of advice for coping with a dangerous world? Few would argue that we should be deliberately negligent in evaluating food aid, or that ldcs should be encouraged to trust in big brother. The problem is that observers who adopt the approach of 'guilty until proved innocent' do not always apply it to other forms of aid, and frequently dispense with it altogether when considering development strategies more attractive to their own prejudices. As a result, the different modes of aid and strategies for development are not judged on the same basis. Aid is inherently a balance of probabilities affair and those who support it do so because they believe that on balance the advantages outweigh the disadvantages. If Botswana, Lesotho, Tunisia and Upper Volta are anything to go by, the same applies to food aid.

The result of overkill by the critics, thus far at any rate, has not been to temper the claims of food aid supporters but rather the reverse. Not only do donors make quite unwarranted claims for the impact of food aid on, say, nutrition, but they link it to every passing development fad and fancy: food aid and basic needs, food aid and rural development, food aid and habitat. The object is to make food aid *respectable*. This is unfortunate, since respectability may not be conducive to effectiveness. Possibly the most dangerous of these strivings for respectability is the one which tries to link the supply of food aid to desirable rural development activities simply because they are desirable and not because they can easily utilise food aid. In this the donors find support from the critics. After concluding that any positive effects of food aid will be 'a pleasant surprise' the authors of *Food First* argue that to maximise its potential for good 'food aid should be used as payment for work that directly contributes to creating the preconditions for food self-reliance.'[14] This is a fundamentally misguided approach: food aid should be used in activities that can use it effectively and are not destabilised by it. This book has played down the administrative difficulties of handling food aid, but there is no doubt that it is not an easy type of resource to utilise. It is typical that many of the most promising avenues for rural development require very delicate control. It is possible that they cannot successfully accommodate even the rigidities of financial aid, let alone the problems of food aid. To be sure, there is nothing inevitable about this – the area development projects in Lesotho, for example, appear to utilise food for work more successfully than do other agencies – but the starting point for deciding use should be the comparative advantage of food aid rather than the desirability of the various possible projects.

This is not to argue that food aid donors should pay scant regard to the development strategies of their recipients. The extent to which donors should or can influence recipient policies, particularly in such sensitive areas as income distribution, is a matter on which observers have widely varying opinions. However, if it is considered legitimate for donors to use their aid for this purpose, it may be better simply to concentrate food aid on countries with 'good' policies and to deny it to 'bad' countries than to risk undermining by inappropriate injections of food aid the very projects that are considered desirable.

The comparative advantage of different types and uses of food aid will depend on the characteristics of the donor and of the recipient. Project food aid demands continuity of supplies and will benefit from a donor presence on the spot; these are not as essential with bulk food aid. The World Food Programme, CRS and CARE can provide continuity and a local presence; the EEC cannot. This suggests that there should be some specialisation among the donors, with the EEC concentrating its bilateral efforts on bulk supply for open-market sales, and channelling food aid that it wants to supply for projects via the multilateral and voluntary agencies. Such specialisation is difficult politically, however, so long as some methods of disbursing food aid are held to be inherently superior to others simply because they link directly to fashionable projects.

Similarly, different types of food aid are suited to different types of recipient. Project food aid tends to require a greater administrative capacity on the part of the recipient than does bulk supply. On the other hand, medium-income states with a good administrative infrastructure may find certain types of food aided project, such as food for work, socially unacceptable to large sections of the population. Neither mode of food aid is inherently superior in all circumstances. Bulk supply, especially if it substitutes for commercial imports, gives the recipient the greatest flexibility, which may be considered a good or a bad feature depending on the views of the observer and the policies of the recipient. Project food aid is less flexible, but it may encourage recipient governments to undertake works that would otherwise have been neglected, and since many projects provide income to rural people they may reduce migration to urban areas. However, this advantage of the project approach should not be exaggerated. If a recipient is genuinely attempting to implement a desirable rural development or basic needs project it can be helped just as well through the counterpart funds generated by open-market sales as by direct injections of food aid into the projects. Similarly, if a recipient government is clearly opposed to a certain policy it will easily be able to divert project food aid away from its intended purpose. Indeed, even if the recipient is merely indifferent to the policy, project food aid may not achieve its aim unless buttressed by financial aid.

The ways in which food aid should be used will therefore vary according to the political, social, and economic characteristics of the recipient and also, as noted above, the attributes of the donor. Whatever approach is adopted, it is easy to expect too much of food aid. It cannot normally create employment *and* produce valuable works *and* improve nutrition *and* be efficient *and* reach the poorest. Some trade-offs are necessary. But given that different approaches have different effects and that both donors and recipients have a multiplicity of objectives, there is enough flexibility in the various modes of food aid to enable recipients to use it simultaneously for several different ends.

We may conclude with a perhaps obvious, but nonetheless often overlooked observation. Food aid is unlikely to have a negative effect and may well have a positive impact if supplied in good time and in the form of locally acceptable commodities to a food deficit country with energetic agricultural development policies and as part of a broader package of measures designed to assist a poverty-oriented development strategy. It is likely to have a negative impact if supplied under the opposite circumstances. Since most recipients fall somewhere in between these two extremes, the decision whether or not to provide food aid will depend on a delicate judgement. In this food aid is no different from any other kind of aid.

Notes

1. See Bibliography: Lappé and Collins (1977), p. 335. Emphasis in original.
2. Except, of course, as a truism if 'dumping' and 'large' are defined so as to apply only to situations where domestic producers are hit.
3. Although there is some feeling that the Sahelian governments are using *emergency* food aid to avoid taking decisive action.
4. See Bibliography: IFPRI (1977), p. 17.
5. *World Food Programme News,* Rome, Oct-Dec. (1977), p. 3.
6. See Bibliography: this issue is taken further in Jones (1976a).
7. See Bibliography: Jones and Tulloch (1974), p. 4.
8. The phrase is V.M. Dandekar's.
9. See Bibliography: Singer and Maxwell (1978), p. 3.
10. *International Herald Tribune,* 29 November (1976).
11. Arguably this situation may change following greater donor emphasis on reaching the poorest.
12. See Bibliography: George (1976), p. 192.
13. See Bibliography: Lappé and Collins (1977), p. 342. Emphasis in original.
14. Ibid., p. 342.

APPENDIX

Currency Equivalents

This book refers to several currencies all of which have changed their parities frequently over the period covered, and not all of which are freely convertible. Conversions can therefore be misleading, and only give a general idea of the magnitudes involved. Below are the rates of exchange for the main currencies used in the book for those who want to undertake the exercise. Since 1976 Botswana has used the Pula as currency. However, throughout most of the period covered by this book, it used the South African Rand, as does Lesotho.

Conversion Table for Currencies Used in Book

Country	Currency	Rate expressed as	1960	1965	1970	1971	1972	1973	1974	1975	1976	1977
Botswana Lesotho	Rand	Dollars per Rand	–	1.396	1.390	1.398	1.302	1.444	1.472	1.366	1.150	1.150
Upper Volta	CFA franc	CFA franc per dollar	246.85	246.85	277.71	277.03	252.21	222.70	240.50	214.32	238.98	245.67
Tunisia	Dinar	Dinars per dollar	0.42	0.52	0.52	0.52	0.48	0.42	0.44	0.40	0.43	0.43
EEC	Unit of account	Dollars per E.u.a	–	1.022	–	1.048	1.122	1.229	1.191	1.241	1.118	1.140
UK	Pound	Dollars per pound	2.804	2.803	2.394	2.434	2.502	2.452	2.339	2.222	1.806	1.746

Sources: IMF International Financial Statistics; EEC.

BIBLIOGRAPHY

Anderson, M.A. (1977a) *CARE Pre-school Nutrition Project: Phase II Report* (CARE, New York, August 1977)

Barnum, H. (1971) 'Simulation of the Market for Food Grains in India', *American Journal of Agricultural Economics,* vol. 53, no. 2, May (1971), pp. 269-74

Basutoland (1960) *1960 Agricultural Census Basutoland* (Agricultural Department, Maseru, 1963)

BCEAO (1976) *Indicateurs Economiques H.V.,* no. 238 (Banque Centrale des Etats de l'Afrique de l'Ouest, April 1976)

Belli, P. (1971) 'The Economic Implications of Malnutrition: the Dismal Science Revisited', *Economic Development and Cultural Change,* vol. 20, no. 1 (October 1971)

Benoit, H. (1974a) *Pour une Stratégie en faveur de l'enfance et de la jeunesse tunisiennes* (IDET-UNICEF, July 1974)

Berg, A., Scrimshaw, N.S. and Call, D.C. (eds) (1973) *Nutrition, National Development and Planning* (MIT Press, Cambridge, Mass. 1973), cited in Maxwell (1977a)

Berg, E. (1975) *The Recent Economic Evolution of the Sahel* (Centre for Research on Economic Development, University of Michigan, Ann Arbor, 1 June 1975, mimeo.)

Botswana (1976a) *The Rural Income Distribution Survey in Botswana 1974/75* (Central Statistics Office, Gaborone, June 1976)

Botswana (1976b) *National Development Plan 1976-81* (Ministry of Finance and Development Planning, Gaborone)

Botswana (1975a) *Botswana Project 324 Expansion: Quarterly Progress Report 1 July 1975 to 30 September 1975* (Gaborone)

Botswana (1975b) *Education Statistics 1975* (Central Statistics Office, Gaborone, December 1975)

Botswana (1974a) *Medical Statistics 1974* (Central Statistics Office, Gaborone, 1975)

Botswana (1974b) *A Study of Constraints on Agricultural Development in the Republic of Botswana* (Ministry of Agriculture, Gaborone; FAO, Rome, November 1974)

Botswana (1972a) *Report on the Population Census 1971* (Gaborone, 1972)

Botswana (1972b) *Report on Village Studies: Moshupa, Manyana,*

Molepolole (Gaborone, 1972)

Condette, M. (1970a) *Tunisie: Assistance conjointe UNESCO –
UNICEF à l'enseignement – Rapport d'évaluation 1969-70*
(UNESCO, Paris, June 1970, mimeo.)

CRS (1977a) *Program Plan Fiscal Year 1977* (Catholic Relief Services,
Ouagadougou)

CRS (1974a) *Field Bulletin No. 21* (Catholic Relief Services, USCC,
Office of the Pre-School Health Program, Nairobi, 15 August 1974)

CRS (1974b) *Field Bulletin No. 20: An Evaluation of the
CRS-Sponsored Pre-School Health Program in Lesotho* (Catholic
Relief Services, Regional Office, Nairobi, 15 June 1974)

Dandekar, V.M. and Rath, N. (1970a) *Poverty in India* (Indian School
of Political Economy, Poona, and Ford Foundation, New Delhi,
1970), cited in Maxwell (1978a)

Delorme *et al.* (1977). Delorme, H., Chabert, J-P. and Egg, J. *Les Aides
Alimentaires de la CEE et de la France* (Institute Nationale de la
Recherche Agronomique and Fondation Nationale des Sciences
Politiques, Paris, September 1977, mimeo.)

DEMS (1973) *Report to the Ministry of Local Government and Lands:
Pre-project training courses for Supervisors and Leaders; Primary
Schools and Rural Health Facilities Development Project*
(University of Botswana, Lesotho and Swaziland, Department of
Extramural Studies, Francistown, September 1973)

Dudley, L. and Sandilands, R.J. (1975) 'The Side Effects of Foreign
Aid: The Case of Public Law 480 Wheat in Colombia', *Economic
Development and Cultural Change* vol. 23, no. 2, January (1975),
pp. 325-36

EEC (1974a) *Memorandum on Food Aid Policy of the European
Economic Community: Communication from the Commission to
the Council* (Commission of the European Communities, Brussels,
ref: COM (74) 300 final, 6 March 1974)

FAO (1977a) *Monthly Bulletin of Agricultural Economics and
Statistics*, FAO, Rome, vol. 26, no. 11, November (1977)

FAO (1972a) *FAO Principles of Surplus Disposal and Consultative
Obligations of Member Nations* (Food and Agriculture Organisation,
Rome, 1972)

FAO (1955) *Uses of Agricultural Surpluses to Finance Economic
Development in Under-developed Countries – a Pilot Study in
India*, Commodity Policy Studies No. 6 (Food and Agriculture
Organisation, Rome, 1955)

Fisher, F.M. (1963) 'A Theoretical Analaysis of the Impact of Food Surplus Disposal on Agricultural Production in Recipient Countries', *Journal of Farm Economics,* vol. 45, no. 4, November (1963), pp. 863-75

George, S. (1976) *How the Other Half Dies: The Real Reasons for World Hunger* (Penguin Books, Harmondsworth, 1976)

Ginor, F. (1963) *Uses of Agricultural Surpluses; Analysis and Assessment of Economic Effects of the US Public Law 480 Title I in Israel* (Bank of Israel, 1963)

Goering, T.J. (1962) 'Public Law 480 in Colombia', *Journal of Farm Economics,* vol. 44, no. 4, November (1962), pp. 992-1004.

Grissa, A. (1973) *Agricultural Policies and Employment: Case Study of Tunisia* (OECD Development Centre Studies: Employment Series No. 9, Paris, 1973)

Hamilton, A.G. (1975) *Rural Consumer Food Preference and Grain Storage Survey: an Interim Report* (Gaborone, July 1975, mimeo.)

Holtham, G. and Hazlewood, A. (1976) *Aid and Inequality in Kenya* (Croom Helm/ODI, London, 1976)

IFPRI (1977) *Food Needs of Developing Countries: Projections of Production and Consumption to 1990* (International Food Policy Research Institute, Research Report 3, Washington, December 1977)

INS (1976a) *Projection de la consommation des ménages à l'horizon 1981 et 1986* (Institut National de la Statistique, Tunis, 1976).

INS (1976b) *Bulletin Mensuel de Statistique,* (Institut National de la Statistique, Tunis) no. 261-264, September-December (1976)

Isenman, P.J. and Singer, H.W. (1977) 'Food Aid: Disincentive Effects and their Policy Implications', *Economic Development and Cultural Change* vol. 25, no. 2, January (1977)

ISMOG (1977) *Studie Voedselhulp Europese Gemeenschappen* (Instituut voor Sociaal-economische Studie van Minder Ontwikkelde Gebieden, Amsterdam, May 1977)

Jain, S. (1975) *Size Distribution of Income: a Compilation of Data* (World Bank, Washington, 1975)

Jones, D. (1977) *Aid and Development in Southern Africa* (Croom Helm/ODI, London 1977)

Jones, D. (1976a) *Food and Interdependence: The Effect of Food and Agricultural Policies of Developed Countries on the Food Problems of the Developing Countries* (Overseas Development Institute, London, 1976)

Jones, D. and Tulloch, P. (1974) 'Is Food Aid Good Aid?' *ODI Review,* no. 2, 1974

Joy, J.L. (1973a) 'Food and Nutrition Planning', *Journal of Agricultural Economics,* xxiv, 1, January (1973), p.p. 165-93

Kansas State University (1974). Pfost, H.B., Dahl, R., Thornburrow, W. and Steinke, K. *Study of the Tunisian Grain Marketing System,* Report no. 47, Food and Feed Grain Institute, Kansas State University, Manhattan, (Kansas, 1974)

Khatkhate, D.R. (1962) 'Some Notes on the Real Effects of Foreign Surplus Disposal in Underdeveloped Countries', *Quarterly Journal of Economics,* vol. LXXVI, no. 2, (1962), pp. 186-96

Klaasse Bos, A. (1978) 'Food Aid by the European Community: Policy and Practice', *ODI Review,* no. 1, 1978

Lappé, F.M. and Collins, J. (1977) *Food First: Beyond the Myth of Scarcity* (Houghton Mifflin, Boston, 1977)

Lesotho (1976a) *Second Five Year Development Plan 1975/76-1979/80* (Kingdom of Lesotho, Maseru)

Lesotho (1973a) *Appropriation Accounts, Revenue Statements and Other Public Accounts for the Year Ended 31 March 1973* (Maseru).

Lesotho (1970a) *1970 Census of Agriculture Report* (Bureau of Statistics, Maseru, December 1972)

Levinson, F.J. (1974) *Marinda: an Economic Analaysis of Malnutrition among Young Children in Rural India* (Cornell/MIT International Nutrition Policy Series, Cambridge, Mass., 1974), cited in Maxwell (1977a)

Mann, J.S. (1967) 'The Impact of Public Law 480 Imports on Prices and Domestic Supply of Cereals in India', *Journal of Farm Economics,* vol. 49, no. 1, February (1967), pp. 131-46

Marres, P.J.Th. and van der Wiel, A.C.A. (1975) *Poverty Eats My Blanket* (Under Government Printers, Maseru, May 1975)

Maxwell, S. (1978a) *Food Aid, Food for Work and Public Works,* Discussion Paper No. 127 (Institute of Development Studies, Sussex, March 1978)

Maxwell, S. (1977a) 'Food Aid and Supplementary Feeding: Impact and Policy Implications' (Institute of Development Studies, Sussex, unpublished paper, November 1977)

Mettrick, H. (1969) *Food Aid and Britain* (Overseas Development Institute, London, 1969)

Morton, K. (1975) *Aid and Dependence: British Aid to Malawi* (Croom Helm/ODI, London, 1975)

OECD (1976a) *Development Co-operation – 1976 Review* (Organisation for Economic Co-operation and Development, Paris, November 1976)

OECD (1974a) *Development Co-operation – 1974 Review* (Organisation for Economic Co-operation and Development, Paris, November 1974)

OECD (1974b) *Food Aid* (Organisation for Economic Co-operation and Development, Paris, 1974)

Purvis, M. (1963) 'Some Observations on the Effects of PL 480 wheat sales', *Journal of Farm Economics,* vol. 45, no. 4, November (1963), pp. 858-62

Rath, N. and Patvardhan, V.S. (1967) *Impact of Assistance Under PL 480 On Indian Economy* (Gokhale Institute Studies No. 48, Poona, 1967)

Reutlinger, S. and Selowski, M. (1976a) *Malnutrition and Poverty: Magnitude and Policy Options,* World Bank Staff Occasional Paper No. 23 (Johns Hopkins University Press, Baltimore, 1976)

SCF (1976) *Save the Children Fund Newsletter* (Maseru), June (1976).

Schneider, H. (1975a) *The Effects of Food Aid on Agricultural Production in Recipient Countries: an Annotated Bibliography* (OECD Development Centre, Paris, 28 August 1975, mimeo.)

Schultz, T.W. (1960) 'Value of US Farm Surplus to Underdeveloped Countries', *Journal of Farm Economics,* no. 42, December (1960), pp. 1031-42

Scrimshaw, N.S. and Gordon, J.E. (1968) *Malnutrition, Learning and Behaviour* (MIT Press, Cambridge, Mass., 1968), cited in Maxwell (1977a)

Seevers, G.L. (1968) 'An Evaluation of the Disincentive Effect Caused by PL 480 Shipments', *American Journal of Agricultural Economics,* vol. 50, no. 3, August (1968), pp. 630-42

Shaw, J. (1970) 'The Mechanism and Distribution of Food Aid: Multilateral Food Aid for Economic and Social Development', *Journal of World Trade Law,* vol. 4, no. 2, March/April (1970)

Singer, H. and Maxwell, S. (1978) 'Food Aid to Developing Countries: A Survey', *World Development* (forthcoming)

Singer, H. (1978a) *Food Aid Policies and Programmes: a Survey of Studies of Food Aid,* doc. WFP/CFA: 5/5-C (World Food Programme, Rome, March 1978)

Sommer, A. and Lowenstein, M.S. (1975) 'Nutritional Status and Mortality: a prospective validation of the QUAC stick', *American Journal of Clinical Nutrition,* vol. 28, no. 3, March (1975), pp. 287-92

SPEAF (1976) *Etude de factibilité – Approvisionnement des GMV en céréales, fabriqué des biscuits et d'aliments pour bébés,* vol. 1 (Ministère du Commerce, du développement Industriel et des Mines/

SPEAF, Brussels, August 1976)

Srivastava *et al.* (1975). Srivastava, Uma K., Heady, Earl O., Rogers, Keith D. and Mayer, Leo V. *Food Aid and International Economic Growth* (Iowa State University Press, Iowa, 1975)

Srivastava, U.K. (1968) 'The Impact of Public Law 480 Imports on Prices and Domestic Supply of Cereals in India: Comment', *American Journal of Agricultural Economics,* vol. 50, no. 1, February (1968), pp. 143-5

Stevens, C. (1978a) 'Food Aid and Nutrition: The Case of Botswana', *Food Policy,* vol. 13, no. 1, February (1978), pp. 18-28

Stevens, C. and Speed, J. (1977) 'Multi-partyism in Africa: the Case of Botswana revisited', *African Affairs,* vol. 76, no. 304, July (1977), pp. 381-7

Thomas, J.W., Burki, S.J., Davies, D.G. and Hook, R.M. (1976) 'Public Works Programmes: Goals, Results, Administration', in *Policy and Practice in Rural Development,* ed. Guy Hunter, A.H. Bunting, Anthony Bottrall (Croom Helm/ODI, London, 1976)

Tunisia (1976a) *Tunisian National Nutrition Survey 1973-75 Preliminary Report* (Tunisian National Institute of Nutrition and Food Technology, Tunis, June 1976)

Tunisia (1976b) *Retrospective et projections Préliminaires* (Ministère de l'Agriculture, Tunis, January 1976)

Upper Volta (1976a) *Réforme de l'Education – Dossier Initial* (Ministère de l'Education Nationale et de la Culture, Direction de la Planification, Ouagadougou, 1976)

Upper Volta (1975a) *Rapport Annuel 1974-75* (Ministère du Plan, du Développement Rural, de l'Environement et du Tourisme, Direction des Services Agricoles, Ouagadougou, July 1975)

Upper Volta (1972a) *Plan Quinquennal de Développement Economique et Social 1972-76* (Ouagadougou)

USA (1975a) *Development Assistance Program FY 1975, Upper Volta and Niger* (Department of State, Washington, March 1975)

USDA (1977a) *Food for Peace Fiscal Year 1975: The Annual Report on Activities Carried Out Under Public Law 480, 83D Congress, As Amended During the Period July 1, 1974 Through June 30, 1975* (United States Department of Agriculture, Washington, 9 February 1977)

World Bank (1975a) *Lesotho: A Development Challenge* (International Bank for Reconstruction and Development, Washington, October 1975)

WFP (1976a) *Studies of the Role of Food Aid in Relation to Trade and Agricultural Development in Botswana, Lesotho and the Arab Republic of Egypt,* doc. WFP/CFA: 1/10 Add 1 (World Food Programme, Rome, April 1976)

WFP (1976b) *The World Food Programme and Employment,* doc. WFP/CFA 1/15-A (World Food Programme, Rome, February 1976).

WFP (1976c) *Food Aid and Habitat,* doc. WFP/CFA 1/15-B (World Food Programme, Rome, February 1976)

WFP (1975a) *Feeding of Primary School Children and Vulnerable Groups: Interim Evaluation Report,* doc. WFP/IGC: 28/11 Add A4 (World Food Programme, Rome, August 1975)

WFP (1975b) *The Contribution of Food Aid to the Improvement of Women's Status,* doc. WFP/IGC: 27/15 (World Food Programme, Rome, February 1975)

WFP (1975c) *Upper Volta 366 Secondary School Feeding: Progress Report,* doc. WFP/IGC: 27/10 Add A5 (World Food Programme, Rome, February 1975)

WFP (1975d) *Upper Volta 462 - Feeding of Hospital Patients: Progess Report,* doc. WFP/IGC: 28/10 Add A6 (World Food Programme, Rome, August 1975)

WFP (1975e) *Upper Volta 446: Kou Valley Settlement - Progress Report,* doc. WFP/IGC: 27/10 Add C7 (World Food Programme, Rome, February 1975)

WFP (1975f) *Resources of the Programme - Report by the Executive Director,* doc. WFP/IGC: 28/4 Add 1 (World Food Programme, Rome, September 1975)

WFP (1974a) *Upper Volta 243: Construction of Wells, Reservoirs and Small Dams - Terminal Report,* doc. WFP/IGC: 25/11 Add B3 (World Food Programme, Rome, February 1974)

WFP (1974b) *Lesotho 351 Institutional and Livestock Feeding: Terminal Report,* doc. WFP/IGC: 25/11 Add C8 (World Food Programme, Rome, February 1974)

WFP (1973a) *Ten Years of World Food Programme Development Aid 1963-72* (Food and Agriculture Organisation, Rome, 1973)

WFP (1973b) *Two Projects for the Feeding of Primary School Children and Vulnerable Groups in Lesotho and Swaziland: Interim Evaluation Report,* doc. WFP/IGC: 24/10 Add 42 (World Food Programme, Rome, August 1973)

WFP (1973c) *Lesotho 544 - Feeding of University Students, Boarding School Pupils, Hospital Patients and Youth Service Trainees,* doc. WFP/IGC: 24/10 Add 44 (World Food Programme, Rome,

September 1973).

WFP (1973d) *Lesotho 352 - Self Help Public Works: Report of the Interim Evaluation and Project Formulation Mission,* doc. MISC/73/3 (World Food Programme, Rome, August 1973)

WFP (1971a). WFP/FAO Nutritional Division *Strategies for Establishing National Supplementary Feeding Programmes,* cited in Maxwell (1977a)

WFP (1971b) *Upper Volta 366 - Secondary School Feeding: Interim Evaluation Report,* doc. WFP/IGC: 19/9 Add 21 (World Food Programme, Rome, February 1971)

WFP (1969a) *Terminal Report: Upper Volta Price Stabilization Scheme,* doc. WFP/IGC: 16/8 Add 14 (World Food Programme, Rome, 10 October 1969)

WHO (1974) 'Malnutrition and Mental Development', *WHO Chronicle,* vol. 28, no. 3 (March 1974) pp. 95-102

Witt, L. (1975) *Impact of Food Aid on Agricultural Development* (State Department, Washington, mimeo.)

Wood, R. and Morton, K. (1977) 'Has British Aid Helped Poor Countries? Five African Cases', *ODI Review,* no. 1, 1977

World Bank (1976a) *Public Works Programs in Developing Countries: A Comparative Analysis,* (World Bank Staff Working Paper No. 224, Washington, February 1976)

INDEX

acceptability 14, 77f., 150, *see also* taste changes

additionality 117-19, 198, 202-3

administration 19, 48, 62, 78, 81, 83, 86-8, 118, 140-2, 203, 207f.

Africa 15, 19, 31ff., 35, 39f., 42ff., 48, 136, 199, *see also individual countries*

agriculture: in dcs 13, 26f., *see also* surpluses; in ldcs 13f., 17ff., 30, 45f., 49-53; 61, 81, 107-8, 123-9, 144, 166-7, chap. 9 *passim*, 197f., 200-2, 204, 208, *see also under individual countries,* food for wages, food for work

aid, concept of 13-15, 206; costs of 61-3; criticisms of 14-21, 147, 199-202, 206; disaster 38; financial 13ff., 17, 19, 50, 61ff., 117-8, 142, 197, 202-5, 207f.; objectives 23, 67-8; politics of 204-5; project 17, 38-40, 61, 67f., 75-131, 179-81, 183, 188-95, 198, 203, 205, 207f.; psychology of 206-9; rules 45-6, 72-3, 204; shunting 167, 198; tying 17, 57-63; valuation 23-4, 26, 32, 43, 45, 57-63, 68, 78, 80, 149, 179f., 193-4, *see also* emergency relief

America, Latin 18, 32, 35, 42, 136, 179, *see also individual countries*

Anglo De Beers Forest Services 108

animal feed 31, 71, 77, 135, 169f.

Argentina 168

Asia 18, 20, 31ff., 35, 40, 42ff., *see also individual countries*

balance of payments 33, 46, 51, 56, 73, 102, 166, 184

Bangladesh 33, 38, 45, 83

basic needs 206, 208

Belgium 21

Ben Salah, Ahmed 51

blended foods 23, 26f., 40, 59-60, 88, 90, 92, 97, 105, 147ff.

Botswana 48-50, 52-4; and counterpart funds 82; and food for nutrition 68, 86-7, 164, 199,

Botswana–*contd.*
MCH 60, 96-7, 140, 146, 179-80, 193, primary school lunches 60, 90-1, 138, 179-80, 193; and food for wages 124-6, 129, 189, food for work 104-5, 111-3, 120, 180, 188, 192-3, 195, and agriculture 124-6, 129, 188f., 192-3; and institutional feeding 77-81; commerce 179-80; Council of Women 86; education 139, 147, 180; income distribution 139-40

Bourguiba, President 51

breast feeding 148

Britain 13, 16, 21, 48, 52, 55, 202

bulk supply 17, 61, 67-75, 80-1, 117, 168-79, 183-8, 203f., 207f.

calorie/protein debate 60, 90, 149-50

Cambodia 15

Canada 25f., 40-1, 43-4, 50, 68f., 71, 82, 168

Catholic Relief Services (CRS) 30, 57f., 85, 87f., 92, 94ff., 104ff., 143f., 147, 153ff., 193f., 207

cereals 23f., 26, 33f., 35-6, 43f., 49, 68-76, 149f., 168-79, 184-6, 199f.; International Grains Arrangement 33, *see also* sorghum, wheat

China, People's Republic of 124

Church World Service (CWS) 30

civil servants 56, 55f., 98, 177

Colombia 142, 152

colonialism 48, 146

commerce 144, chap. 8 *passim*

Common Agricultural Policy (CAP) 32, 60, 202

Consultative Subcommittee on Surplus Disposal (CSD) *see* surpluses

consumption, additional 76, 81, 123, 143-5, 162, 164, 166, 171, 180, 186, 188-9

continuity 147, 161, 188, 202-3, 207

co-operatives 51, 72, 82, 127-9, 169

Co-operative for American Relief Everywhere (CARE) 30, 87f., 94, 99, 142ff., 150ff., 160f., 207

Costa Rica 142